Also by Elizabeth Warren and Amelia Warren Tyagi

The Two-Income Trap: Why Middle-Class Parents Are Going Broke

ALL YOUR WORTH

The Ultimate Lifetime
Money Plan

ELIZABETH WARREN

AND AMELIA WARREN TYAGI

*f*P

FREE PRESS

New York London Toronto Sydney

The names and identifying characteristics of certain individuals referenced in this publication have been changed.

This publication contains the opinions and ideas of its authors. It is sold with the understanding that neither the author nor the publisher is engaged in rendering legal, tax, investment, insurance, financial, accounting, or other professional advice or services. If the reader requires such advice or services, a competent professional should be consulted. Relevant laws vary from state to state. The strategies outlined in this book may not be suitable for every individual, and are not guaranteed or warranted to produce any particular results.

No warranty is made with respect to the accuracy or completeness of the information contained herein, and both the authors and publisher specifically disclaim any responsibility for any liability, loss or risk, personal or otherwise, which is incurred as a consequence, directly or indirectly, of the use and application of any of the contents of this book.

fP

FREE PRESS
A Division of Simon & Schuster, Inc.
1230 Avenue of the Americas
New York, NY 10020

FREE PRESS and colophon are trademarks
of Simon & Schuster, Inc.

Designed by Katy Riegel

For information regarding special discounts for bulk purchases,
please contact Simon & Schuster Special Sales at 1-800-456-6798
or business@simonandschuster.com

Manufactured in the United States of America

1   3   5   7   9   10   8   6   4   2

Library of Congress Cataloging-in-Publication Data is available.

ISBN 0-7432-6987-X

It is time to stop worrying
and start living.

Contents

PART TWO: POWERFUL TOOLS

ALL YOUR WORTH

Getting Started:
The Truth About Money

The rules of the game have changed.

Somewhere in your bones, you already know this. Hard work and good intentions are no longer enough. Security, comfort, lasting prosperity—you want it, you work hard for it, and yet the worry remains. Real financial peace seems so hard to achieve.

You can't count on good old-fashioned hard work the way your parents did. Go to school, get a good job, do your work, don't go crazy with spending, and everything will work out, right? Not anymore. That advice may have worked in your parents' day, but today you have to be *smart* with your money. Not just a little smart, but super smart. You have to learn the new rules—the rules nobody told you and nobody talks about. And you have to learn them fast.

Just for a moment, forget what you know about money. Forget about your bills. Forget the size of your paycheck. Forget your shopping trips and the shoes you just bought. We want to give you a new perspective on your money, a different way to think about it. We want you to explore new possibilities.

What if we told you that this book could show you how to cover your bills, without worry or fear? No more bounced checks. No more anxiety about how you'll make it through the month. Just the power to pay your bills on time, and then to relax in security and comfort.

Now, what if we told you that on top of showing you how to conquer your bills, this book could show you how to have some money for fun? No living like a Scrooge. No asking yourself every minute, *"Can I really afford this?"* Just some cash in your pocket for plain old just-because-you-feel-like-it *fun*.

And now, suppose we told you that in addition to all of this, you could still have money to save? Money to get *ahead,* each and every month. Enough money so that you could finally start to dream a little—and make real progress toward those dreams. Enough to build some *real* wealth.

And what if we said you could do all this without counting pennies, without carrying around a calculator, and without thinking constantly about money? In fact, after a little up-front work, you could stop thinking about money altogether, and spend your days focusing on the things that really matter.

Would you keep reading?

Is This Book for You?

At this point, you may be thinking, "Aw c'mon. I've looked at these financial books before. All windup and no delivery. They take your $26 and leave you no better off." All those get-rich-quick schemes that assume you have thousands of dollars lying around, just waiting for the right investment. All those chapters on how to buy stock options, how to choose a vacation home, how to plan your estate so that your kids can inherit millions without paying taxes. Who are they kidding?

Or maybe you bought one of those "Billionaire Tells All" books, which promised to unlock all the secrets to becoming fabulously wealthy. And here you are, still trying to figure out how the heck you're supposed to "make your money work for you."

And then there are the lectures on what *they* think your problem is. *"Stop taking expensive vacations." "Shift to a better mutual fund."* But what if you haven't taken a real vacation in ages? What if you don't have two nickels for a mutual fund, or maybe you aren't quite sure what a mutual fund is?

We'll let you in on a secret: *Those books are not written for you.* They are written for people who already have plenty of money, people who don't worry about making ends meet. Oh sure, the store is glad to take your money, but those books are written for people who are already rich and who want to get just a little bit richer. So, where is *your* book?

Right here. *All Your Worth* is for anyone who ever worries about money. For anyone who works hard and plays by the rules, but discovers that the rules have changed. For anyone who wants to build wealth, but isn't sure how to get started. In short, this book is for anyone who wants to get control of his or her money once and for all, to stop worrying and start living a richer, fuller life.

> This book is for anyone who wants control
> of his or her money, once and for all.

If you have already solved all your money problems, if you are secure about your future and never worry about money, if all you want is a book to help you get a little richer, then keep shopping. This isn't your book. But if you are like the rest of us, and if you are ready to take charge of your money, then this is your chance to make some profound changes in your life.

BUILDING YOUR WORTH OVER A LIFETIME— A PLAN THAT WORKS

We want to be clear right from the start: We are not going to tell you how to get rich working ten minutes a day. We are not going to claim that you can live like a millionaire on $20,000 a year. And we are not going to pretend that you can retire at age 32. We figure you are too smart to believe that kind of twaddle anyway.

We are also not going to say that if you'll just shift to generic toilet paper and put $5 a week in the bank, all your problems will instantly disappear. A few pennies here and a few pennies there, and the next thing you know, you will be debt-free, investment-rich, and lighting cigars with Donald Trump. Nope, we're not selling that brand of snake oil.

In fact, you won't get any count-your-pennies advice here. And for a very good reason: Penny-counting advice is downright dangerous. That's right—*dangerous*. Trying to count every penny won't solve your financial problems. But it *will* distract you from the real issues. (It will also provide you with lots of opportunities to fight with your loved ones and make everyone miserable!) This book skips the pennies and goes straight to the heart of the matter—getting real control over your dollars.

Here's a little secret that the other financial books won't tell you: Savvy money managers don't spend a lot of time looking for ways to save a few pennies. They charge right ahead to the big-ticket items, looking to make high-impact changes in the shortest period of time. They don't sweat the small stuff. And neither will we.

> Savvy money managers start
> with the dollars, not the pennies.

We're going to work on the big stuff, not the pennies. This means that what we're going to do is completely different from those other books. But we'll do it anyway. Why? Because it *works*. It will take some effort at first, but once you get going, you can manage your bills *and* start some serious wealth creation.

How can we be so sure this will work? Because *All Your Worth* isn't based on gut reasoning or lucky guesses. It is based on more than twenty years of intensive research, drawing on the experiences of literally thousands of people from across the country.

This book doesn't waste time lecturing you on problems someone dreamed up. It focuses on the *real* issues that regular people struggle with every day. And it offers workable, lifetime solutions designed to help ordinary people get control over their money once and for all.

> *All Your Worth* is based on more than
> twenty years of intensive research.

THE ORIGINS OF *ALL YOUR WORTH*

One of us (Elizabeth) is a professor at Harvard Law School. I have spent decades writing academic books and teaching an entire generation of law students about the rules of money. I have gone before the United States Supreme Court, the White House, and Congress to talk about those rules. I have raised so much noise on television, on radio, and in the newspapers about financial trouble in America that I was named one of the Fifty Most Influential Women Lawyers in America. But I have spent a lot of my time out of the spotlight, giving advice to people—friends, family, folks who participated in our various studies. These "What can you do right here, right now" conversations have become a big part of my life.

The other of us (Amelia) is a financial consultant, with an MBA from the Wharton School at the University of Pennsylvania. I started my career as a consultant with McKinsey & Company, where I advised some of the largest corporations in America. Then I left the big-business world to cofound HealthAllies, a new kind of company dedicated to helping families get more affordable health care. Today I spend my time writing or speaking on the radio about finance, and working with people who want to get control of their money.

We are also mother and daughter, two women who come from a long line of hardscrabble Okies. Shortly before I (Elizabeth) was born, my father lost the family's life savings to a crooked business partner. During my growing-up years, Daddy sold carpeting at a department store and worked as a maintenance man for an apartment complex. I got my first job at 9, rocking a neighbor's colicky baby in the afternoons so his mama could get a few hours of sleep. By age 11 I was taking in sewing, and at 16 I worked the mail desk at an insurance office. My college financial aid applications classified my family as "poor," although I never thought we were any worse off than our neighbors.

I was married at 19, and Amelia was born three years later. She spent her early years tagging along while I went back to school. We lived on a budget that was so tight that I still remember crying with relief when my mother-in-law offered me one of her dresses to wear to a job interview. (She was seven inches shorter than I am, so you can imagine how ungainly I looked!)

I (Amelia) spent a lot of my childhood in a moving van, as my mom moved from place to place, finishing law school and then taking teaching jobs at various colleges. First New Jersey, then Texas, then Michigan, then Pennsylvania, and finally off to Massachusetts. I ended up going to nine public schools over twelve years, so I certainly know what it's like to adapt quickly! I headed back to Pennsylvania for graduate school, where I met the man who would later become my husband. He and I now have a 3-year-old daughter, which makes me a working mother of a preschooler. (That also makes Elizabeth a grandma—her favorite job so far!)

Together we have written one best-selling book about families and money, *The Two-Income Trap*. That book told the story of how the new rules of money have trapped millions of decent, hardworking families, who struggle financially every day. We showed that even though today's families are working harder than ever, many are in *worse* financial shape than their parents were.

The book caused a sensation. Within days of publication, the phone started ringing—reporters, advocacy groups, even a presidential candidate called. Mostly they wanted to talk about ways the law could be improved to help families. We explained the policy recommendations in *The Two-Income Trap,* and then we walked on with hopeful smiles on our faces, cheered by the idea that we might have helped bring about some important changes.

But there were other conversations, ones that didn't leave us smiling. For some people, *The Two-Income Trap* did more than raise some public-policy issues; it touched a raw nerve. We would be going about our business, and then, out of the blue, someone—a neighbor, a caller to a radio program, a mom dropping off her son at preschool—would pause and say quietly, "You're not just talking about money, you know. You're describing my entire life." And then the voice would drop to an urgent whisper. "*No one knows how much I worry about money. What should I do?*"

Of course, we gave the best answer we could. But how much could we really say in the grocery store checkout line or in the ninety seconds allowed to a radio caller? Over time, those conversations began to haunt us. Whenever we had a quiet moment, we would think about the people who had asked us for help. Sure, America needs policy changes, and in time maybe we'll get some laws that make more sense. But in the meantime, what should people *do*?

At first we thought the answer would be really easy—just find a couple of good books we could recommend. So we started looking for a great book that would help ordinary people get control of their money.

And we looked.

And looked.

Everywhere we went, we found pretty much the same thing. Plenty of books on the difference between bull and bear markets, and lots of tips on how to find a great deal in potato futures. In other words, we found oodles of advice for people who are financially secure and just want to make a little more money. But what about people who *aren't* so secure? What about the people who stopped us in the grocery store, the mothers at the preschool, and the guys at Home Depot? Where was the advice for them?

It didn't exist. So we developed *All Your Worth.*

BALANCING YOUR MONEY

So what is the secret to riches? Why do some people get ahead, while others constantly struggle? Our research led us to a very simple and incredibly powerful financial principle that you won't hear anywhere else—*balance*.

What is balance? Doctors recommend it all the time. A balanced diet, with grains, proteins, and plenty of fruits and vegetables. A balanced lifestyle, with enough work, enough play, enough exercise, and enough sleep. This book will help you get your money in balance, to find that same long-term, sustainable approach to your finances.

A lot of budgeting starts at the edges and works in "Cut back here" and "trim over there." That's a little like planning a diet by saying "cut out cookies" and "no sugar in your coffee." This approach may (or may not) work for slight modifications, but it is not a comprehensive lifetime plan. And if you don't have a master plan, then trimming a few expenses in one place while you overspend elsewhere won't do you any more good than cutting out doughnuts while you gorge on cupcakes.

We start by approaching your money in a whole new way. No complicated lists. No spending diaries. Instead, we will help you analyze your spending by dividing it into three simple categories. There is one category for your regular monthly bills, a second category for the money you can spend "just for fun," and a third category for savings. And just like a balanced diet that lets you choose between chicken and fish, *All Your Worth* lets you make lots of choices within each category—so long as the overall category doesn't get too heavy or too light.

When your money is in balance, you have designed your finances so that you *always* have enough to cover your needs. This means that you always have enough to pay your bills without worry.

Balance also means that you always have something in your pocket for a little fun. This isn't about giving up doughnuts and nacho chips forever. This is about enjoying life, each and every day.

And, most important, balance helps you build wealth and create a brighter future for yourself. Day by day, dollar by dollar, you build real riches—with a plan that's easy, steady, and strong.

> When your money is in balance,
> you always have enough to pay your bills,
> have some fun, *and* save for your dreams.

And here is the best part of all. Once your money is in balance, you can stop worrying about it. Managing your money becomes automatic. And so it moves into the background of your life, where it belongs.

Balancing your money isn't about making money the King of Your

Life. You know and we know that money isn't the goal in itself, and the pursuit of money is no substitute for putting together a real life. But we also know that if you don't have a solid, workable plan, then money (or the lack of it) can take over your life. It is a great irony: If you don't think smart about money, you'll wind up thinking about money all the time. But once you get it right—once your money is in balance—you can think a lot less about your finances and a lot more about the things that are truly important. *All Your Worth* is about making the most of your worth in every sense of the word—making the most of your financial worth *and* your worth as a human being, so you can live the kind of life you want to live.

6 STEPS TO A LIFETIME OF RICHES

All Your Worth is a simple, easy-to-follow process. There are six steps. Step One will introduce you to the principles of balance, and help you evaluate where you stand today. You will then set some simple, measurable goals for where you want to go. Steps Two through Six will show you how to meet those goals, so you can get your money in balance and start creating some real wealth. At the end of this book are three additional tools that focus on critical areas in your finances, special relationships and special times that can profoundly affect your financial well-being. We'll cover money and your marriage; buying a home; and staying in control if you find yourself in tough times.

Each of the steps builds on the one that came before, so you should read them in order. And be sure to complete *all* the steps. Skipping a step can cause you to miss something you will need later on.

Once you start going through the steps, you will never think of your money in the same way again. You will develop a whole new approach to spending and saving. We guarantee this will transform your finances. And by the time you reach the last step, you just might transform your life.

WILL IT WORK?

At this point, the skeptic in you is probably asking: Will this really work? Is this another get-rich-quick book? Is this the same fix-the-problems-that-I-don't-have advice? Is this just one more setup for failure? Or could this really help me change my life?

All Your Worth will *work*. It won't give your skin a rosy glow and it won't put hair on a bald head (sorry, Dr. Phil!). It will take some thinking and a little effort to set up, but it will help you get your financial house in order. It will let you smile in the daytime and sleep easy at night. And it will work for more than a week or a month. It will work forever.

> *All Your Worth* is a plan for life.

This plan works because it is a lifetime strategy. It isn't based on a quick fix. It isn't a cheap paint job on a crumbling old house or a crazy crash diet. This plan makes sense when you are 20 and when you are 80. It's a plan that works for single people and for couples with more kids than they can count. You will build a solid foundation that accounts for all your worth, and you will create a plan you can live with for life.

So what have you got to lose? Do you want to keep worrying, or are you ready to try something new? Are you ready to start on your path to a lifetime of riches? Are you ready to make the most of all your worth?

PART ONE

6 Steps
to a Lifetime of Riches

1

Step One:
Count All Your Worth

Ah, to have *enough*. Enough money to pay the bills. Enough to have a little fun. Enough to put something aside for the future. Enough to feel some real confidence. Sounds good, doesn't it?

Have you ever wondered why one person can manage just fine on $40,000 a year, while another person is in big trouble on $140,000? The second person isn't spending wildly on trips to Vegas or bathing in grande lattes at Starbucks. And the first person isn't wearing 20-year-old hand-me-downs. So what's up?

The difference comes down to one simple, but very powerful, idea: Get your money in balance.

What is balance? You've heard of a balanced diet, with enough of each of the basic food groups. Balancing your money follows the same general idea. The right amount of this, the right amount of that, and not too much of any one thing—and you have the formula for a sustainable, lifetime plan. When your money is in balance, you spend just the right amount on each of your major expense categories. You allocate a certain amount to what you *need*, like your house and your insurance. That's a little like the meat and potatoes—the stuff that fills your belly and keeps you from going hungry. You also allocate a certain amount to savings, so you can get ahead, each and every month. That's like your vitamins and your exercise program—it's the stuff that helps you get stronger and healthier, so you'll be better off tomorrow than you are today. And last comes the money that's just for fun. This is for a trip to the movies and a new set of speakers (and an occasional ice-cream cone!), because life is about more than just boiled vegetables.

All Your Worth balances your money into these three categories:

1. Your Must-Haves (the things you need)
2. Your Savings (the money you save)
3. Your Wants (the stuff that's just for fun)

This is just like a diet where you look at your carbs, your protein, and your fat intake. In fact, it is even simpler than a diet, because we won't get into complex versus simple carbohydrates or polyunsaturated fats. There are just three categories, and every dollar that you spend falls into one of these three categories.

We'll explain each category in more detail later on, but for now understand this: Getting these three categories right will be the key to getting your money into balance. It's that straightforward.

If something gets out of balance, you can spot the results pretty fast. If you start to go hog wild on potato chips, the effects will show up on your hips. Likewise, if you blow too much on designer clothes or a brand-new luxury car, you'll feel the pinch in your wallet right away.

When you get your money into balance, your money worries fade away. It's like a balanced diet: If you know you should have four servings of meat, you don't worry about whether it's okay to order the roast chicken. Likewise, if you know it's okay to spend a certain amount on fun stuff, you don't have to constantly ask, "Can I really afford this?" You already know what is okay, so you can relax and enjoy your money.

> Balancing your money
> is the key to having enough.

Step One will help you master the principle of financial balance. By the end of this step, you'll know where you're starting from and where you need to go. As any good general will tell you, knowing exactly where you're headed is half the battle—and this is only Step One! So let's get started.

THE MUST-HAVES:
WHY THE OLD ADVICE NO LONGER APPLIES

You may already have a sense of where your spending is out of balance, in which case this will be pretty easy. On the other hand, you may not have a clue—and that's okay too.

Later in this chapter we'll use a step-by-step process to help you determine your exact financial balance. For now, let's get a quick sense of your starting point.

SELF-TEST: ARE YOU HEAVY ON THE MUST-HAVES?

We start with the Must-Haves, which are the heart of your Balanced Money Plan. Later on, we'll give you exact guidelines for figuring out what counts as a Must-Have, but for now, just think of these as the basic bills you need to pay each and every month like your mortgage and your car payment. Respond with True or False to the following statements:

I worry about having enough money to cover my regular bills, like my electric bill.	True	False
It seems like most of my money goes to things I can't control, like rent or car payments.	True	False
By the time I pay my big bills, there is hardly anything left over.	True	False

(continued)

The cost of living for just the basics—housing, car, insurance—seems way out of reach.	True	False
I only spend money on things I *need*, but there still isn't enough.	True	False
Even though I never buy anything extravagant, I don't have anything in savings.	True	False
I can't think of anything in my budget that I could really cut back on.	True	False

How many statements did you agree with? If you marked "True" more than once, you are probably heavy on the Must-Haves. For you, the old financial advice no longer applies.

What do we mean by "the old advice"? We bet you have heard it before. Your mother-in-law, some expert on TV, or your significant other says something along the lines of, "You're in trouble because you buy too much stuff. If only you wouldn't buy those designer jeans (or restaurant meals or satellite TV) all your problems would go away." The advice is nearly always followed by that self-righteous little shrug, the one you can see even over the telephone, the one that seems to say, "If only you weren't so superficial and silly. Oh well, I guess not everyone is as enlightened as I am." Sound familiar?

We're going to let you in on a secret. For an awful lot of folks, that old mother-in-law advice is just plain *wrong*.

But before we explain why the old advice is wrong, we need to start by saying that it *used to be right*.

Remember how we told you back on the very first page of this book that the rules have changed? This is one of those rules. Back when your parents were young, it was a pretty reliable rule that if they held regular jobs and lived regular lives, their money was pretty much in balance. Why? *Because your parents just couldn't spend all that much on their basic monthly bills.* If they earned a middle-class income, the odds were good they could afford a middle-class home without much stretching—and they could buy that home on Dad's salary alone. Your folks didn't have to hire a whiz-bang accountant to figure out what they could afford. All they had to do was walk down to the local bank to apply for a mortgage. If your parents tried to buy a home that cost more than they could manage, the bank just wouldn't lend them the money. Mom and Dad and their friends didn't have to worry too much about getting in trouble because it just wasn't *possible* to take on a mortgage that was more than they could afford.

The same held true in other areas. If your dad wanted to buy a car that was more than he could really afford, he couldn't get the car loan. If your mom wanted to rent an apartment that was out of balance with your family's income, the landlord wouldn't rent it to her. If your parents wanted to take out a loan—say, for an addition on the house or just to make ends meet for a while—they had to meet with a banker, face-to-face, to explain why they wanted the money. The banker would have asked for pay stubs, tax returns, and all kinds of financial records, so he could evaluate the prospects for repayment. And if things looked out of balance, the banker would have rejected the loan.

As a result, in those days it was really, really rare to spend too much on the basic monthly bills. Why? It's not because your parents' generation was smarter or thriftier or "more in touch with what matters." No, things were different in your parents' day *because the rules were different.* Your parents lived in a time when the government strictly regulated the banking industry. The amount of interest a lender could charge was tightly limited, so banks had to be very careful to lend money only to people who could comfortably pay them back. As a result, in your parents' generation there were no "zero-down" mortgages. Almost no one was "house poor," spending too much on a home or apartment. There were no offers on TV to "cash out" your home equity. No one had a car payment the size of Texas, and car leases hadn't even been invented.

The rules were different in other ways. Tuition at State U was less than $1 a day, so no one started out life with a six-figure student loan. Once someone found a job, if they worked hard, they could pretty much count on keeping that job until it was time to collect a gold watch at retirement. No one trembled in fear over the prospect of mass corporate layoffs that swept out even the hardest-working employees, and "downsizing" referred to the size of a lady's dress, not the size of the workforce. The boss generally picked up the tab for health insurance and a pension, so no one spent half their salary on medical care, and not too many people fretted about getting by after retirement.

So when your parents say that all you need to do to be secure is to work hard and lay off the T-bone steaks, keep in mind that *they were once right.* When they got married, it was a pretty safe assumption that if someone earned a decent living, drove a typical car, and lived in a regular neighborhood, then the money would work out just fine. Back in their day, if someone was struggling financially it was probably because they were blowing too much cash on silly stuff.

But the rules of the game have changed.

The old guarantees no longer exist. In today's world, you *can* get a mortgage that is too big for you—and the banks will *help* you do it. You *can* get a car lease that chews up half your income. You *can* wind up with a student loan bigger than some home mortgages. And as sure as the sky is blue, you can rack up credit card debt without blinking an eye, even if you don't have 50 cents to make the payments.

Does that mean it's impossible to keep your money in balance today? Of course not! But it means that you can't take things for granted the way your parents could. *You* have to understand the new rules. Because unlike your parents, you can't count on the mortgage lender, or the car dealer, or the landlord, or your boss, or even the so-called financial experts to protect you. You have to protect yourself. And that starts by getting your money in balance.

BRETT AND BRANDI: NEVER ENOUGH

Just ask Brett and Brandi Caldwell. The day I (Elizabeth) met Brandi, I thought she would wear a hole right through her shirtsleeve where her right hand kept rubbing her left arm. She explained that she and Brett both work hard—really hard. Brett takes overtime whenever he can. They don't go to movies, and they never eat out. They haven't taken a vacation since their honeymoon in Mexico, which was nearly five years ago.

They were desperate to get out of debt, but whenever they started to pull out of the hole, something *always* went wrong. The baby got another ear infection that she just couldn't shake. Brett's car broke down. The insurance came due. Every month, the credit card balance got a little bigger, as they fell a little further behind. Confused and hurt, they found themselves feeling a little suspicious of each other. If they weren't spending extravagantly, what in heaven's name was *wrong*?

They tried scrimping even more. Brandi started cutting the kids' hair, and Brett climbed up on the roof to replace the flashing around the fireplace. They turned down the heat and told the kids to put on sweaters. Brandi scoured the newspaper for coupons, joking that she would make a casserole out of three-day-old roadkill if it were on sale at the grocery store.

Nothing seemed to help. There was never *enough*.

When their 4-year-old was invited to a birthday party, Brandi cruised the aisles at the discount store. But Tessa was desperate to have the $18 princess tea set for her "best friend ever." In the car on the way home, the little girl refused to look at the $4.88 plastic doll that Brandi had bought over Tessa's tearful protest. After a long silence, she asked her mother quietly, "Why can't we ever do anything *nice*?" Brandi later told me:

> That's when I lost it. I was bone tired. Tired of always coming up short. Tessa is such a good kid, and she just wanted a stupid birthday present for her best friend and I didn't have the money. I started to cry and I couldn't stop. It was so bad I had to pull off the road . . . I'm not a crier. I'm really not. But she's just a little girl.

Brett and Brandi came to my office laden with files and bills, ready for a marathon session of let's-figure-out-the-money. After we went over some numbers, I leaned back and told them they were spending too *little* on the extras. They were stunned. I explained that their real problem had nothing to do with birthday presents or haircuts; their real problem was that they were spending way, way too much on their basic monthly bills. Brett and Brandi had bought a "starter" home, even though they didn't have two nickels for a down payment, which meant they were paying for two mortgages (to make up 100% of the home price). Then there were payments on the new SUV, which Brett had bought to replace the pickup when the transmission died. They had signed up for the most expensive health insurance that Brett's company offered and they were still making payments for a new washer and dryer. By the time they were finished covering the things they *had* to pay for, there wasn't enough left over for a trip to Baskin-Robbins, let alone savings for a rainy day.

The key for Brett and Brandi was to focus on the big picture and to figure out where their money was out of balance. They needed to concentrate their energies on the big-ticket items, and to forget about the little things for a while. It took some coaxing, but Brett finally agreed to sell the monster SUV, replacing it with a six-year-old Taurus. Brandi buckled down and reshopped the homeowners' insurance and the car insurance, and she signed up for the lower-cost HMO. Brandi laughed that she got so carried away with shopping for insurance bargains that Brett started calling her the Money Queen. Brett jumped in with, "Seriously, this is hard work and Brandi is the best." They aren't in the clear yet, but Brett and Brandi are sleeping well for the first time in years—and they have enough for a nice birthday present every now and then.

Does Brett and Brandi's story sound familiar? Maybe you never spend a nickel on anything you don't absolutely *need,* and yet you barely make ends meet. If that's where you're starting from, don't worry—you are not alone. In the new rules of money, millions of people have gotten caught in the same situation. Keep reading; we'll show you the way out.

IN THE HOLE: TOO MUCH ON WANTS

Of course, maybe your problems are nothing like Brett and Brandi's. You may be one of those people whose basic costs are pretty well under control, but you still find it tough to put anything away at the end of the month.

SELF-TEST: DO YOU OVERSPEND ON WANTS?

Respond with true or false to the following statements:

When I go shopping, I'm never quite sure how much I can afford to spend on things.	True	False
When I see something I really want, I just buy it, even if I don't have the money.	True	False
I never know where all the money goes.	True	False
I buy things, and then after I get them home I worry that I couldn't really afford them.	True	False
Worrying about money sometimes takes the pleasure out of outings that are supposed to be fun.	True	False
When holidays or birthdays come up, I'm not sure how much I can afford to spend.	True	False
I probably spend too much on clothes, restaurant meals, and/or going out for fun.	True	False
I work hard, so I buy the things I deserve.	True	False

How many of these statements did you agree with? If you marked True more than once, you are probably overspending on your Wants.

You may have stumbled into another new rule of money: Even as it has gotten easier to get in trouble with your basic monthly bills, it has *also* gotten easier for your spending on "extras" to get out of control.

In your parents' day, when your mom wanted to buy something she didn't really need, like going out for dinner and a drive-in movie, she had to wait until she had enough to pay for it. Why? Not because she was especially prudent or thrifty. She had to wait because she had no choice. If she didn't have the money, she couldn't buy what she wanted. No cash, no movies. Period. When your mother was young, Visa and MasterCard were not flooding mailboxes with "preapproved" sky's-the-limit credit cards for every man, woman, child, and family dog. There were no all-purpose credit cards for ordinary middle-class folks, so your mother bought only what she could pay for on the spot.

Today it is so amazingly *easy* to get out of control with the stuff you don't really need. Your mother probably kept all her spending money in her wallet. If she wanted to know if she could afford to see the new Charlton Heston flick, all she had to do was open her purse and start counting. But in this age of plastic, you need a calculator just to figure out whether you can afford a hamburger. How much did you charge on the Visa? How much on the MasterCard? How much did you put on the debit card or the gas card? And how much did your mate charge? Sheesh! Who can keep up with all that? It is so much *easier* just to slap down the plastic, and wait until the end of the month to find out how it all adds up. And that's when the worry creeps in. You hope you will be able to pay it all off, but you fear there just may not be enough.

Monica, a 26-year-old native of Birmingham, Alabama, knows what that worry tastes like. She would shake her head at a story like the one Brandi and Brett tell. She lives in a modest apartment—comfortable, clean, and cheap. She has the usual things—cell phone, DVD player, two cats who think they own the apartment. Nothing exotic. She's a dependable person, the kind who holds the door for strangers and works late at the office when a deadline hits. She sang in choir throughout high school and college, and she still loves to sing at church and in community groups. A bit insecure about her weight, Monica dresses carefully and has her hair professionally cut and colored. She remembers everyone's birthday, and she gives little presents in between times to co-workers, to family, to neighbors—small, funny things that made her think of them. She's a soft touch for kids selling stuff for school fund-raisers, and she can always be counted on for a donation to an animal refuge or a homeless shelter.

Monica tried budgets, the same way she tried diets. She would keep track of every nickel and cut out all the extras, but it never lasted. Something *always* came up—a friend from college came to town, her brother's car broke down. Besides, she could never quite figure out the point of writing down everything she spent. What was she supposed to do with all those lists? So Monica rocked along, never taking more than a nervous sideways glance at her bills.

On Mother's Day she bought her mom a corsage and made reservations at a nice restaurant. Her mom and dad had a great time, and when the bill arrived, Monica snapped it up with a flourish—"for all you've done for me." Her mother smiled and patted her hand. A few minutes later the waiter returned, the corners of his mouth turned down. "Perhaps there has been a mistake, but the card was refused." Monica jerked the offending piece of plastic out of his hand and dived back into her purse. As she fumbled through her wallet, more than half a dozen credit cards spilled across the table. Her dad was dumbstruck by the number, but her mother was quicker. She reached out and picked up the Visa that had landed closest to her, and handed it to the waiter. "No, not that one!" Monica almost shrieked. Monica's mother looked stunned—why on earth was her daughter yelling at her? And then the realization hit her like a slap in the face—this card was also over the limit. Everyone was quiet as Monica paused and looked intently at each card, almost as if she were considering which tooth to have drilled. After some hesitation, she handed a card to the waiter. It passed, and the family filed out in silence. When they got into the car, her mother began tentatively, "Monica, I don't want to interfere—" Monica cut her off quickly. "Don't. Just don't. I'll work this out."

The morning after Mother's Day, Monica was ready to go on another crash diet—and she wanted our help with the details. We knew it wouldn't last more than a week or two, and then she would be back in the same spot. We offered Monica something easier—and far more lasting. We offered to help her get her money balanced for life.

In a little over an hour, we helped Monica create a plan that would leave her with a sizeable portion for Christmas presents and movies with her girlfriends, while still making sure she had plenty left over to start paying off her credit card balances and building up some savings. When we checked in with Monica a few months later, she was still working her way out of debt, but she said she'd never felt better. "I feel light as a feather now. I didn't realize how much those bills weighed."

ONE STEP FORWARD, ONE STEP BACK:
NOT SAVING ENOUGH

Any rich person will tell you: It's not how much you make, it's how much you keep. Saving is what protects you from that rainy day, and it's what makes your future brighter. Saving is the road to wealth creation.

Of course, you know this. And so you work hard. You don't buy the designer coffee beans. Your house is not the finest in the city—or even on the block. And yet, does it seem that you can't quite get ahead? Is your savings plan a "next month we'll do it" because this month never works out?

SELF-TEST: DO YOU STRUGGLE TO SAVE?

Respond with True or False to the following statements.

I work hard, but I still don't save much.	True	False
I carry a balance on my credit cards most months.	True	False
I don't have a plan for regular saving.	True	False
I worry about having enough for retirement.	True	False
If I lost my paycheck for three months, I don't know what I would do.	True	False
When I have to deal with small emergencies (e.g., car trouble, extensive dental work), I have to use my credit cards or pay the bill off over time.	True	False
I don't have a real plan for saving for college for my children.	True	False
I owe money to a friend or loved one.	True	False

When I make a major purchase, like a new sofa or a dishwasher, I need to pay in installments.	True	False
I try to save, but I worry about whether it's enough.	True	False

If you marked "True" for more than one of these questions, you are struggling to save enough. Maybe you are putting something away, but you worry about whether it's enough. Or maybe you're caught on that endless get-ahead-fall-behind treadmill, where you never create any *real* wealth.

You may think that building savings is just a matter of "buckling down" and using your "willpower." That's certainly the impression you get from a lot of financial experts (and from your mother-in-law!).

But the truth is, having enough money for savings has little to do with willpower. Instead, it is about *balance.*

At the beginning of this chapter, we told you that there are only three categories for your money: Must-Haves, Wants, and Savings. If you spend too much on one thing, then something else will be short-changed. This leads to a simple but very powerful insight: *If you aren't saving enough it is because you are spending too much on your Wants or your Must-Haves (or both).*

If you're struggling to save, you should find this extremely comforting. Why? Because once you get your Must-Haves and your Wants into balance, you will start saving *automatically.* You can do it without breaking a sweat. No more worrying about whether you're saving enough. No more "buckling down." Just a simple, automatic plan for saving a certain portion of your paycheck, every single month.

Keep reading to determine exactly where your money is out of balance, so you can start developing your own plan to create some real wealth.

THE BALANCED MONEY FORMULA

For Brett and Brandi and for Monica and for everyone else who can't seem to get ahead, the key is the same: Get the money balanced—

enough for the Must-Haves, enough for Wants, and enough for Savings. Brett and Brandi and Monica were tilting in different directions, but they were all out of balance and in danger of crashing financially. No matter how hard they scrambled, they just couldn't get caught up, couldn't build toward the future, and couldn't stop worrying. But once they saw what was wrong and brought their money into balance, they started to get ahead. They learned that they finally could have *enough*.

That's how the Balanced Money Formula works. There is always enough for each of the three categories. Must-Haves, Wants, and Savings each follow a preset formula, so that they are always balanced against each other.

So what's the formula? Here it is:

- Must-Haves: 50%
- Wants: 30%
- Savings: 20%

THE BALANCED MONEY FORMULA

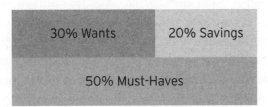

Simple, direct, and effective. Here is the bull's-eye, the center of a lifetime plan for your money.

Testing yourself against the Balanced Money Formula is a little like checking your cholesterol against the recommended levels. It helps you flag when something is wrong, and it shows you where you need to take a closer look at your money choices. When Brett and Brandi compared their spending to the Balanced Money Formula, it became immediately obvious that they had a Must-Have problem. They were spending nearly 80% of their money on Must-Haves, so getting their Must-Haves under control was their path to balance. Monica was in a very different place. She had committed just 40% to her Must-Haves, but her Wants were eating up more than 60% of her income. For her, getting control of the Wants was the key to success. Different problems, but they both come back to balance for the solution.

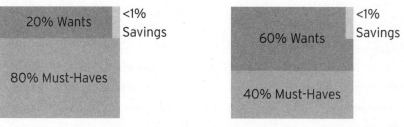

Brett and Brandi: Out of balance on Must-Haves

20% Wants

<1% Savings

80% Must-Haves

Monica: Out of balance on Wants

60% Wants

<1% Savings

40% Must-Haves

Is it ever all right to deviate from the 50/30/20 formula? Yes, there are special times in life when you may shift away from the basic pattern. If your income dips—say, your hours are cut or you take a few months off work to care for a sick family member—then nearly all your money would go to Must-Haves, while you would cut back on Wants and Savings until things got back to normal. And there can be special circumstances that may cause a permanent shift away from the Balanced Money Formula. An independent contractor supporting a family might decide he needs to put even more into Savings to protect against the times when business is slow. Or an older couple with a passion for travel and a fully paid mortgage might choose to go light on the Must-Haves so they could go heavier on the Wants. We will talk later about special situations, but for now keep this idea front and center: The Balanced Money Formula is the right place for most people most of the time, and it is a good place to aim for in your lifetime money plan.

Why 50% for Must-Haves?

That's the first question most people ask. The Must-Haves get only half your money? Half? How can that be? Are we saying you live on only half your money? Not exactly. We're saying you should limit the *hard-*

core commitments to *at most* half of your income. Remember, Must-Haves are the things you will have to pay no matter what.

But you may still wonder, if these are Must-Haves, why don't they claim 60%? Or even 80%? After all, how can it be wrong to spend money on things you *Must Have*?

Why 50%? There are three simple reasons.

1. It is sustainable. Anyone can live on rice cakes—for a day. Anyone can hold her breath—for fifteen seconds. And anyone can spend *everything* on the rent and the car payments—for a very short time. *All Your Worth* is not about getting straight with your money for a month; it's about getting straight *for life*. A diet that works for only a day is as worthless as lipstick on a pig. A spending plan that works for only a month is worth even less.

Spending 50% of your income on Must-Haves is sustainable. It leaves you with plenty of money for the rest of your life. Enough for fun, and enough for the future—enough to last a lifetime.

2. It is safe. When everything is going well, you should have money for what you Must Have *and* for what you Want. But let's face it, over a lifetime, things don't always go according to plan. Sometimes the rain falls and you don't have an umbrella.

Money balance is the key to keeping you safe when things go wrong.

Suppose you get laid off. That's no fun to think about, but we all know it could happen. If your Must-Haves take only 50% of your income, then how would you fare? A lot better than you might think. With Must-Haves at 50%, your unemployment check could cover your needs for several months. (In most states, unemployment insurance covers roughly 50% of your previous salary, up to certain limits.) Knowing you can cover the basics should take some of the terror out of the pink slip! Likewise, if you were in a serious accident and you couldn't work, most disability policies would cover about half of your salary, and so your basic needs would be met. And if you are married, keeping your Must-Haves at 50% means that you could get by on only one paycheck for a while.

Keeping your Must-Haves down to 50% gives you something that is so incredibly valuable: *flexibility*. If your Must-Haves creep higher—say, to 70 of 80%—there just isn't much room to maneuver. There's not any space to scale back, nowhere you can cut if you need to. But if you can get by on 50% of your income, you have the flexibility to cut back on your spending whenever you need to. You are in control. You can manage an unexpected expense like a car accident or a leaky roof. You'll be okay if your boss cuts your hours. If you keep your Must-Have expenses under 50%, you can stay light on your feet, ready to roll with the punches.

3. *It has been tested over time.* We go back to 50% for the Must-Haves because that number worked for Americans for a long time. A generation or so ago, most families spent half (or less) of their incomes on the Must-Haves. As a result, most people were able to put money away, each and every month. Unlike today, saving was the norm. We go over the details in *The Two-Income Trap*, but the bottom line is this: Bankruptcy rates were low, foreclosures were rare, and few people even knew what a repo man did for a living. Getting rich, little by little, was commonplace; people did it every day. People also *worried* less—a whole lot less. They knew they could make it to the end of the month, and they knew they had plenty of money for a rainy day. So they slept easier and smiled more. Not a bad model for us to learn from today!

Why 30% for Wants?

Why 30% for Wants? Because you deserve some space where you can relax and enjoy yourself! This is what life is all about, the right-now reward for all your hard work.

This is the place for all the treats and extras, the things that give life spice. A new set of speakers, plane tickets to Grandma's, aerobics classes, Christmas presents, and on and on. These are bought with "fun money," the free money set aside for your Wants.

Unlike the Must-Have category, which is very restrictive in what gets included, Wants is a totally open field. Maybe your fun money goes to Duran Duran CDs and Kevin Costner films. Maybe you prefer origami lessons and Swedish massages. Maybe you think other people's Wants are boring or dumb or icky, while your Wants are cool, sensitive,

EXAMPLES OF WANTS

Cable TV	Movies	Madonna CD
Lite beer	Dinner at Olive Garden	T-bone steak
Cleaning service	Babysitter for a night out	Trip to Six Flags
Haircut	Purple nail polish	Dog grooming
Pair of Nikes	New hamster	Birthday present
Home computer	Car wash	Soccer camp
New sofa	Deep-tissue massage	Pot of begonias
Gap T-shirt	Save the Whales donation	Espresso machine
Elks Lodge dues	Karate lessons	*People* magazine
Krispy Kreme	X-Men video game	Tattoo

or socially responsible. Be that as it may, the fact remains: *You can spend your fun money on anything you want*. Anything at all; it doesn't matter one bit. If you want to spend it piercing your belly button and playing the slots in Vegas, we won't raise an eyebrow.

The fun is almost unlimited in choices. Dresses or Ding Dongs, dog treats or daffodils—whatever strikes your fancy. There is only one rule: The Wants category has a lid—and the lid is clamped down tight. There is no limit on how you spend fun money, but when it is gone, it is truly gone. No fudging around the edges. No borrowing against next month's fun money. No nibbling out of the Savings. You can safely spend this much, but no more.

> You can spend your Wants money on anything that strikes your fancy, so long as you stay within 30% of your income.

A spending cap can sound so dreary, full of denial and no-no-no. But this cap is all about liberation, not deprivation. When you know that it is okay to spend because the limits have been worked out, then you really can enjoy your money.

Setting aside a specific amount for your Wants is the key to breaking the cycle of crash-diet budgeting. It puts an end to those fits of good intentions when you suddenly declare you Must Clamp Down On All Extra Spending Immediately. Talk about the road to misery! It's like telling yourself that since you need to lose weight, you Must Never, Ever Eat Anything But Raw Vegetables. It's impossible to live like that for very long, so either you deny yourself all the time and feel lousy, or you splurge and feel guilty. Either way, you are perpetually caught between the two sides to the trash compactor: misery from constant denial and guilt from having fun. You always feel bad about your money and, since you're never quite sure how to get caught up, you don't get any closer to a real solution to your problems. The Balanced Money Formula helps you break that cycle.

By figuring out *now* what is a Must-Have and what is a Want, you make it very easy to follow the golden rule of financial responsibility: *Pay your Must-Haves first.* The Wants should never, ever compete for money with your Must-Haves. In other words, when everything goes well, there is money for Must-Haves and Wants. But if something goes wrong, the Wants are the first thing you cut. There is no money for a trip to Las Vegas or a new set of speakers until the car payment and the rent are paid. You already know this, but saying it out loud today makes it a lot easier to cut right to the chase should the need ever arise. If that rainy day ever comes, you'll know right where to head for shelter.

The Balanced Money Formula helps you create a prominent place for the money you spend on your Wants. No guilt, no worry, just fun. It's grounded in reality, because it starts with what you earn each month. It's safe, because you spend it *after* you've set aside enough for your basic needs. And it's worry-free, because you've given yourself 100% permission to spend it. You'll be surprised how much more fun this spending can be.

20% for Savings—Are We Kidding?

Savings comes at the end of the Balanced Money Formula, rather than at the beginning. That isn't because Savings isn't important. It is! Savings comes at the end so you know *how* to find the money to save. *All Your Worth* makes Savings really, really easy. Think about the formula: 50% for Must-Haves and 30% for Wants. That means that the 20% for Savings is automatic; it just happens. Once you get the plan in place and you bring Must-Have and Want expenses into line, you will have your 20% left over for Savings. No need for a Herculean "we have to tighten our belts so we can save for a house (or the kids' college or whatever)." No boom-and-bust bank account. Just a simple, steady, month-by-month plan to build your wealth.

So why 20%?

So you can stop worrying

Maybe you've felt it. The rush in the pit of your stomach when you hear the pinging sound in your car, and you wonder how you'll ever pay the mechanic. The tightness in your chest when the plumber tells you it will be $185 to fix the shower. The rock-hard knots in your back when you realize that the check you mailed to the electric company will probably bounce.

These are the feelings of not having any Savings. And when you start to save—when you really sock it away, month after month—these feelings stop. You can put these feelings in a box and mail them to the moon, because they won't be with you anymore.

Setting aside 20% of your income will put some money in the bank *fast*. You will build a cushion that is there when you need it. This cushion will let you end—once and for all—the worry over life's little financial emergencies. It will take a lot of the sting out of things that go wrong, because you will know that you can manage. When you have some money in the bank, you can *relax*. In other words, Savings isn't just about living better tomorrow—it is about living better today.

So you can pay off your past

If you are like most Americans, you're probably carrying a balance on your credit card. And then there are those old medical bills, and maybe an IOU to your sister. Your debts worry you, and you know you should pay them off. But where do you find the money?

Your 20% for Savings will go toward your future, but it will also go toward paying off your debt. With 20% for Savings, you know exactly where the money to pay off your debts will come from. No more hold-your-breath-until-Visa-is-paid. And no more credit card balances that linger for years! Just a rock-solid plan for you to pay off all your past debts. Fast. Because it's time to get on with building your future.

So you can grow older in comfort

You may want to spend your golden years learning karate, or writing the great American novel, or just fishing with the grandkids. No matter what your dreams are, *All Your Worth* will help you save enough to spend those years in comfort and dignity. According to the smartest economists out there, that takes a *minimum* of 10% of your income to get ready for retirement.

The Balanced Money Formula earmarks 20% for Savings so you will have enough to save for retirement *and* have plenty left over for all your other dreams.

So you can build riches to last a lifetime

When you get your money in balance, you start building a powerful habit. You create a pattern of saving, month in and month out. And that's the real secret to wealth creation. It doesn't come from sudden, heavy-duty lifting. Instead it comes gradually, a dollar at a time. It's a little like staying in shape. You don't run 100 miles one day a year; you run a few miles, each and every week. And so *All Your Worth* shows you how to put aside 20% of each and every paycheck so you can start building real wealth, one dollar at a time.

HOW DOES YOUR MONEY STACK UP?

Okay, the moment has arrived. You are about to do something most people have never done: take stock of your money.

Are you feeling a little nervous about this? Does it sound like it might help, but it may be a little hard? Okay, let's pause for a minute and go back to something we said earlier: No one can live a real life counting every penny. No one can have any fun if every smoothie and every new shoelace has to be recorded in some journal. That isn't living. And we won't ever ask you to do that.

Instead, we're going to ask you to do something far more interesting—and far more powerful. We want you to get the big picture on where you are spending your money. A big, one-time snapshot, so you can answer the question once and for all: Where is your money going? We'll do this once, and then we'll help you put the insights you gain into a plan that will work day after day.

It is time now, to figure out how your money adds up. So take out a pencil and get going!

Getting Started: What You Make

Your earnings are the backbone of your lifetime Money Plan. To calculate "What You Make," enter all the money that comes in on a regular basis in Worksheet 1. For most folks, this is just a month's worth of your (and your partner's) take-home paychecks.

WORKSHEET 1. AFTER-TAX INCOME
Income
Monthly income, after taxes (Include child support, tips, and all other sources of income. If income is variable take the average of several months.) $ _____

HELP FOR WORKSHEET 1

What if my income varies from month to month? If your income varies, just do your best to estimate what comes in on average. You may want to calculate the average across several months, so you can account for the ups and downs. Or you can pull out last year's tax return, and divide your total income by 12.

What if my taxes aren't deducted from my check? Estimate the taxes you will pay at tax time, and deduct them from your regular monthly income. If you need help, look at last year's tax return.

What if I get extra income from a side business or from working overtime? Estimate what you take home on average (after taxes, of course), and add it in with the rest of your income.

What if my employer deducts health insurance premiums from my check? If your employer deducts health insurance premiums, enter in your total income *before* those deductions are taken. (The same goes for deductions for disability and life insurance.)

What if my employer contributes to a retirement plan or pension? Add the amount of your employer's contribution in with your total income. (If the contributions are made once a year, just take the annual amount and divide by 12.) Technically, these contributions aren't part of your take-home paycheck, but they build toward your lifetime Savings, so we want to be sure to count them now.

What if I can't get an exact number? Just do your best! The point here is to get a reasonable estimate of your after-tax income, so you can get started balancing your money. There won't be a team of accountants knocking on your door, so relax!

The Basics: Your Must-Haves

Before you tally up your Must-Haves, let's get clear on what they are. The list is surprisingly short: A place to live, utilities, medical care, insurance, transportation, and minimum payments on your can't-escape legal obligations. This is the core, the amount that you must pay every month, in good times and in bad.

Where did this list come from? We put forth three simple guidelines to decide what qualifies as a "Must-Have":

1. Could you live in safety and dignity without this purchase (at least for a while)?
2. If you lost your job, would you keep spending money on this?
3. Could you live without this purchase for six months?

The first two questions force you to look at what really matters. If you lost your job and had to live on a tiny unemployment check, you would still pay your mortgage. You wouldn't (we hope!) go on a trip to Disneyland.

The third question is for those things that seem like Must-Haves, but really aren't. Consider a basic example: clothing. Unless you live in a nudist colony, you "must have" clothes to step outside your door. But the odds are you have a closet full of clothes. Would you *like* a new pair of shoes? Sure. Do you want to walk around in those old lime-green pants? No. But *could* you wear your old shoes and green britches and still be warm and safe for another six months or so? We bet you could.

Are we saying you should never buy new clothes or CDs? Of course not. We're just saying that this category, the Must-Haves, is only for the necessities. A place to live, because you need that for your basic dignity (and because you've made a long-term legal commitment to a lease or mortgage). Insurance and medical care, because you need those to stay safe and healthy. Car payments so you can get where you need to go, and an allowance for gas for your regular back-and-forth. Child care may be another Must-Have, if you need it to get a paycheck. And your can't-escape legal obligations, like student loans, child support payments, and anything you've signed a long-term contract for.

"Wait a minute!" you might be saying. "What about my credit cards?" If you are like most Americans, you are probably carrying a balance on your credit cards. Because this situation is so common we're going to treat payments on your credit cards differently. We know they're a legal obligation that you "must" pay. But the goal of *All Your Worth* is not to keep making minimum monthly payments forever; the goal is to get rid of these debts altogether. So leave them out of the Must-Haves; they will go in a separate category later on.

Putting food in the right category is also a bit tricky. Obviously you "must have" food to live. On the other hand, if you're like most of us, you could probably cut way back on the amount you spend on food. You could stop eating out, stop buying beer and frozen dinners, and live on beans and rice (or something similarly cheap) if you really had to. So food isn't a fixed obligation the way your mortgage or car payment is. This means you have to think of food as straddling two categories: A small amount to cover your basic nutritional needs should go with the Must-Haves. All the rest—the restaurant meals, the beer and soda, the PowerBars, and the T-bone steaks—fits in the Wants category.

Now it is time to calculate your Must-Have Score. Enter all of your monthly Must-Have expenses in Worksheet 2.

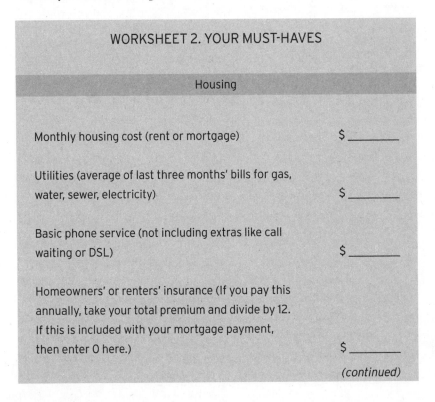

WORKSHEET 2. YOUR MUST-HAVES

Housing

Monthly housing cost (rent or mortgage) $ _____

Utilities (average of last three months' bills for gas, water, sewer, electricity) $ _____

Basic phone service (not including extras like call waiting or DSL) $ _____

Homeowners' or renters' insurance (If you pay this annually, take your total premium and divide by 12. If this is included with your mortgage payment, then enter 0 here.) $ _____

(continued)

WORKSHEET 2. YOUR MUST-HAVES *(continued)*

Property taxes (If you pay this annually, take your
total bill and divide by 12. If this is included with your
mortgage payment, then enter 0 here.) $ _____

Medical Care

Health insurance (If your employer provides your
insurance, then enter the amount that is deducted from
your paycheck. If your employer pays the full premium,
then enter 0 here.) $ _____

Monthly total of what you pay out of pocket for recurring
medical expenses (e.g., regular prescription drugs,
medical supplies) $ _____

Transportation

Monthly car payment or lease payment $ _____

Car insurance (If you pay this annually,
divide your bill by 12.) $ _____

Gas, average monthly expense $ _____

Other transportation costs to get you to work
(e.g., parking, bus, or subway fare) $ _____

Insurance

Monthly payments for other insurance (e.g., life insurance,
disability insurance, long-term-care insurance) $ _____

Food	
Basic food needs (USDA rule of thumb: $180 a month for a single adult; $650 for a family of four)	$ _____

Legal Obligations	
Student loan (monthly payment)	$ _____
Ongoing contractual obligations (Enter monthly bill for anything that you have a long-term contract for, such as cell phone, gym membership, child care, satellite TV, appliance payments.)	$ _____
Other ongoing legal obligations (e.g., child support or alimony payments)	$ _____

Total	
Total Monthly Must-Haves	$ _____

Must-Have Score	
Must-Have Score = Total Monthly Must-Haves ÷ After Tax Income (from Worksheet 1) × 100	$ _____ %

HELP FOR WORKSHEET 2

Where should I put my credit card payments? Don't worry about credit card payments yet; they will go in another section.

I hire an occasional babysitter or enroll my kids in after-school activities. Does this go with the Must-Haves? If you've signed a long-term contract, then it's a Must-Have. Likewise, if you need the child care so you can earn a paycheck (or look for a job), then it is a Must-Have. But if it is something your family *could* live without, then it's a Want.

I spend a lot more than $180 a month on food! The goal is to give yourself a basic budget to cover your essential food needs; you're not trying to record what you actually spend every month.

I'm still making monthly payments for my washer/dryer. Where does that go? Monthly payments for appliances, furniture, and anything else that you've signed a contract for go under "Ongoing contractual obligations" in the Legal Obligations section.

Sometimes I pay extra on my mortgage. Does that go here? No, we will have a place for extra payments later on.

I pay my cable bill every month; where does that go? Since you *could* live without cable TV (we hope!), it doesn't belong with the Must-Haves (unless you signed a long-term contract, it goes with Legal Obligations). Assuming you could cancel cable TV whenever you want, it should go with the Wants, which we will cover later on.

I took a home equity loan to pay off my credit cards. Where does that go? Monthly payments on your home equity loan or second mortgage belong with your housing costs.

What about Christmas and birthday presents? I have to get my kids a gift! These are not regular monthly expenses. And if you lost your job, this is probably something you wouldn't spend money on (or at least not very much money). So it belongs with the Wants, not the Must-Haves.

The last line in Worksheet 2 shows your Must-Have Score. This is the amount of income you have committed to your Must-Have expenses every month.

Understanding Your Must-Have Score

Under 35%: Must-Have Safety Zone

You are keeping the Must-Have spending under tight control. You have left yourself lots of flexibility, and lots of room to have some fun and to save for the future. Overspending on Must-Haves is not a problem for you. Two gold stars!

35-50%: Must-Have Balance

Your Must-Have spending is well balanced. You have made substantial commitments, but your spending plan can comfortably leave room for Savings and for fun. Good balance—and a gold star!

50-65%: Must-Have Danger Zone

Do you scrimp on the fun stuff, but still find that you're not saving as much as you should? That's because your Must-Have commitments are too big for your income. The warning lights are flashing. Step Three will help you examine your Must-Haves more carefully. We will help you decide where to trim, and show you how to protect yourself if you decide to stay heavy on the Must-Haves. It may seem a little challenging, but don't worry—you don't have too far to go. And once you get your Must-Haves in balance, the hardest part is over. You will be able to relax and start building some real wealth.

More than 65%: Must-Have Crash Zone

Do you find that whenever the car breaks down or Christmas rolls around, you wind up putting everything on the credit card? Do you find yourself worrying over every penny, but still not having enough to pay the bills? Did Brett and Brandi's story sound familiar? It should! You are drowning in big commitments. You are spending so much on your monthly Must-Haves that you hardly have enough left over to buy a six-pack of paper towels, let alone save something for your future. Even the smallest hiccup can seem like a major disaster because there is no extra money to handle anything that goes wrong. You shot through the Danger Zone many warning lights ago, and now you are deep in the highest risk area—the Crash Zone. You need to get your Must-Have spending under control immediately.

Pay special attention to Step Three, which starts on page 70. It is the step that will make the most difference in your life. Some of the choices may be tough, but cutting your Must-Haves is the *only* road to financial peace for you. Don't keep cruising and telling yourself everything will work out. You are driving down the freeway of life at 200 miles per hour with no seat belt, no steering wheel, and no brakes. You need to make some changes before you crash.

Special Circumstances

We understand that you may have special circumstances, and there are times in life when your money may not stay in perfect balance. When a new baby comes or a job disappears, when you go back to school or someone gets sick, things naturally get out of kilter for a while. That's okay; *All Your Worth* is designed to last a lifetime, and that means it is flexible enough to handle the ups and downs in life. Keep reading; in the upcoming chapters, we will talk more about special circumstances and when it may be okay to stretch beyond 50%.

Saving for the Future: Where You Stand

It's time to move on to the next element in the Balanced Money Formula—your Savings. We know this is slightly out of order, but we'll hit the Wants in a little while. For now, it's time to take the measure of how much you are getting ahead (or falling behind).

The Savings category actually includes two kinds of money. The first is all the stuff that usually comes to mind when you hear the words "saving for the future," like money for a retirement account or a regular bank account. The second kind of Savings is debt repayment. You may not think of paying off your debts as saving for the future, but that's what it is. Consider your car loan. If you put $500 in the bank, you'll have $500 in Savings you can call on later. But if you pay off $500 on your car loan, then that's $500 extra (plus interest) you'll have in your pocket later on. Paying off your debt is another way to get ahead, and it is just as important as putting cash into the bank. Every time you pay down principal on a loan you are building your Savings for the future.

Enter your traditional savings and your debt payment into Worksheet 3.

WORKSHEET 3. SAVING FOR YOUR FUTURE

Part 1: Savings

Traditional Savings

Monthly contributions to a retirement account (If you make an annual contribution, divide the total by 12. If your employer contributes to a retirement account or pension, include that amount here too.) $ _____

Other Savings (Enter the total of any other monthly saving, such as a college savings account or a passbook savings account. If your Savings varies from month to month, add up all your Savings from the past year, and divide the total by 12.)   + $ _____

Debt Payment

If you make extra payments (beyond the regular monthly payment) to pay off the principal of your mortgage, car loan, or student loan, add up the extra payments you make each month. (If your payments vary from month to month, include all the extra payments for the last year and divide by 12. Do not include credit card payments here; they will go later.)   + $ _____

(continued)

WORKSHEET 3. SAVING FOR YOUR FUTURE *(continued)*

Part 1: Savings

New Savings

Add up your Traditional Savings and Debt Payment
from above.   = $ _____

Part 2: Credit Card Debt

Credit Card Debt

If you regularly carry a substantial balance on your
credit card, calculate the amount by which your balance
is growing or shrinking: (credit card balance one year
ago − today's balance) ÷ 12. If your balance has
been increasing, this will be a negative number. If the
balance has been shrinking, this will be a positive
number. If you don't usually carry a balance, or if your
balance is fairly small (less than $200) enter 0. $ _____

Part 3: Monthly Savings Score

Total Monthly Savings

Total Monthly Savings = New Savings
(from Part 1) + Credit Card Debt (from Part 2). (If you
entered a negative number in Part 2, you should subtract
your Credit Card Debt from your New Savings. If your
debt is growing faster than your savings, your Total
Monthly Savings number will be negative. This means
you are spending more than you are saving.) $ _____

Monthly Savings Score

Monthly Savings Score = Total Monthly Savings ÷
After-Tax Income (from Worksheet 1) × 100
(Remember, if the Total Monthly Savings subtotal
is negative, then this number is negative too.)   _____ %

HELP FOR WORKSHEET 3

What if the amount I save varies a lot from month to month? Calculate the total amount you saved over the past year and divide it by 12. If you don't know how much you saved over the past year, just do your best to estimate your average Savings over the past few months.

I carry a balance on my credit card. What should I enter in Part 2? The goal is to calculate how much your credit card balance is growing or shrinking every month. Suppose your balance was $900 one year ago, and it is $1500 today:

Balance from one year ago of $900 − current balance of
$1500 = −$600
−$600 / 12 months = −$50/month.

In this example, you would enter −$50 next to Credit Card Debt. This means your credit card balance has been rising by an average of $50 each month.

If you don't know your credit card balance from one year ago, just find a statement from a few months ago, and calculate the average amount by which your balance has been rising or falling each month.

I pay my credit card balance most months—do I need to enter anything for my Credit Card Debt in Part 2? No. Only people who carry an outstanding balance month after month need to fill in their credit card balance. If you pay off your balance every month (or almost every month), you can just enter 0 next to Credit Card Debt.

(continued)

HELP FOR WORKSHEET 3 *(continued)*

I took out a home equity loan to pay off my credit card balance. Does that count as Savings? No! You still owe the money, although now you owe it to the mortgage company instead of the credit card company. So your debt is still the same.

My savings and debts are all over the place—I'm confused! The goal here is to help you get a snapshot of whether you're getting ahead or falling behind each month. Don't get too caught up in trying to get this perfect; we'll help you get where you need to go.

The last line in Worksheet 3 shows your Monthly Savings Score. This is the percentage of your income that is going to Savings. This is the amount by which you are getting ahead—or falling behind—on a monthly basis.

Understanding Your Monthly Savings Score

20% +: Super Big Saver

Congratulations, Big Saver! You are socking it away. This keeps you safe, and it will make it possible for you to turn some big dreams into big reality. Set off some firecrackers!

12-20%: Strong Saver

The future is clearly important to you. You are carving out a good-sized slice of your money for Savings, and you've made the future an important part of your day-to-day spending plan. Good job! You are well into the Safety Zone. Keep aiming at 20% for your future, so you get on the road to building some real wealth.

6-12%: Solid Saver

You've made a solid start on putting your future first, and you're way ahead of most of your neighbors. You need to push a little harder, but the good news is that you're already on the right path.

0-5%: Starving Saver

Does it seem that every time you get ahead, something happens to pull you back? Do you want to save, but it just doesn't work out? Does it seem like you have put all your dreams on hold? You know how important it is to save, but you aren't giving yourself enough room for real progress. Now is the time to dig in and push hard on your other expenses, so you can find the money to build your lifetime security. Stick with it—*All Your Worth* will help you start building real wealth.

Less than 0%: In the Hole

Are you falling behind instead of getting ahead? Are you worried that real trouble may be just around the corner? Does it seem like the hole just gets deeper, and there's no way out? This is a scary place to be, and we are going to help you break free. You can find your way out of debt and learn how to *stay* out of debt, once and for all. This is the first step in building a future you look forward to instead of one that makes you want to cover your head.

We know that 20% for Savings may still look like a lot of money. For some of you, it may seem as far off as having cities on Mars—and about as crazy a dream. But don't worry, we're not going to shake a finger and then leave you on your own. Instead, we're going to start by helping you get control over your Must-Haves and your Wants. By the time we're ready to focus on your Savings, the money will already be there!

SPENDING ON YOUR WANTS: WHERE YOU STAND

You may be feeling a little nervous about this part, afraid that we'll ask you to account for every last ice-cream cone and pinball game. Well, don't worry. You don't have to run around with a notebook writing down everything you buy. The calculation for what you spend on Wants is the simplest one of all.

WORKSHEET 4. YOUR WANTS

All your money	100%
— Must-Have Score (last line in Worksheet 2)	— _____%
— Monthly Savings Score (last line in Worksheet 3. If this was a negative number, you should *add* it here instead of subtracting.)	— _____%
= Wants Score	= _____%

The last line in Worksheet 4 shows your Wants Score. This is the portion of your monthly income that you are spending on your Wants.

Understanding Your Wants Score

20-30%: Wants in Balance

Spending on your Wants is under control. You don't splurge on things you can't afford, but you don't deny yourself either. This is a sustainable place for a lifetime of financial peace. Enjoy!

Less than 20%: All Work and No Play

You are spending very little on your Wants. You certainly won't get into trouble spending like this on Wants. Even so, you should ask yourself—are you making enough room for fun? Are you keeping your Wants low because of too many Must-Haves? Life needs to have space just for fun; get into a place where there is room for a little more enjoyment.

More than 30%: Splurger

Does it seem like money flies out of your hands, and you're never sure where it all goes? Did Monica's story sound familiar? It should, because your Wants spending is out of balance. Does this mean you need to cut back? Probably. If you are having trouble putting away enough for the future, then cutting back on your Wants is the right move for you. Step Four will show you how.

A LIFETIME OF BALANCE

Let's take a last look at how your money compares with the Balanced Money Formula. Pull your results from the earlier worksheets to fill in your Balanced Money Score:

YOUR BALANCED MONEY SCORE

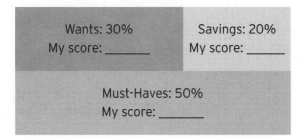

Wants: 30%
My score: _____

Savings: 20%
My score: _____

Must-Haves: 50%
My score: _____

Now you have it all in one place: a summary of where you stand with your money. You can see it all at once—the money you earn, the money you spend, and the money you save is all accounted for. Now you know where you stand.

Remember how we said that understanding the problem is half the battle? Well, now you've won half the battle—and you're only on Step One! It may not feel that way yet, but getting a clear picture of exactly where you are and where you need to go is central to your success.

The following pages will help you get your Must-Haves, your Wants, and your Savings into balance, step-by-step. *All Your Worth* will help you create a lifetime of balance. You know where you are and where you are headed. Now you are ready to take the next steps to seize control over your money and to build a lifetime of riches.

2

Step Two:
Escape from the Thinking Traps

You've learned the Balanced Money Formula. You've measured your own money balance. You know where you need to go. Maybe you're all revved up, ready to start making the most of your worth.

And then again, maybe you're developing a big case of the "buts."

But I live in Chicago (or Los Angeles/New York/Boston/name-the-city) where housing prices are through the roof!
But I have kids!
But my wife doesn't work!
But I'm a waiter (or a sales clerk or an actor or a teacher or a minister or a name-the-job)!
But I'm self-employed!
But my credit card balance is bigger than the national debt!
But the economy stinks!
But I'm too old!
But I'm too young!
But I'm married!
But I'm single!

Okay, now that's out in the open. You have a hundred good reasons why your spending is out of balance. A hundred good reasons why your costs are too high and your income is too low. A hundred good reasons not to change.

And only one reason to change. *Because change is the only way to make things better.*

You didn't pick up this book to be told, "You are right, everything is hopeless." You picked up this book because you thought that maybe, just maybe, *All Your Worth* could help you get straight with your money once and for all.

Getting straight with your money happens in your head, not just your wallet. That's not a bunch of psychobabble. It is the plain and practical truth. Because if you tell yourself "I can't do this because . . . ," then of course you can't do it. Getting your money in balance is like anything else in life: You must believe in your ability to succeed.

When Amelia's brother Alex was a little fellow, he announced (at the ripe old age of 6), "I don't swim," and that was that. We could spend an afternoon at the municipal pool, and he wouldn't even get his bathing suit wet; two rounds of swimming lessons hadn't made a dent. But we were moving so I (Elizabeth) could take a new teaching job, and we would be staying at a place with a pool. It was just plain dangerous to have a 6-year-old who could fall in and sink like a rock, and I was getting desperate. So, with the move less than a month away, I took Alex to a neighborhood teenager who posted a notice at the grocery store promising to teach any child to swim.

When we showed up for the first lesson, the girl eyed Alex silently for a long time. Then she said, "I'm not sure he'll be able to swim; I'll need to measure him." I started out of my chair—I wasn't paying this girl to tell my son he couldn't swim!—but she shook her head quietly. Then, like a surgeon gathering her instruments, the girl took out a tape measure, a scale, and a notepad. She measured his height and the span of his arms, and she weighed him. She told Alex to touch his toes, and then stretch his arms high in the air. When the exercise was over, she sat quietly, writing line after line in her notebook. As the minutes ticked by, Alex stared intently at her pencil, convinced that his future lay in her notebook. Finally, the girl lay down the pencil and looked at Alex.

"Not every boy is cut out for swimming, Alex. But *you*—you rate very high on the swim-ability matrix. You have the makings of a *fine* swimmer." Alex's little chest puffed out proudly, as a grin crept across his face. He strode to the edge of the pool, and slowly stepped into the shallow end, keeping his cool as the water rose to his thighs, then his chest, then his neck. And (you guessed it) within the week, he was swimming like a fish.

We can't guarantee that you will succeed. But we *can* guarantee that unless you *believe* that success is possible, nothing will change. If you persuade yourself that you are destined to fail, then that's one prophecy that will come true for sure. *All Your Worth* asks for some hard work and some lifelong changes, and that can't happen if you quit before you start.

We won't hit you with a bunch of gobbledygook or ask you to "get in touch with your inner millionaire." Instead we are going to lay out a very simple, two-part approach to help you get ready for success.

First, you'll identify the negative-thinking traps that may be preventing you from accomplishing all your goals. Second, you will learn how to assess the role that negative-thinking traps play in your life, and then banish them, once and for all. That's it—find the traps and get rid of them.

That may sound simple, but the effect is incredibly powerful. If you believe that you are in control of your future and you *can* get straight with your money, then there is no telling just how far you can go.

IDENTIFY YOUR NEGATIVE-THINKING TRAPS

There you stand, ready to try something new. And then "BAM!"—a trap you didn't even see grabs you by the leg, and stops you dead in your tracks. You don't change anything—not because something happened in the real world, but because something happened in your head. A self-destructive belief—a negative-thinking trap—takes hold, and persuades you that you are destined to fail.

Negative-thinking traps develop a momentum of their own. Living with debt and fear can become a habit, rather like smoking or overeating. It's something you get used to, something you build into your daily routine. After a while, you begin to believe there is no other way. Even if there are material changes in your life—you get a raise, the babies grow up—you don't even notice that things could be better, because you hold so tightly to the belief that failure and anxiety are an inevitable part of your life.

It's time to identify your negative-thinking traps. We're going to help you name your traps, one by one. The amazing thing about this exercise is that so long as the traps stay carefully concealed in the shadows, they are powerful. You can't move for fear of getting caught. But once they are uncovered, once you can see them and poke at them a little, their power seems to fade away. After a while, they are nothing more than rusty reminders of an earlier life you have long since left behind.

Here we identify several of the most common negative-thinking traps so that you can begin to uncover them, exposing them to the bright lights and ending their powerful hold.

All-or-Nothing

> I'll never stick to a budget.
> My credit is ruined, so why bother?
> I always carry a balance on my credit card.

Never. Always. Forever. These are the hallmarks of all-or-nothing thinking.

All-or-nothing thoughts add up to one thing: If I can't be perfect, there's no point in trying to be better. One little mistake, one little stumble, and it's all over but the weeping. Quit at the first misstep. Sound familiar?

Over the years, we have seen the concept of financial balance provoke an attack of all-or-nothing fatalism in otherwise reasonable people. *"I'll never cover my Must-Haves on half my income!" "I can't save $2, let alone 20%!"*

Maybe you feel the same way. Maybe you looked at that 50-30-20 formula, and you wanted to throw this book against a wall and shout, "I can't do that!"

If that's how you're feeling, then please listen very carefully. *All Your Worth* is a *lifetime* plan. It is about moving toward a better place, no matter where you start. It is about setting a clear goal while managing the ups and downs that are a part of every life. *All Your Worth* is *not* all-or-nothing.

Getting your money into perfect balance may not be possible for you, at least not right this minute. Maybe you signed a bunch of long-term contracts that you can't get out of. Maybe you are out of work. Maybe you have been robbed. We get it. There may be real circumstances that prevent you from hitting the 50-30-20 goal immediately.

What then?

Remember your mama's advice: *Just do your best.* If you can't save 20%, can you save 15%? If you can't get your Must-Haves down to 50%, can you get them down to 55%? Getting your money in balance is one of those things where close really does count.

> If you can't get your money into perfect
> balance, get as close as you can.

Consider Ross Pennen. After he added up all the numbers, Ross looked at me (Amelia) with his jaw set. "Nope, can't do it." Before I could say a word, he rushed ahead. He had to pay child support, and rent was high, and he was at 58% on Must-Haves, and balance might work for other people but not for him. When he finally paused for a breath, I quietly asked, "Could you do 54%?" Ross was clearly taken aback. "But I can't do 50." I pushed back, "Try 54%." He resisted a little longer ("But it's supposed to be 50!"). Eventually he agreed to give it a try. Within two months, he had pulled his Must-Have expenses to 54%. More important, he trimmed his Wants from 42% to a dead-on 30%—something he would never have tried if he had insisted on all-or-nothing. Now, after more than a decade of living paycheck to paycheck, he is socking away a steady 16% of his income every single month.

I met up with Ross a little over a year later. He was still somewhat combative, and his tendency for perfectionism hadn't disappeared. But there was a certain pride that I hadn't seen before:

> I got a daughter who's a junior at Colorado State. I always told her I didn't have any money, so after a while she just stopped asking. But I started saving up, and I finally sent her something. Just a thousand bucks, but I'm proud to finally help her out a little, y'know? . . . I look at where I used to be, and I go "Damn, I'm glad I'm not there anymore."

Think of it this way: If you can change a 60-40-0 budget to a 55-30-15 plan, you will be *much* better off. Granted, you won't be perfect. But you *will* start getting ahead, each and every month. Moreover, with those kinds of numbers, in a few years you will be in a better place than the overwhelming majority of Americans. And *that* will be something to be proud of.

Money Is Too Hard

> I don't understand finance.
> I'm no good at math.
> Money makes me nervous.
> My financial situation is just too complicated.
> Other people understand money better than I do.

If you agreed with any of these statements, then you are telling yourself that money is too hard for you. There is a good reason to feel shaky about your money skills. A whole world out there is telling you that they get it—and you don't. The business news networks chatter about stock futures and commodity indexes until it sounds like they are speaking Klingon. The financial page runs on about a dip in the exchange rate of the yen and a rise in euros as if everyone in the world knows what they're talking about. The unspoken message is always the same: Money is *hard.*

And maybe the people around you—even people you love very much—have given you the message that money is too hard for you.

Women hear this all the time. In high school, we got steered into home economics, while the boys took *real* economics. Fathers and husbands told us not to worry about money, that they would handle it.

Of course, women are long past the days when they batted their eyelashes demurely while some man offered to "take care of everything." But we still hear lots of variations on the too-hard-for-me theme from women (and plenty of men). I (Amelia) was scheduled to appear on a local news channel, and the station sent a camerawoman to film me at home. Lucie was smart and capable, the sort of in-charge person who gets things done. As we visited during setups and take-downs, she started asking questions about money. She was an independent contractor, and her credit cards were in a tangle. After she ducked a couple of my pointed questions, Lucie laughed sheepishly and said, "You know, I'm just the artistic type. I can't really do numbers." I watched her maneuver the camera for a few more minutes, and then I asked, "How do you figure out the right lighting for the shot?" She launched into a complex explanation that left me in the dust. At the third mention of an orange card and some kind of calibration, I cried, "Wait! You know stuff that is really complicated. If you can hold down this job, I guarantee you can straighten out your spending." She laughed in surprise, but quickly resumed her "I-can't-do-it." But when the shoot was over, she asked if we could schedule a time to come back to work on her financial plan.

Truth was, Lucie didn't need much hands-on help from me. Once she had worked through the basics on her own, she was flying. She called a few weeks later to say thanks, and remarked, "This isn't very hard, you know. You just have to be determined."

Lucie was right: Money isn't that hard. Getting straight with your money can be *challenging*—in the sense that you may have to make some difficult choices and break some long-standing habits—but it isn't *complicated*. You don't have to be great at math, and you don't have to understand a lot of specialized financial terms. Heck, you don't even have to like finance. Getting your money into balance is less about whether you're left-brained or right-brained, and more about your willingness to put in some effort and stick with it.

Take it from us. One of us (Amelia) received a degree in finance from one of the finest business schools in America. The other of us (Elizabeth) is a Harvard law professor who teaches business and commercial law to some of the smartest future lawyers in America. We know this stuff really well, and we're here to tell you that you don't have to be a Wall Street whiz kid to make smart decisions with your money. Most of the complicated financial products, convoluted analyses, and twenty-letter words you hear on the business channel are important to people who are trying to run giant companies, and maybe to a few multizillionaires. But all that jargon and all those complicated calculations aren't particularly relevant for a typical, hardworking person who just wants to take control of her money and build some wealth.

Knowing the ins and outs of advanced finance is a little like knowing how to speak Pashto. If you want to be the ambassador to Afghanistan, then speaking Pashto could be really important. But if you aren't planning any travel to that part of the world, you can live a rich, full life without speaking a single word of Pashto. The same general idea goes for money.

If you still think money is too hard for you, then pause for a moment and probe exactly how helpless you are. Do you stand at the checkout line at the grocery store and pull out all your money and tell the clerk, "Gee, take whatever you want"? Do you see a sale for 30% off and think, "Huh, I wonder what that means?" Do you say to your employer, "Just pay me whatever you want. I can't tell the difference anyway"? Of course not. You stick up for yourself and make smart decisions every single day about money.

Most of what you really need to know to get straight with your money is about as complicated as a trip to the grocery store. You need to be able to comparison shop, so you can tell the difference between a good deal and a bad deal. You need to be able to do a little basic addition and subtraction (or punch numbers into a calculator), so you can figure out how much you are spending. You need to be able to make out a list and stick with it until you get everything done. And you need to be able to ask a question, in case there is something you can't find on your own. That's about it. You don't need to know a lot of fancy new vocabulary words. You don't have to be a whiz at trigonometry. You sure as heck don't need to know the difference between equity swings and stock swaps.

> Getting straight with your money is about
> as complicated as a trip to the grocery store:
> You need to comparison shop,
> add and subtract, stick with a plan,
> and ask questions—nothing more.

One last point about money competence: If a newscaster, an insurance agent, or even your beloved spouse ever makes you feel stupid about money, then all we can say is, *they* are wrong, not you. Turn off the TV, find a new agent, and tell your mate to treat you with the respect you deserve. Because, really and truly, if you are smart enough to earn it, you are more than smart enough to spend it wisely.

Finger-Pointing

My financial troubles are primarily the fault of my
    boyfriend/girlfriend/spouse/ex-spouse.
My basic obligations cost more than I can possibly afford.
My job doesn't pay enough for me to make ends meet.
I'm just not lucky about money matters.
My ex doesn't pay enough support (or: support takes too much
    out of my paycheck), so I can't be financially secure.
Housing in this area is so expensive that I can never get my
    finances straightened out.
My kids just cost too much; I'll never be able to get ahead.

Hey, but maybe these statements are all true! Maybe your ex really is a jerk who doesn't make his support payments, and maybe a one-bedroom condo in your area really does cost more than the Hope diamond. If that is reality, where is the trap?

The trap is in the hidden message: You are telling yourself that you are off the hook. The financial problems you face are someone else's doing, and therefore it's all out of your hands. You are telling yourself there's nothing you can do. And if there is nothing you can do, then you have a free pass to sit on your duff.

Finger-pointing can become a vicious habit. Today it's housing prices, tomorrow it's the kids, the next day it's because the grass is green and the sky is blue. Reason piled on reason explaining why the problems are out of your control, and why you shouldn't bother trying to fix them.

The truth is that there will *always* be a reason why you can't balance your money. There will *always* be someone or something that you can point your finger at. And the reasons will *always* be good reasons. And yet, you know and we know, so long as you stay focused on why everyone and everything else is to blame, you will miss the opportunity to make things better.

Move past the finger-pointing. Just give it up. Even if the reasons are true. It might really be true that your boss doesn't pay what you deserve, that your ex is a first-class stinker, and that you get allergies from watching the Weather Channel on TV. But truth isn't the issue.

Move past the blame because it isn't *helpful*. In fact, it is worse than not helpful; it is downright destructive. Success can't rain down on you so long as finger-pointing is your umbrella.

How do you get beyond finger-pointing?

First, take a minute to get it out of your system. Tell your 4-year-old that it's high time she got a job. Find an ad for a really overpriced condo, and use it to clean up after the dog. Go in the closet and call your boss a penny-pinching slave driver (but not too loudly, of course). When you finish, say out loud, "Enough. I'm done with the blaming. This is useless and it hurts *me*."

And then change the subject. Try substituting a sentence about something you can do to make your financial situation *better*. Your answer may be really bold ("I am going to look for a better-paying job!") or really modest ("Maybe the generic toilet paper isn't so bad"). The point here is not to put pressure on yourself to solve all your problems in one bite. Just stop focusing on whatever you're pointing your finger at, and get your focus back where it belongs—on yourself, and what you plan to *do*.

If you want to get straight with your money, then there are no free passes. There is no oh-well-there's-nothing-I-can-do. Because there is *always* something you can do. *All Your Worth* shows you some smart moves you may not have thought about. Maybe you can't make things perfect, but you can *always* make things better.

Waiting for the Money Bunny

> As soon as I start making a little more money, everything will work out.
> I'm healthy, so I'll be fine without insurance.
> I figure my income will keep going up, so there's no reason for me to worry about the future.
> I can pay my debts any time I want; it's not really a problem.
> I'm young; I don't need to worry about money yet.
> I'm not worried about saving for retirement; something will work out.
> I don't want to think "small" by saving just a little bit at a time.
> I think a lot about winning the lottery.

Ah, if only. If only you win the lottery. (Sure, the odds are 1 in 7,000,000, but someone has to win, right?) If only your no-good bum of an ex gets a great job and starts paying the child support on time. (Which is even less likely than winning the lottery!) If only your crazy Uncle Travis has a bunch of stock certificates in the attic, and he leaves them to you in his will (even though you haven't called him in ten years). If only the Easter Bunny hides an IRA in the bushes, and pays off the car loan while he's at it . . .

We never saw the Easter Bunny, but we sure loved to sit back, imagining all the candies and colored eggs he would soon drop off. There they would be, treats nestled all around just waiting for us to pick them up. Maybe you plan your financial life the same way—just waiting for something or someone to arrive with baskets of money that will shoo away any bad news.

On the surface, it can sound so positive. You tell yourself that your fantasies and daydreams are just an expression of a sunny disposition.

You say, "I believe in myself and my potential." What could be wrong with that?

Nothing—in small doses. A dash of optimism or a moment of idle daydreaming is perfectly fine. Heck, we're not too proud to admit that we've passed a few minutes here and there imagining what we would do if we got a gazillion bucks. The issue is not whether happy fantasies pass through your mind, but whether you let those fantasies guide your actions—or, more to the point, guide you to *in*action.

Money fantasies can become another excuse not to act. If someone or something else is going to make your problems disappear, there's no need to do anything.

Deep down, you probably know that your money fantasies aren't healthy, at least not when they stand between you and the progress you know you need to make. But when you're feeling nervous about your money, it can be so tempting—and so comforting—to spend your time fantasizing about winning the lottery instead of confronting stone-cold reality. If money fantasies are so alluring, how can you shoo them away?

Remember what the Easter Bunny brought: extra treats. No one ever said you could count on the basics to come your way without some work and planning. So here's the way to keep the fantasies in perspective—use them as extra treats. If you have been saving and then you win the lottery, throw a giant party (and invite us)! If your daughter becomes a star cellist and wins a big college scholarship, then celebrate and use her college fund to take a great cruise! And if you buy health insurance and never even catch the sniffles, count yourself as one of the luckiest people on the planet. In other words, if you want to live a better life, you have to agree to let the bunny bring the gumdrops, while you supply the meat and potatoes.

If you still find those money fantasies a little too attractive, just think about this: How much more comfortable would you be with a nice fat bank balance? How nice would life be if you knew that the ringing phone wasn't a bill collector, because you were caught up on all your payments? How much better would you sleep if you knew you were making real progress toward a brighter future? These are the fantasies that you can turn into reality. And we'll show you how.

Counting the Pennies

You have made the commitment: It is time to get straight with your money! So where do you start? First you spend an hour finding the paperwork to redeem the $10 rebate on your new CD player (where is that darned form?). Then you blow another half hour waiting on hold to dispute a $4 charge for a call to Illinois that you are *sure* you never made. Then you spend an hour poring over your FICO credit report, deciphering all those abbreviations because you read somewhere you're supposed to check it every month. (No changes since last month!) And then you spend 45 minutes shredding all your trash (and unjamming the shredder). As evening approaches, you give yourself a big pat on the back—you just spent the *whole day* getting your money into shape! Right?

Wrong. You didn't save any real money, and you didn't make any lasting changes. You just spent a day counting pennies. Sound familiar?

You may be thinking that Grandma always told you to watch your pennies, so what's wrong with that? Everything—if it takes your eye off the dollars.

You have only so much time and energy to focus on money. You need to work, to fix the car, to take care of your kids (or your cat or your girlfriend), and do a zillion other things besides getting straight with your money. There just isn't *time* to chase down every possible financial detail to perfection. There are only so many money minutes in your day, and you have to spend them wisely. If you use them up trying to save $5 instead of $500, you won't get very far.

We once counseled a man who watched every penny—to the exclusion of watching his dollars. Roberto was a fanatic sale chaser, driving miles out of his way to pick up milk at whatever store was having a special. He also kept the most meticulous financial records we have ever seen, carefully photocopying every receipt, filing every bill, and recording every purchase in his computer. He even went so far as to *burn* his old records, figuring that he would never, ever be a victim of identity theft from some guy digging in his trash and finding a form with his name on it. And you know what? Roberto owed thousands of dollars to the IRS because he hadn't gotten around to filing his tax returns in the last three years. He didn't have car insurance (which was illegal) or health insurance (which was dangerous). And he hadn't saved a nickel for retirement. Every week Roberto spent hours saving pennies and updating his financial records. But when it came to what really mattered, his financial house was built on sand.

So what's the alternative to counting the pennies?

Follow the steps in *All Your Worth*.

The steps in this book are designed to keep you focused on the important stuff. Your time is precious, and we won't ask you to waste it chasing after pennies. We will help you stay focused on the dollars. Just stick with us, and don't wander off into double-coupon land.

Once you've completed all the steps in *All Your Worth*, if you still want to go after that $3 rebate, go right ahead. But if you'd rather go spend $3 on a triple-fudge ice-cream cone, we promise not to tell Grandma. You will have made a lot of smart choices about budgeting your time *and* your money, and you will deserve a reward.

BREAK FREE FROM THE TRAPS

We hope by now that you're feeling invigorated, ready to shake off the negative-thinking traps standing between you and success. But there is a chance that today's enthusiasm may be lost to tomorrow's doubts. So now is the time to get ready and to develop a plan of action in case those traps reappear.

If you feel the tug of a negative-thinking trap, follow 3 steps:

1. Identify the trap

Traps have the most power when they are hidden. If you find yourself feeling discouraged, or if you feel like you are just not making the progress you should, look for the trap. When you keep promising yourself that you'll take care of the insurance but it just never happens, look for the trap. When you pull out the papers but you don't seem to get anything accomplished, look for the trap.

Once you identify the trap, it will immediately lose much of its power. And when the trap loses its power, fighting your way out of it becomes much easier. If you find yourself glancing at the enrollment forms for your retirement account and thinking, "My kids will probably take care of me, so I don't really need to save for retirement," that's the time to stop and ask yourself: Have you just fallen into a trap? Are you waiting for the financial Easter Bunny? The trap will lose a lot of its bite just from exposure. Finger-pointing, all-or-nothing thinking, waiting for the money bunny—call it out. Whatever you are thinking, whatever it is that keeps you from changing, flip on the lights and give those thoughts a name.

2. Remember your goals

You are clear about your goals: You want to get straight with your money, to stop the worry and get on the path to a richer life. If you find yourself getting hung up with your old negative-thinking traps, ask yourself: *Are these thoughts helping?* Are your fantasies making your future brighter? Does telling yourself that you are not smart enough make you any better off? Is your all-or-nothing perfectionism really getting you closer to your goal? Is obsessing over discount toothpaste really making you richer? If the answer is no, then you have a rock-solid reason to banish them from your head.

3. Put up a fight

Now comes the time to argue. When you've identified the negative-thinking trap, argue with it. Point by point, tell yourself why your thinking trap isn't right.

Fight with yourself! Call out the negative-thinking trap. Say its name, and then identify the effect it has on you. Tell yourself out loud how this trap is keeping you from acting. Then pop it right in the teeth. Tell the truth—you are capable, you are committed, you are going to take hold of your present and plan your future.

Lucie, the camerawoman who asked Amelia for help, said that talking out loud to herself helped her tackle her credit card debt:

I'd say, "Okay, Lucie, you can hold a 75-pound camera steady in the middle of a hurricane. You know how to change the spark plugs in a Chevy. You can say the names of the presidents in order. Anyone smart enough to do that is smart enough to take on money."

Lucie said that she was doing great until one day the guy she shared an office with came in without her noticing. "I had just announced in this really loud voice, 'Damn it, I can hang wallpaper!' Richie goes, 'Uh, I didn't know you want wallpaper in here, but don't get mad. I'll pay half.' "

Take a moment right now to write down the negative-thinking traps you fall into. Next to each trap, write down your rebuttal. We've entered some of the most common traps to help get you started.

EXERCISE: FIGHT YOUR NEGATIVE-THINKING TRAPS

If you fall into this trap . . .	Tell yourself . . .
Money is too hard; I just can't do it.	I'm smart enough to run a house or earn a paycheck, so I'm smart enough to manage money wisely.
It's someone else's fault that I'm in financial trouble.	I will do everything in my power to make my financial future as good as it can be.
I have a million financial things to take care of—I'll never get it all done!	I'll focus on the most important things, and let the little stuff go.
Everything will get better when _____ happens to me.	Everything will get better when I take action.
I'll never get to 50-30-20, so why bother trying?	I may not be perfect, but I can make things better.
Trap: _____ _____ _____	Rebuttal: _____ _____ _____

Trap: _____   Rebuttal: _____
_____   _____
_____   _____
Trap: _____   Rebuttal: _____
_____   _____
_____   _____

Don't hold yourself back. You can be the most effective, most energetic fighter on your own behalf. You just have to do it.

MAKE THE COMMITMENT

Are you ready for change? Not just a little interested, but really committed? Are you ready to *believe* you can swim to the other end of the pool? Do you know that you can arm-wrestle with your checkbook and win? Because that's what this step is all about. It's time to get rid of the negative-thinking traps and the excuses for staying put, so that you are really, truly ready to make the most of this opportunity.

What will it take to change? You won't have to perform any magic tricks, and there won't be any mission-impossible assignments. You just have to commit to do your honest-to-goodness *best*.

If you are ready to get serious, then write it down. You signed a contract for your cell phone—three long years. You signed for the car loan—four years. You signed for the credit cards, the gym membership, and the PTA bake sale. You make deals all the time. So now make a deal for yourself.

Here are some terms for your contract. Put a check mark next to each statement you are ready to commit to. And if the spirit moves you, add some more that are very special to your circumstances. And when you're finished, sign your name at the bottom. This is one of the most important commitments you may ever make, so take it seriously.

YOUR CONTRACT WITH YOUR FUTURE

*Check all
that apply*

I am ready to commit the time to shop for a better deal on
the things I need.   _____

I am willing to take steps to make sure that I will never be a
victim of any person or company that wants to rip me off.   _____

I am willing to forgive myself and others (my spouse, my ex,
my parents) for past financial mistakes, and to work from this
point forward to make my future secure.   _____

I am willing to make my financial well-being a top priority
in my life.   _____

I am willing to talk straight about money, and not fool myself
into believing things that I know in my heart are untrue.   _____

I will be alert to any negative-thinking traps, and I will work to
root them out.   _____

I know that I must take responsibility for my financial future,
and I am committed to making permanent changes.   _____

I will do my best to follow the steps in *All Your Worth*.   _____

Signed _____   Date _____

Are you ready to sign up? Is your commitment real?

If you checked off most of these statements and you committed yourself to follow through, then you are on the road to healthy change. You are willing to work hard, and you are committed to creating a better future. Congratulations (and keep it up)!

If you found yourself skipping past many of the statements, or shaking your head "no," then you aren't committing to change. If you don't want to sign and date this, you may still be sitting on the fence. Maybe you are stuck in one of the negative-thinking traps, telling yourself that things will work out somehow or that if you can't be perfect, there's no point in trying hard. Or maybe it just seems more comfortable not to change.

If you're still sitting on the fence, ask yourself: Can you commit to do more? In this world where nothing is certain, there is one thing we can absolutely promise you: Tomorrow will come. We want you to get ready for it! We want you to have the best possible chance for a good tomorrow. Make the commitment for yourself and for your future.

In the next chapters we will walk you through the step-by-step process to get your money in balance. Some of the steps may come easily, and some may be harder. Whenever you hit a roadblock, go back to your contract. Remind yourself of what you committed to on this very day. Keep asking yourself: What can I do to get over this hurdle? What can I do to make things better? The goal here is to make your money—and your life—the best it can be. So get out there and take a step toward a better future.

3

---■---

Step Three:
Count the Dollars, Not the Pennies

Clip coupons. Get the generic cereal. Buy your pasta in bulk. Take a brown-bag lunch. Watch out for the lattes. Everywhere you go, the same old advice. *Watch your pennies.*

Well, it's time to stop counting pennies, or at least to put it on hold for a while. Why? Is it bad to save a bit here and there? Of course not. But if you are like most people, you have only so many minutes you can devote to worrying about your money. And we want you to spend those precious minutes where they count the most: *your dollars.* Instead of spending your time on how to squeeze a few nickels out of small purchases, it's time to focus on the really big expenses, where an hour on the phone can save you thousands of dollars.

This step starts with an incredibly simple premise: *Dollars are worth more than pennies.*

Of course, this isn't exactly breaking news. But stop and think about it. When you add up all the time you spend making decisions about how to spend your money, what gets the most time? If you're like most people, you spend hours every month thinking about the prices of the little stuff. A pair of shoes, a pound of tomatoes, a bottle of wine—you look at the price tag, you comparison shop. You weigh your options, thinking twice before you buy.

Now think about the big-ticket items. Your home or apartment. Your car. Your insurance. Sure, you probably thought hard about those purchases . . . once. But when was the last time you thought about them? You probably just write those checks, month in and month out, without thinking about whether you're getting the most for your dollars.

If you are overspending on these big monthly bills, then money is draining out of your pocket a lot faster than you can replace it by getting double coupons on your frozen vegetables. This step—the foundational step for getting straight with your money—will help you get your big Must-Have purchases into balance.

The monthly Must-Haves are the very heart of your money plan. The Must-Haves claim more money than anything else you buy. They keep your life dignified and secure. The Must-Haves are the first, last, and most important purchases, around which all other money decisions are arranged. Balancing your Must-Haves will create the bedrock upon which you can build your entire money plan, for the rest of your life.

BUT I NEED THIS STUFF?

It seems so sensible. Prudent. Maybe even a little conservative.

You spend your money on the things you *need*. Who could fault you for that?

No one goes on television or writes a book that criticizes people for spending too much on the basics. Oh sure, someone may chide people for buying an oversized McMansion or a brand-new Lexus. But the real point is that those things are more than anyone really needs—fancy, oversized, expensive stuff that normal people could easily do without. Who says you shouldn't spend all your money on a normal house and a normal car?

We do.

It doesn't matter if you are living in a regular house. It doesn't matter if you are driving an average car. It doesn't matter if all of your Must-Haves seem perfectly ordinary and no different from those of your neighbors. Because you can't use your neighbors as a guide. Why not? *Because most of your neighbors are not building wealth.* They probably owe money on their credit cards, and they don't have any plans for a better future. They may not talk about it, but the odds are high that they worry about money. A lot.

In recent years, worry over money has become normal. Living out of balance has become normal. Surveys show that fighting over money with the people you love has become normal. Which all adds up to one very important point: *Normal isn't good enough.* If you want to build real wealth and make the most of your worth, then you need to have a plan that is *better* than normal. And that starts with getting your Must-Haves into balance. So even if this seems hard or strange or just "not normal," we want you to tackle your Must-Haves head-on.

Imagine, for a moment, what it will be like to get your Must-Haves into balance. Think of this as like that little mental vacation you take when you imagine what you would look like if you lost ten pounds or how it would feel to cook dinner in a remodeled kitchen. Take a short money vacation: Imagine what it would feel like to have plenty of money in the bank. Picture yourself shopping for clothes or taking a little weekend trip. Does it seem easier, more relaxed, maybe even a little more fun? Now pull up a second vision. Imagine how much safer you would feel if you knew you could miss a few months of work, and you'd be able to cover the rent or the mortgage. And now try one more thought. Imagine yourself socking away some money, month after month. Think about a nicer house, travel, college for the kids. Think about your dreams, think about getting closer to them each day. Sounds good, doesn't it? Keep that feeling in the front of your mind as you pull your Must-Have expenses into balance because that's what you can turn into reality.

This step will require some real effort, but there is some really good news too: *Once you get this right, you won't have to do it again for a long, long time.* Your monthly Must-Haves are recurrent payments—payments that stay roughly the same, month in and month out (and even year in and year out). So once you get them straight, they stay straight. Which means you can put them on the back burner where they belong, and quit worrying.

> Once you get your Must-Have expenses right,
> you won't have to worry about them
> again for a long, long time.

Even better, your savings from getting the Must-Haves into balance will come back to you, month after month. That extra money will be yours, automatically. That means there will be more money for fun, and more money for your future. And less time spent worrying about money, so you can focus on what really matters—the rest of your life.

So roll up your sleeves, get out your pencil, and get ready to go. It's time to save some dollars.

1. Set a Goal

Getting your Must-Haves aligned is about balance. Not too much, and not too little. Step One showed you what the right balance is for most people—spending about 50% of your take-home pay on Must-Haves, so you have 30% for Wants and 20% for Savings.

Calculate your Must-Have target in Worksheet 5.

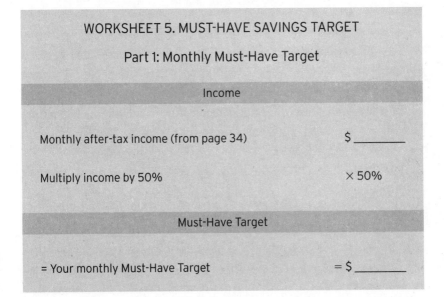

WORKSHEET 5. MUST-HAVE SAVINGS TARGET

Part 1: Monthly Must-Have Target

Income	
Monthly after-tax income (from page 34)	$ _____
Multiply income by 50%	× 50%
Must-Have Target	
= Your monthly Must-Have Target	= $ _____

The last line in Part 1 is your ideal spending amount for your monthly Must-Haves. Compare this number with your current monthly Must-Have expenditures (from page 39) to find out how much you need to save. If your current Must-Haves are less than your target, this means you are spending less than 50% of your income on Must-Haves. You don't need to make any cuts in your monthly Must-Haves, so you can skip Part 2 of this worksheet.

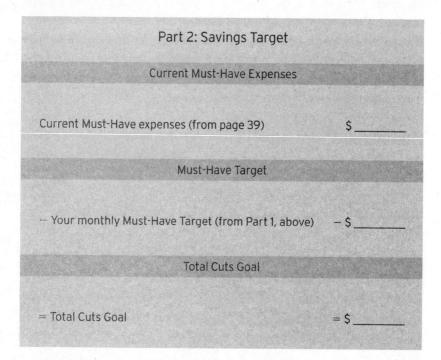

Part 2: Savings Target

Current Must-Have Expenses

Current Must-Have expenses (from page 39) $ _____

Must-Have Target

— Your monthly Must-Have Target (from Part 1, above)   – $ _____

Total Cuts Goal

= Total Cuts Goal   = $ _____

The last line in Part 2 of Worksheet 5 shows you what you're working toward—the total cuts you want to find.

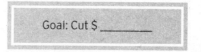

Goal: Cut $ _____

Keep the number in front of you because it is your goal: This is the amount of money you want to squeeze from your Must-Have expenses, so you can get your monthly spending into balance. Every time you make a cut in your Must-Have expenses, put it toward that goal.

Does your goal seem like a big number? Stick with it. We will help you get there, step-by-step. And if you ultimately decide that you want to stay a little heavy on the Must-Have expenses for a while, we will show you the steps you need to take to protect yourself.

What if you are already spending less than 50% of your income on Must-Haves? Congratulations! Your Must-Haves are in balance with your income, so you have one less thing to worry about. Even so, go ahead and follow the next section, which focuses on places to save money without cramping your style. After all, there's no reason to keep putting money in someone else's pocket if you can keep it for yourself!

2. Cut the Easy Stuff

When you are cutting back on expenses, start in the easiest places—the spots where you can make cuts that you will never feel. The price comparisons may take a little time, but the results are the best—all gain, no pain. Your day-to-day living will feel the same, but you can keep more of your money.

Lower Your Insurance Costs

Yes, insurance sounds boring. We don't know any little kids who zoom around the living room pretending to be insurance reps. And shopping for insurance sounds like about as much fun as cleaning the gutters in a rainstorm. Even so, *saving* money sounds good, right? And talk about a place where the saving is easy! A couple of phone calls, and you can save month in and month out, *for years.*

The big secret of insurance is that most people are paying too much—way too much. The companies just keep pocketing the profits. Homeowners' insurance, life insurance, car insurance—you name it, most people just overpay. If you haven't shopped in the last two years, you probably pay too much. If you only got one quote before you signed up, you probably pay too much. If your real estate agent arranged for the insurance when you bought the house, you probably pay too much. And if you have a deductible less than $500, you probably pay too much.

Let's start with a quick review of which types of insurance you need. Car insurance and homeowners' (or renters') insurance are the most obvious. Health and disability insurance are also a must, but they're a little trickier (and most people get them at work), so we'll talk about them in a separate section later on. If you have dependents, you need life insurance. And if you're over 55, long-term-care insurance may also be a good idea.

Shopping for insurance isn't hard. You don't have to drive anywhere, and you don't have to try anything on. Hop online for some quotes or pull out the yellow pages and call a couple of agents. They will be eager to quote you the price for a new policy.

Here are some tips for saving on your homeowners'/renters', life, and car insurance bills:

• *Consider buying all of your insurance from one company.* Some companies give big discounts if you carry your homeowners', car, disability, and life insurance in the same place. Ask.

• *Ask about other discounts.* Insurance companies offer all kinds of discounts—some of which might surprise you. Discounts for non-smokers. For burglar alarms. For smoke detectors. For reaching the age of 65 (or 55). For paying annually instead of monthly. Amelia even got a discount because her husband has a degree in engineering. (We're still trying to figure that one out.) So be sure to ask for a list of *all* the discounts; maybe you'll discover that having naturally curly hair will pay off once again.

• *Take the largest deductible you can.* Choose something that would hurt to pay—not enough pain to make you cry, but enough to make you say "ouch" out loud. Over the long run, insuring against the little things, like $200 damage from a hailstorm or a $150 ding in the parking lot, costs more in premiums than you actually get back. Besides, filing a small claim usually costs you more than it's worth in the long run, because the insurance company can use your claim as a reason to raise your rates. Here's the general rule: Take the biggest deductible they offer (typically $1000 for auto insurance and $2500 for homeowners' insurance). If you don't have enough in the bank to cover a deductible that large, don't worry; we'll help you get there soon.

- *Get at least 5 quotes.* The goal is to save money, so don't take the first offer you get. And don't just get a bunch of quotes from a single agent, who may have an incentive to steer you to a certain insurer. Keep shopping until you get quotes from at least five different sources.
- *After you get your quotes, contact your current insurance company.* Tell them your lowest quote and ask if they can beat it. Sometimes you can get a good deal without the bother of switching.
- *Credit rating affects your insurance quotes.* If your credit rating is low, make a commitment to shop for insurance again after six months of clean living, and to shop again after six more months. As your credit rating climbs, your insurance premiums will drop. Remember, insurance plans aren't like cell phone contracts: If you find a better deal, you can switch whenever you want.
- *Watch out for the extras.* You need car insurance in case you get into an accident; steer clear of add-ons like roadside assistance and free rental cars. Likewise, you need a check when your house burns down, not when the faucet leaks or the dishwasher breaks. Don't sign up for the little stuff. It is nearly always a bad bargain.
- *Choose the lowest premiums you can find—from a reputable company.* Insurance companies are all pretty much the same, so long as they're high-quality companies. To judge the quality of a particular insurer, find its rating from an independent judge like A. M. Best, Moody's, or S&P. (These ratings are available online, or you can ask the insurance company to tell you.) So long as an insurer has a good rating, get the lowest quote you can and don't worry about which company sponsors the fastest car at Indy.

Get Rid of the Insurance You Don't Need

Now that you are spending less on the insurance you need, it is time to get rid of the insurance you *don't* need. This advice may surprise you; after all, it seems so responsible to buy insurance—so why not buy more? But insurance is like anything else that's for sale: Sometimes it's worth the money, and sometimes it isn't. Below are the most common insurance rip-offs that you should stay away from:

• *Credit disability insurance (or credit unemployment insurance).* Credit card companies now offer insurance on their own credit card balances. These are bad deals squared! They say they will cover you if you lose your job or get seriously ill, which sounds pretty good. But— and this is a very big "but"—these policies are incredibly expensive and offer very flimsy benefits. Most of these policies do nothing more than let you skip your monthly payments on the balance you were carrying at the time you got sick or lost your job. This means that if you don't carry a balance, the policy is completely, totally useless.

Even if you do carry a balance on your card, the company doesn't pay it off; they just suspend interest (for a while), without giving you any new credit to cope with the costs of losing your job. (And some of these policies don't even suspend interest payments; they just sock you with a bigger bill down the road!) This kind of "insurance" is a real sucker's bet. If you're carrying it, drop it today—and demand a refund for the unused portion.

• *Credit card loss protection.* The FTC has identified credit card loss protection as one of the top three scams in America, taking in more than 3 million people in the last year. This insurance promises to cover your losses if your card is stolen and the thief goes on a spending spree. Sounds good, but here's the catch: Federal law *already* limits your loss to $50 per card! You might as well buy an insurance policy to cover you if you drop a bag of groceries on the sidewalk—sure, it is a nuisance, but you don't stand to lose much money.

• *Identity theft protection.* This is the latest scam, primarily marketed by credit card companies. (Hmm, notice any pattern about insurance marketed by credit card companies?) Sure, the protection sounds good, but stop to ask yourself: Can a company really prevent thieves from using your personal information to their advantage? Of course not. The benefits of most of these policies add up to little more than someone making a few phone calls on your behalf if you become a victim. Do you want to pay big bucks each and every month, just so someone may someday make a couple of phone calls? Nope. If you have identity theft insurance, dump it.

• *Specialty life insurance products.* Life insurance is there to replace your income and to provide for your dependents if something happens to you. Sounds simple, but there are an awful lot of insurance peddlers who are making fat profits by making things seem a whole lot more complicated than they actually are.

- *Insurance for kids.* Gerber Life and other companies have made a booming business out of preying on the fears of young parents, and, in our opinion, they deserve a face full of strained peas for doing this. Kids don't earn income, and they don't have dependents, so they don't need life insurance—plain and simple. If you want to put something aside for your kids, put money in a college savings plan or buy a savings bond. Put your money into something they can use later on. But don't waste your money on a life insurance policy.

- *Cash-Value insurance.* Also known as "whole life" or "universal" life insurance, this is ordinary life insurance with a savings plan tacked on. Cash-value insurance is quite expensive, and it requires you to hand over control of your savings plan to an insurance company that usually gets mediocre returns. These policies also tend to charge very high agent fees, which usually wipe out any tax savings or other benefits. Most experts agree that you'll get a lot better results if you just buy ordinary term life insurance—and invest the difference on your own.

- *Mortgage life insurance.* This pays off the mortgage on your home if you die. That sounds good, but it costs *three times* more than an ordinary life insurance policy with similar benefits. You would be better off taking the same money and buying more life insurance, which could pay off the mortgage *and* leave a lot left over for your loved ones. If you have mortgage life insurance, call and cancel right away.

- *Accidental death insurance.* This is life insurance—with a twist. It only covers you if you die in an accident. Since only 5% of deaths are from accidents, odds are very high that your loved ones would never collect a dime. Pass it up.

- *People with no dependents.* If you don't have dependents, cancel your life insurance. If no one is counting on you to take care of them, then don't pay an insurance company for protection that no one needs.

• *Odd insurance.* All kinds of companies offer all kinds of odd bits of insurance. The phone company will insure your phone jacks—for a monthly fee. The pest control company will insure your house against termites. The dishwasher manufacturer will sell you an extended warranty. The travel agent will sell you flight insurance in case the plane crashes. Some companies will even sell you alien-abduction insurance. Most of these policies are way overpriced for what you get. Unless you have some special reason to believe you are vulnerable (like your basement is full of tangled old phone lines or there's a flying saucer that hovers over your house), don't waste your money.

Get a Discount on Your Student Loans

Still paying off that degree in medieval history? Many student loan issuers will give you a discount if you are careful to pay on time, or if you authorize monthly transfers from your bank account. For example, Sallie Mae (the nation's largest issuer of student loans) will slice 2 percentage points off the interest rate on certain loans if you have made your payments on time for the past two years. Ask your student loan issuer if you can qualify for any discounts; it is worth a phone call. But watch out for private banks that offer to consolidate your student loans; they may lower your monthly payment, but usually at the cost of keeping you in debt longer than necessary. The goal is to get a cheaper interest rate *without* prolonging your payments.

Reshop Your Mortgage—But Be Careful

If you haven't checked your mortgage rate in the past year or so, then it is worth shopping. This may be your single biggest opportunity to shave money off your Must-Haves without changing a thing about how you live. But be warned: This can be dangerous territory. The rules of the game are changing fast, and there are a lot of companies (including some with very big names) that are doing their best to cheat you. So keep alert and watch your step.

Here are the 6 rules of mortgage refinancing:

1. *Arm Yourself Before You Call.* You can save a lot of time in the long run and make things a lot easier if you get ready before you start shopping.

- *Clean up your credit report.* The mortgage lender will start by ordering a copy of your credit report, so your best bet is to clear up any errors ahead of time. Order a copy of your credit report from each of the three big credit bureaus: Equifax, Experian, and TransUnion. (Depending on where you live, you can get your report for free or for a very low fee.) Steer clear of anyone who offers to clean up your credit report for you; they charge a lot of money, and most of them don't do any good anyway. This is strictly a do-it-yourself job.

    If you find any errors, notify the credit bureau immediately. Here are some common errors to look out for: mistakes in your name, Social Security number, and other personal information; accounts that are not yours; bankruptcies that are more than 10 years old, and other negative information that is more than 7 years old (by law, the credit bureau is required to remove that information); credit inquiries that are more than 2 years old; missing notations when you've disputed a charge; list of credit card and mortgage accounts that are in good standing; closed accounts that are incorrectly listed as open. According to a recent poll, 1 in 4 credit reports contains an error serious enough to keep you from getting a good loan, so be sure to take the time to check your credit report before you apply for the mortgage.

- *Gather your financial information.* Gather your pay stubs, tax returns, bank statements, and the like. You'll need this before you can finalize your applications, so you might as well gather it ahead of time. You can usually get a more accurate quote if you have all the information at the time you apply.

- *Find out your current mortgage balance.* This should be listed on your monthly mortgage statement. If you've thrown that out, then call the mortgage company and ask.

- *Learn how much your house is worth.* The lenders will need to know this so they can calculate a "loan-to-value ratio" (which tells them how much equity you have in the house). The more equity you have, the better your interest rate. Eventually you will need an official estimate of the value of your house, but having a general sense ahead of time can help you with your shopping. So check out the open houses in your neighborhood and take a look at the real estate section of the newspaper so you get a ballpark estimate of what your house is worth.

2. *Get multiple quotes.* Before you buy something big—say, a washing machine or a new television—you probably check prices at two or three stores. Well, your mortgage probably costs 200 times more than your washing machine, so you should talk to 400–600 mortgage companies, right? Okay that's a bit much, but you get the point—shopping hard for a mortgage can save you far more money than shopping for pretty much anything else. So put in the time to get it right. Here's our rule of thumb: Five quotes before you quit. Five different mortgage companies with lots of information and plenty of range to compare. And if the quotes are all over the place, then you may want to get five more. The bottom line is that the time you spend here pays off big-time.

3. *Never forget that the mortgage broker does NOT work for you.* The mortgage broker, like an insurance broker, gets you price quotes from a lot of different places, and gets a commission for his services. So far, so good. *But,* mortgage brokers (unlike most insurance brokers) often get extra commissions from the lender if they talk you into taking a mortgage with a higher interest rate than you actually qualify for. That's right: They get kickbacks for steering you to a bad deal. And it's perfectly legal, so you'd better beware.

Yes, it is your money. Yes, you choose which lender will have your mortgage. Yes, the broker will tell you that he "checked with all the banks" and that he found you "a great deal." But the fact is, mortgage brokers are a lot like car salespeople. The more you pay, the more they make. A recent study at Harvard Law School showed that people who went to mortgage brokers paid, on average, over $1,000 more than people who went directly to the mortgage lender.

Does this mean you should never use a mortgage broker? Not necessarily. There are some reputable brokers who will give you a perfectly fair quote. (And there are some mortgage companies that will steer you to a bad deal if you *don't* use a broker.) But you should never count on a lone broker, a single Web site, or just one lender to show you all your options. The lesson is straightforward: *You* must get on the phone and get quotes from several different sources. If you're not sure if a particular company is a mortgage broker, just ask. And keep asking questions until you are sure you have the best deal.

4. *Do not increase the amount of money you borrow.* There are lots of people (including a number of so-called financial experts) who will tell you that it's smart to "cash out" your home equity and take on a bigger mortgage. Well, we're here to tell you it isn't smart. In fact, it is just plain dangerous. You are not "cashing" anything. You are just borrowing money that you will have to pay back someday—and you are doing it in the most dangerous way possible. If something goes wrong and you can't pay, the mortgage company gets to take away your house. Later in this book we will talk about home equity loans in depth, but for now just remember this simple rule: When you refinance your mortgage, don't let the bank talk you into taking on a single dollar of new debt.

5. *Watch out for fees, points, and other fine print.* Picture this: a team of lawyers fanning out through a forest to lay bear traps, which they carefully cover over with leaves. Then switch the image: The forest is really just a mortgage agreement, and the leaves are just words to cover up what they are doing. But the traps are real, and you need to make sure that they aren't in your contract. Here's a list of the questions to ask, along with the answers you want to hear:

- *What is the interest rate?* By law, every mortgage lender must quote you the annual interest rate. (You may also be quoted the Annual Percentage Rate, or APR, which lumps certain fees into the total cost.)

   Once you have the annual interest rate, you can make an apples-to-apples comparison on the interest rate, which is probably the most important part of the loan. Here's a rule of thumb: Unless you have recently declared bankruptcy or have *really* bad credit (and we're not talking about a couple of late payments), if someone wants to charge you more than the average market rate (which is listed in the newspaper and available at www.freddiemac.com), this is probably a bad deal.

- *How many points are on the loan?* A "point" is just jargon for an extra fee of 1% of the total amount of the mortgage loan. Generally speaking, there is a tradeoff between points and interest rate: A loan with fewer points will have a slightly higher interest rate, and vice versa. If you think you will sell the house or refinance again in the near future, then your best bet is usually to avoid the points and pay the higher rate.

  Regardless of how long you plan to stay in the house, you should steer clear of any mortgage that charges more than 1–2 points. Don't assume that all big lenders charge about the same fees. Not long ago, when most companies were charging less than 1 point on refinancing, Wells Fargo reportedly charged some customers as much as *10–12* points!*

- *What are the closing costs, origination costs, and other fees?* Ask for a "Good Faith Estimate" of closing, origination, and other costs, and use this information when you do your comparison shopping. If the fees are unduly large, or if the estimate is in a range that is too wide to be useful (for example, we heard of one company that tells people that the fees are anywhere from $0 to $12,000!), walk away. This isn't a company you can trust for the next 30 years.

- *How long is the payoff period?* The typical mortgage payoff period is 30 years. But if someone tries to steer you to a 40-year loan or an "interest-only" loan (where you *never* pay off your mortgage!), run the other way. And if you have a relatively short time left to pay on your mortgage—15 years or less—get a 10-year or 15-year loan, rather than a 30-year. Lower monthly payments are great, but not at the cost of keeping you in debt for more years than necessary.

- *Is this a fixed or variable rate?* If rates are low, then it is a good idea to lock in the rate for as long as you plan to live in your house. You will pay slightly more for a fixed-rate loan, but the

* Ken Shimamoto, "Wells Fargo Woes," *Fort Worth Weekly,* 2003.

security is worth it; the rate on a variable loan can go up at any time. If you think you will stay in this house for the rest of your life, get a 30-year fixed-rate mortgage. If you are pretty sure you will move on in a few years, you might consider a mortgage that is fixed just for the first 5 or 7 years, which tends to be cheaper than a 30-year fixed loan. Brokers call such mortgages ARMs, for adjustable rate mortgages. At the end of the 5- or 7-year period, the rate can vary, but by then you will have sold the house and moved on. But stay away from any ARM that lasts less than 5 years; the risk that rates will rise while you're still living there is just too high. And if you're not really sure whether you'll move or stay put, your safest bet is still a 30-year fixed loan. It costs a little more, but 30 years of easy sleeping is well worth the price.

- *Is there a balloon payment?* If the answer is yes, walk away. A "balloon payment" is a giant payment that will be required of you at some point in the future (on top of your usual monthly payments). These are notorious scams that have cost countless homeowners tens of thousands of dollars in extra fees, and many have even lost their homes.
- *Is there a prepayment penalty?* If the answer is yes, walk away. If you need to sell your home, or if you want to refinance to obtain a better rate in the future, a prepayment penalty leaves you at the mercy of your mortgage company—paying extra for the privilege of paying off your loan.
- *Is there a Yield Spread Premium (YSP)?* This is industry-speak for the kickback that gets paid to brokers for steering you to a bad deal. Ask if the loan has a YSP. If the answer is yes, walk away. And if you can't get a straight answer, run away. These aren't people you want to deal with.
- *Do I have to take out Private Mortgage Insurance (PMI)?* When you buy a home with a small down payment (less than 20% of the purchase price), most lenders require that you take on Private Mortgage Insurance (PMI). If you get in trouble and the bank forecloses, the PMI will pay the mortgage company off. It doesn't benefit you and it doesn't help you hold on to your

house, so it's really only there to help the mortgage lender, not you.

If the lender tells you that you have to buy PMI, try another lender. If you have built up some equity and your credit is good, some lenders will waive the PMI requirement even if you haven't hit the magical 20% mark.

If PMI is a must, then be sure to ask what the cost is, and use this as part of your comparison shopping. If the lender tells you that your loan includes "single-premium PMI," then run the other way. Single-premium PMI charges you an up-front "single premium" for a period of coverage (typically five years), which you have to pay even if you sell the house. Single-premium mortgage insurance is such a rip-off that several consumer groups have advocated outlawing it altogether.

6. *If you are over 60, or African-American, or Latino, shop even harder.* Here's a tough reality that no one wants to talk about: African-Americans, Latinos, and older Americans are specifically targeted for high-priced mortgages. Take it straight from the mortgage lender's mouth; when a loan officer at a major bank was asked how she decided which customers to hit with extra fees, here's what she said:

> If someone appeared uneducated, inarticulate, was a minority, or was particularly old or young, I would try to include all the [additional costs] CitiFinancial offered.*

In other words, this company's lending agents routinely steered families to higher-cost loans whenever they thought there was a chance they could get away with it, and they thought they could get away with targeting certain groups. This wasn't an isolated incident; one study showed that on average, people who live in *high-income* African-American neighborhoods get charged *more* for their loans than people who live in *low-income* white neighborhoods.

This isn't fair. This isn't right. Most of the time, it isn't even legal. But the fact is, you need to protect yourself. Get some of your quotes

---

* Paul Beckett, "Citigroup's 'Subprime' Reforms Questioned," *Wall Street Journal,* July 18, 2002.

online or over the phone, so a banker can't try to steer you to a bad deal based on the color of your skin or the gray in your hair. If you live in a neighborhood that is predominantly African-American or Latino, be sure to get quotes from banks outside your neighborhood. And, whatever else you do, get more quotes than you think you need. We know that's a lot of work, and, as we said, it isn't fair that you should be put out because of other people's prejudice. But sharks are preying on your community, and you don't want to get eaten alive. So do what is necessary to protect yourself and your loved ones.

When you have made up your mind and decided to take the plunge, request that the "HUD-1" be sent to you the day *before* the closing. The HUD-1 is a form that lists every single expense, and every mortgage lender is required to provide one. You can look it over on your own time, and you can compare it with the estimate the bank had given you. If you see new costs, or if you just don't like something, walk away. And if something has changed on closing day, don't sign anything. There are scam artists who make their money off bait-and-switch mortgages, so don't get caught. I (Amelia) have a close friend who discovered a prepayment penalty buried in her loan contract when she showed up on closing day. When she refused to sign, the mortgage broker pulled a separate set of papers out of his briefcase. As it turned out, he was carrying *two* sets of mortgage papers, on the off chance that he could get away with tacking on some extra charges at the last minute!

So be ready to walk away. You already have a mortgage, so you can take your time. There is too much money at stake to go forward with people you don't have confidence in.

Even after you sign, federal law gives you three days to cancel the deal and get all your money back. These are your rights. Refinancing a mortgage is a big deal. Getting it right—or wrong—could make a big difference in how much money you have over your lifetime. So be tough.

Refinancing is hard work, and it can be costly, so you don't want to do it very often. But if you are very careful and you shop around, you can save a lot of money. Think of refinancing your mortgage as a temporary job. You'll do some extra work for a couple of weeks, and you'll continue to collect the rewards for years to come. Now that's the best temping gig you'll ever get!

If You Are Renting, Negotiate a Better Deal

What if you rent and you need to cut your Must-Have expenses? Is there anything you can do? No guarantees, but there are some things you can try that may cut your costs.

If your landlord tries to raise the rent, that's a particularly good time to negotiate. Do a little comparison shopping, so you know whether your rent is in line with other apartments in the area. And be sure to check out the tenant laws in your area; many cities limit how much your landlord can raise your rent in a single year.

Once you've done your research, talk to your landlord (or write a note, if talking face-to-face gets all the butterflies fluttering in your stomach). Sometimes a landlord would rather take a lower rent than deal with another vacancy. Handle this diplomatically—explain that you are trying to bring your budget in line, you really like the place and would like to stay, but the cost is just a bit more than you think you can safely manage.

Another possibility is to offer your services in exchange for a break on your rent. Many landlords run small operations—a few houses, a small apartment building—with no big, professional staff to run the place. Landlords will sometimes reduce the rent for a tenant who sweeps out the common areas, handles simple maintenance jobs, or paints vacant apartments. Or maybe your landlord provides something that you could do without? If your apartment comes with two parking places, could you offer to give one back—for a reduced rent? The circumstances will vary from place to place, but you get the idea. Keep your eyes open, and you may be able to trim your monthly rent.

Dump the Long-Term Contracts

"First month free!" "Save $10 a month!" "No payments until January!"
For one of us (Amelia) it was a gym membership. Not far from

where I lived, the gym was so bright and cheerful, just chock-full of new equipment. And a 2-year contract wasn't all that long, right?

You can already guess how this story goes. For the first couple of months I went to the gym regularly, diligently swimming laps and attending aerobics class. Then I twisted my ankle. Then my boss asked me to work late for a few weeks. Then summer rolled around, and it seemed so much nicer just to head to the beach.

I tried getting out of the contract. No dice. I got mad, and being young and a little hotheaded, I just quit paying. So the gym sent a collections agency after me. They put a black mark on my credit report, and I ended up paying the balance anyway (a year after the membership had ended!). Eight years later, I *still* got hassled about that gym membership when my husband and I applied to refinance our home mortgage. What a nightmare!

It was painful, but I learned a lesson worth all $380 of that stupid gym membership: *Don't sign a long-term contract for things that aren't Must-Haves.* It's okay to buy your home, your car, or your college degree on a monthly payment plan, but for anything else, it is a really bad idea.

> Don't sign long-term contracts for things
> that aren't absolutely essential.

Wherever possible, get rid of the long-term contracts. If you're in the middle of a 2-year cell phone contract or a 3-year gym membership, let it run out and don't renew. And if you're about to sign new paperwork, don't do it. Get a prepaid cell phone (so you pay only if you use it). Steer clear of long-term commitments to satellite TV. And avoid those long-term gym memberships! Sign up at the YMCA (which typically runs month to month), or just take up jogging.

But you can get such a good deal! We know, they'll give you first-month-free or 10% off or a new green toaster if you'll just sign up for 2 years. But stop and think. *Why* are they offering such a sweet deal? Because they're nice guys? Of course not. They offer all those gimmicks and freebies because they know that without that contract, odds are you'll drop out. You'll stop going to the gym, or quit watching HBO, or just decide the cell phone isn't worth it. In other words, they know you probably won't want their product for the full 2 years and that's exactly why they want to tie you down with a contract.

There's another reason not to sign on the dotted line. Step One laid out three conditions for an expense to be classified as a Must-Have: 1. It is necessary for your basic safety and dignity. 2. You would spend money on it even if you lost your job. 3. You couldn't live without this purchase for six months. So how do these companies turn a Want into a Must-Have? By getting you to sign a contract. Consider my gym membership. I could have lived in dignity without it (although my buns of steel might have turned into buns of Play-Doh). If I had lost my job, I would have dropped that membership in a heartbeat. But when I signed that long-term contract, I just flipped a Want into a Must-Have. Why? Because the minute I signed that contract, I put my gym membership on a par with my car payment and my apartment lease: I became legally obligated to make that payment, *no matter what.* If my hours got cut or if the transmission fell out of my car, that was just too bad. The gym had a legal agreement they could (and did) enforce. When I scribbled my name on the dotted line, the amount that I had to pay every month, no matter what, had just increased.

So here's an important lesson about Must-Haves: Make as few commitments as you can. Many of life's necessities require a long-term contract—your apartment, your student loans, your car loan. But for everything else, just pay as you go.

Are your Must-Haves coming into line? We hope so! We recognize that cutting the easy stuff isn't always a walk in the park. There can be some real research, some tough questions, and lots of notes. But there is a reason we call this cutting the easy stuff: When you make these cuts, your *life* is just the same. You live in the same place, drive the same car, enjoy the same movies, and have just as much fun. The only thing that changes is that you have more money in your pocket. And best of all, once you cut it *stays* cut. Your savings goes on autopilot, month after month. So take the time to get it right, and reap the rewards for a long time to come.

3. Cut Where It Hurts a Little

Still not there? If the feel-no-pain cuts haven't brought your Must-Have expenses into balance, then it is time to turn up the heat. These cuts involve some real changes in your life, so they're tougher than the easy cuts. But if your Must-Haves are still too big, then this may be the best road to financial balance for you.

Get a Roommate (or a Tenant)

Consider an option you may not have thought of: Share your space. Get a roommate. Take in a boarder. Invite a family member to move in.

You may be thinking, "I'm too old for a roommate." Yes, it may be nicer to live on your own. But c'mon, it's also nicer to have enough money for some fun—and something for your future!

If you think you're in the wrong stage of life for a roommate, spend a few minutes thinking creatively. Samantha, an outspoken 44-year-old in the middle of a divorce, desperately wanted to keep her 14-year-old daughter in the same public school long enough to graduate from high school. But there was just no way she could keep up with the mortgage after her husband moved out, and there weren't any afford-able rentals in her upscale suburban school district. So Samantha did something that never would have occurred to her earlier: She took out a personal ad in a local circular. "It felt sort of daring, like I was doing something off-color," she laughed. After a few weeks, she got the perfect call: Jody, another single mom looking for a place to live, also in a good school district. The two women met, and they hit it off instantly. By the end of the month, Jody and her 8-year-old twins had moved into Samantha's house. It was a little crowded, and it took some adjustment to figure out mealtime and bathroom schedules. But both families had a much nicer place to live than either could have dreamed about on their own. And they were able to keep their kids in good schools—while still having something left over for piano lessons and Christmas gifts. It can be a little bumpy, but roommates can work, even for those who are well past their dormitory years.

If you live in a college town, if you live near an employer who hires young workers, or if you live in an area where housing is very expensive, renting out a room could be your ticket to financial stability. Be sure to check out the local zoning ordinances, and read up on lease terms, security deposits, and the like. And keep in mind that taking a roommate or renting a room doesn't have to last forever. You can try it for a year, and see how it works out for you.

Also, consider your extended family. In Europe, where housing costs are much higher than in the U.S., families—even very prosperous families—have always lived two and three generations to a house. An older relative can help with the bills, and may also enrich your life in unexpected ways. Our Aunt Bee lived with us until she was 95, cheering the loudest at every band concert and making cheese grits that were the envy of our Yankee friends. We started living together out of necessity, but we ended up infinitely richer for having knitted our lives so closely together.

Sell Your Car

Yes, you love your car.

Okay, now we have that out of the way. We know that selling your car isn't pain-free, but it's not that bad. You get to live in the same place, eat the same food, wear the same clothes, and you can still get where you need to go. So here are a few tips about getting your car costs under control.

- *Buy used.* Every expert out there will tell you it is a zillion dollars cheaper to buy a used car. If you are worried about the repair costs, you can even get a "certified pre-owned vehicle" that comes with a warranty.
- *Drive it until it falls apart, and then keep driving it.* Drive your car until the odometer flips. Drive it until you're on a first-name basis with your local mechanic. Drive it until you embarrass your kids. And then drive it some more. And laugh all the way to the bank.
- *Never, ever sign a lease.* Yes, they lower your monthly payments. But what's the cost of those lower payments? You keep paying *forever.* And if you ding the car door or put too many miles on the odometer,

they will slap you with extra fees—before they take your car away. In other words, they charge you for the privilege of having no car. It's like Vegas, only the dealer always wins in car leasing. Take a hint from the car companies—they make fatter profits from leases. Why would you want your hard-earned money to make Ford or GM richer?

• *Shop hard for a good rate on your car loan.* You've just picked out the perfect "pre-owned" car, and you're ready to sign on the dotted line. And then the salesman walks in, with a monthly payment number on a little sheet of paper. But where did that number come from? How can you be sure you're getting the best rate? These days, many of the big car makers actually make more money from charging you too much on financing than they do from selling cars! So don't just take the rate the dealer gives you; do some comparison shopping. Get a few quotes from various banks and credit unions, so you can get the best possible deal.

Still not persuaded? Okay, you can keep driving your brand-new shiny machine under one condition: *Your total Must-Haves must be under 50%.* But if your Must-Haves are too high because of your car payments, then it's time to take action. If you have less than a year to go on your loan or lease, hold your breath and stick it out. And if you signed your papers within the past few months, you're probably better off making payments for another year until the amount you owe is approximately the same as the value of the car. (Otherwise, you may be "upside down" on your car loan, which means you could end up paying thousands of dollars to the bank for turning in a car that is worth less than the outstanding balance on your loan.) But as soon as you can, trade that baby in for something cheaper. Because as nice as those quadraphonic speakers may be, they're not as nice as a lifetime of financial peace.

Return the Rentals

If you are renting furniture, appliances, or anything else besides the roof over your head, then *give it back.* Call the lease company, and find out how fast you can get rid of it. No joke. Furniture and appliance leases are notoriously bad deals. They entice you to get something you really can't afford, and then they charge you way, way too much. If giving back the rentals will leave your living room bare, then head to the nearest Salvation Army and get yourself a "vintage" couch to tide you over until you save enough to buy something nicer *with cash.* It will feel a lot better to sleep in a bed and watch a TV that is *yours,* even if it isn't as fancy.

What about rent-to-own? Rent-to-own typically charges you somewhere between 3 and 10 times too much for second-rate furniture and limited-selection appliances. Ask yourself: Will you be finished making payments within a few months? If not, call and cancel the contract. That's the benefit of rent-to-own: You are allowed to give the stuff back and quit paying. Go hit the garage sales. You'll be way ahead in no time.

Trim the Health Insurance Bill

Oh, boy, this may sound like a scary one. After all, it's *your health* we're talking about. It doesn't get any more important than that. Even the never-waste-a-penny financial planners will tell you to "buy the best health insurance you can afford." And here we are talking about trimming your health costs. Have we lost our minds?

You are in luck. One of us (Amelia) spent several years working in the health-care industry, and later founded a company dedicated to helping people get more affordable medical care, so we can pass along a few tricks of the trade.

If you get health insurance through your job

• *Opt for the lower-cost plan.* If your company offers several health plans that cover all your basic medical needs (prescription drugs, maternity, preventive care, etc.), consider enrolling in the cheapest plan. You may have to take the kids to a different pediatrician, and you may have to get "preauthorization" before seeing a specialist. But before you dismiss the lower-cost policy out of hand, *do the math.* It's amazing how many people will let their employer deduct an extra $50 (or more) a month just so they can go to a dermatologist who is twenty minutes closer to home. The National Committee for Quality Assurance

(www.ncqa.org) can give you information on the plan. Ask your benefits planner what she thinks of the cheaper health plan and whether she
has gotten any complaints. If you like what you hear, you can end up
saving a lot of money by opting for the cheaper policy—without sacri-
ficing your health.

• *Take advantage of the Flexible Spending Account (FSA).* If you expect to have at least *some* medical expenses, then the FSA (if you work
for a big company) or HSA (Health Savings Account, which is like an
FSA for small companies and the self-employed) is a no-brainer. These
accounts let you pay your medical expenses *tax-free.* Add up the stuff
you are pretty sure you will pay for out of your own pocket—prescriptions, glasses, trips to the dentist, and so forth. Then have the money
taken out of your paycheck and put into a Flexible Spending Account,
which you draw on to pay these costs. You'll still have to spend your
own money on some of your medical care, but the tax break effectively
gives you a 30% (or more) discount on every medical bill.

• *Do the math with your mate.* If you and your spouse are both offered insurance through your jobs, the best bet is to sit down with a calculator and figure out the most cost-effective approach. Sometimes
putting the whole family under one policy is the best plan. Sometimes
you are better off if you each go it alone. But don't bother with double
coverage (where you get covered by two policies, one from your work-
place and one from your mate's). Insurance is expensive enough, so
there's no point in paying twice.

If you don't have health insurance

C'mon, don't look away. *Everyone* needs health insurance. Young or
old, healthy or sick, it's just one of those things you need to have so that
you can get the care you need—without going broke—in case you get
really sick. Today it doesn't take a major bout of cancer to wipe you out
financially. Without insurance, even an appendectomy or a slipped
disc could put you in the hole for years.

You also need health insurance so you can get the best possible care.
Researchers have found that if you get seriously ill, you are actually
more likely to die from your illness if you are uninsured. It is no fun to

think about, but the truth is that health insurance is one of the best investments you can make in yourself. So here are the answers to the top two excuses for living without health insurance:

1. *I'm healthy.* "I hardly ever get sick." "I never go to the doctor anyway." It has its variations, but "I'm healthy" is the number one excuse for not having health insurance.

Get real! Saying you're too healthy to need health insurance is like saying "I haven't been run over by a car yet, so I don't need to look both ways when I cross the street." Just because you're healthy today is no guarantee that you'll be healthy tomorrow.

But you already knew that. So here is something you may not have given much thought to: If you're healthy, then there is good news! Health insurance will be a lot cheaper for you. In fact, a healthy adult can get a high-deductible policy (which will protect you in the event of serious illness) for as little as $70 a month in some areas. So there is no excuse for not having it.

2. *It costs too much.* You are right. Health insurance *is* ridiculously expensive, and it is hard to find a bargain. But *it's not as expensive as you think.* How do we know? Because the smartest researchers around have found that people nearly always believe that health insurance costs more than it actually does. Why? *Because most people never bother to get an actual quote.* They just assume health insurance costs too much, and they give up before they start.

So here comes your assignment (you knew this was coming): If you don't have health insurance, find a couple of brokers in the phone book and get some quotes.

Here are a few tips for buying health insurance that won't cost more than the Trump Tower.

• *Hold on tight to COBRA (at least for a while).* If you leave your job, sign up for COBRA benefits immediately so you can stay on your company's health insurance policy. If you have an ongoing medical condition, COBRA may be your best long-term bet, since there is no medical prescreening and preexisting conditions are covered. If you're generally healthy, start shopping for a less expensive plan as soon as you can, but stick with COBRA in the meantime. You will get a better deal on your next policy if you can show that you had uninterrupted coverage.

• *Go with a high deductible.* High-deductible policies are generally a *lot* cheaper, because the insurance company doesn't have to pay out every time you catch a sniffle. The deductibles can get pretty steep ($2000 and higher), but you'll be covered if you face a serious illness. And you may be surprised at just how much money you can save. When I (Amelia) bought insurance for my family, I shifted from a fully loaded, zero-deductible plan to a high-deductible plan. When I did the math, I found that even *if* I got really sick and we had to pay the whole deductible (which is a pretty big *if,* since my family is generally healthy), we would still come out ahead—to the tune of $5000 a year!

• *Consider a no-frills plan.* Sure, it is better to have insurance that covers everything, but this is one of those places where some coverage is better than nothing. When push comes to shove, you can save a lot of money by opting for a policy that doesn't cover maternity, prescription drugs, or preventive care. The most important thing is for you to be covered if you become seriously ill.

• *If you have kids, check out Medicaid.* Many states offer free or reduced-cost insurance for families with moderate incomes and for people with certain disabilities. Medicaid isn't just for poor people: In California, for example, a family of four that earns $45,000 a year can get reduced-cost health coverage for their children. A quick search on the Internet will tell you whether you or your kids qualify. The Centers for Medicare and Medicaid Services is a good place to get started, at www.cms.hhs.gov. And if you've served in the military, be sure to check out the services at the VA, which offers high-quality care for little or no money. The benefits include prescription drugs, so even veterans who see private-care doctors may go to the VA for their prescriptions.

• *Try to buy insurance through a group.* Certain professional groups and unions offer preferred rates on health insurance to their members, so look around.

• *A discount card is no substitute for real insurance.* Medical discount cards are increasingly common, especially since Congress is now promoting them for the elderly. These cards can be a great way to save on things like eye exams, prescription drugs, acupuncture, and dental checkups. But make no mistake, a discount card is only a supplement. *You still need real health insurance.*

- *Steer clear of "cancer insurance."* If you stumble upon a policy that covers only certain conditions (cancer is the most common), steer clear. You want a policy that will cover *all* medical problems, not just one or two.

- *Low annual limits spell trouble.* Watch out for scam insurance that has a ridiculously low annual cap, promising to cover everything *up to* $10,000 (or so). I (Amelia) once had lunch with a guy who sold this product. He actually laughed about the employers who offered this so their workers could "feel" like they had health insurance. A clove of garlic would provide about as much protection in the event of a serious illness, since you can blow through your benefits in a single day at the hospital. So check the annual cap. If it's under $1 million or so, keep looking.

Disability Insurance

If you don't have disability insurance, this is another one that needs to become part of your basic package of protection. The fact is, there is a 1-in-4 chance that you will face a spell of disability before you reach retirement age. As if that isn't scary enough, this year more than 300,000 people without disability insurance will go bankrupt. So get covered! If your employer offers it, sign up. If you are shopping on your own, get a few quotes for disability insurance. You may never need it, but if you do, you'll be so glad you have it.

Reshop the Child Care

If you are a working parent, child care may be the only purchase that seems even *more* absurdly expensive—and more sensitive—than your health insurance. We are both mothers, and we understand just how profoundly important it is to find the right fit for your child. We also understand how unthinkable it may seem to shop based on price. And yet, when you put all your big expenditures on the table, child care is too big to skip past.

Start by talking to other parents. Find out where they send their kids, how they like it—and what it costs. It may be a bit embarrassing to ask about price, but most parents are more than happy to share the information (and commiserate about how expensive it is!). Visit a few of the more cost-effective places. Be sure to look into a range of alternatives, like your church or synagogue, the YMCA, and even teaming up with other families. Child care costs vary widely from one neighborhood to the next, so consider going outside of your neighborhood. Check for a mile on either side of the route you drive to work, for example, to see if there is something good in another neighborhood. You may not relish the extra drive time, but for the right price, it may be worth it. And just like with your car insurance, don't forget to ask about discounts. Two kids? Church affiliation? Willingness to help out on the weekends? It may matter. And don't forget to claim your child care deduction when you file your taxes; it can save you big money.

You know in your heart, but it may help to hear it again: You don't have to spend a lot of money to be a good parent. When Amelia turned two, I (Elizabeth) put her in day care when I went back to school. The first arrangement was the most prestigious (and the most expensive) place in town. The day-care center cost us an arm and a leg, but it had beautiful equipment and a staff with advanced degrees, so I figured we couldn't go wrong. But Amelia was plagued by mysterious stomachaches, and she looked like a grim old lady every time I dropped her off—determined not to fuss, but clearly unhappy. After two months of this, I was desperate to find something else, but everyplace I looked was full or it smelled funny or it just didn't feel right. I began to get scared that I would never find anything and I would have to drop out of school. But the ninth place was charmed. Officially designated as a "play group" rather than a day care, it hadn't even made my list. And the facility was plain—just a couple of rooms in the back of a modest church. But the woman who ran the program was one in a million. Lively and full of hugs, Miss King had a way with kids. By the third week Amelia was squealing with eagerness before we had even reached the church parking lot. And here's the real irony: Not only was Amelia happy, the church play group cost about a third of what I had been spending at the fancy facility. Amelia thrived, and I learned a lesson—

a safe place, some crayons and paper, and a caregiver with a ready smile and a mountain of patience is all you need for magic to happen. And without the right person leading the show, all the equipment in the world won't make it happen. It is a lesson I carry with me today when I teach classes at Harvard Law School.

Ultimately, you may decide that keeping your child in the same day care is worth the extra money. But if you don't shop, you'll never know if there was a good alternative that would take a smaller bite out of your paycheck—while still taking good care of your kids.

4. Consider radical surgery

You've taken the easy steps, and even a few not-so-easy steps, and we hope you've reached your goal. But if your Must-Haves still aren't approaching the 50% mark, then it's time to think honestly about some really big changes, changes like taking a new job or moving to a different place. We know that these can be difficult—even painful—changes in your life. And yet we also know that major change may be your only path to real financial peace.

When It's Time for Another Job

Jobs? We've talked about cutting expenses, but of course there are two ways to get your money into balance—you can cut your costs *or* increase your income. There are no hard-and-fast rules on what is right for your situation. Maybe you just need to do a little hunting and find work that pays better. Maybe you need to let go of a foundering business and get a traditional job. Or maybe you need to get more education so you can get the next promotion. The key here is to get it out in the open: Take a long look at your options. Ask yourself the tough question: Do you really, really need more income?

• *Has it been more than two years since you checked out what you would earn in a similar job at a different company?* There is a basic rule in business: Always know what your assets are worth. The same holds true about your job. Know what you are worth to an employer. And make sure you get every penny of it. If it has been more than two years since you checked out what you could earn at a different company, then it is time to do a little hunting. The information you gather may surprise you.

You already have a job, so you can be choosy. Take your time to look around. Check out the online job postings, visit a couple of placement agencies, and tell all your friends that you'd like to find something that pays a little better. You'll find out pretty fast if there is a better job out there.

• *Could you pick up extra part-time work?* This is a great way to turn work experience—and even your hobbies—into extra cash. Do you have teaching experience, or a degree in English or math? You can make good money tutoring kids after school. Are you at home taking care of your children? Take care of the neighbors' kids too. Typing, gardening, hanging wallpaper, taking photographs, and setting up home computers are just a few skills that can translate into extra money.

• *Is it time for more training?* If a degree or specialized training is necessary for you to get a fatter paycheck, then sign yourself up! Getting a degree can be expensive, and studying after-hours can be tiring. But this is the rest of your life we're talking about, and you'll get a payoff for a long, long time.

• *Is it time to go to work for someone else?* There is nothing quite like working for yourself. We've done it, and we know the joy of making your first sale—and the agony of not making the profits you hoped for. It is hard to admit, but even if you work your fanny off, many small businesses don't work out. There is no shame in throwing in the towel and going back to a traditional job. Think about the hours you put in, and ask yourself: Could you earn more at a regular job? Keep in mind, it doesn't have to be forever. You can always use that steady paycheck to rebuild your savings until you can launch the *next* big venture.

• *Are you or your spouse able to work, but not drawing a paycheck?* Maybe you promised your wife she could stay home with the kids when you got married. Maybe you offered to support the family while your husband launched a new business. Maybe you planned to find a new job once the baby got a little older, but somehow it just never happened. A family that is financially strapped and yet has an able-bodied adult who isn't even looking for a job, is, 9 times out of 10, a family that is living out the consequences of a decision that *once* made sense—but no longer works.

So be honest with each other. If you just can't afford a stay-at-home spouse, then say so. Once again, it isn't all-or-nothing. You may find a part-time job that will cover some bills *and* give you plenty of time for life outside of work. You may decide to work for six months or a year, just long enough for your family to pay off some major debts. You may job-share or work as an on-call temp. The point is to get out there and look—and to be creative.

When It's Time to Move

Your house is special. Moving is expensive. Your whole life will change if you can't wave hello to Mrs. Wysong every morning and sit on the back deck in the evening. There are a lot of very good reasons not to move. And yet you need that moment of cold, hard honesty: If you are living in a home you can't afford, you stand to lose that home and everything else you have built up in your life. The fact is that home foreclosures have tripled in less than 20 years. You want to be prosperous for life, not another crash statistic. If your Must-Haves are still way too high, and taking a roommate or getting a higher-paying job just isn't in the cards, then consider moving someplace more affordable. Getting out from under that heavy house payment may be your best chance for building a lifetime of riches.

Is it time to move?

First, consider your circumstances. If you are expecting a major change in the next year or two, then it may be sensible to stay put a little longer. For example, if you plan to get married or shift to another job, then your housing needs (and your household income) may change. Likewise, if you are planning to move to another city in the next year, don't blow your money on moving twice. But if your situation is pretty stable—if you plan to stay in the same job, the same city, the same relationship (or no relationship)—then it may be time to call the moving van.

Next, consider your community. You may be fixated on a single area, but there may be decent housing—and decent neighbors—in less expensive areas. The test is not "Where do I most want to live?" The test is "Where can I live safely?" Check the listings and get in the car and drive around. Once again, you might be surprised.

CHECKLIST: IS IT TIME TO MOVE?

Money Balance

Are your total Must-Have costs (including housing) significantly higher than 50% (after you've made as many cuts as possible)?	Yes/No

Future Plans

Is your income likely to stay about the same or drop over the next few years (i.e., no big raise or promotion on the horizon)?	Yes/No
Are you planning to stay in the same city for the next several years?	Yes/No
Is it likely that your life will be pretty stable over the next few years, with no major changes (such as a new marriage or job)?	Yes/No

Your Area

Is it possible to live in a less expensive home or apartment in your area without compromising your safety and well-being?	Yes/No

If you answered yes to all of these questions, then moving to a less expensive place may be your best option.

• *Should the move be temporary?* If selling your home sounds too difficult—or just too expensive, once you add in the agent fees—maybe there is another option: Consider a temporary move. You could rent out your home and move into a less expensive apartment—just for a while. We have a friend who is a professor at a business school. His family had a huge financial setback, so he rented out his big house with a pool and moved with his wife and teenage daughter into a two-bedroom condo for two years. It was enough to get them back on their feet. He didn't feel embarrassed; he felt smart and careful.

If the rental value of your home is more than the monthly mortgage payment, you could come out ahead financially. You could hold on to your home while salvaging your financial stability. And if your circumstances change in a year or two, you could move back in.

• *What if you have kids in public school?* Be sure to investigate all your options before you rule out a move. Many school districts will permit students to remain enrolled even if the family moves to another district. That may involve extra driving, but if you are cutting the house payment sharply, it may be worth it. And check out whether any of the schools in your area offer open enrollment or magnet programs. This can be a great way to get a good education for your kids without paying an arm and a leg to live in a prestigious district. Don't rely on real estate agents for information; call the school district direct. You might be pleasantly surprised.

• *What about family?* Is this the time to move back in with your folks, or crash on your sister's couch for a while? Family can help, and often they have more space than cash to offer. If you are a grown-up about it—if you try not to impose, if you recognize what a big benefit they are bestowing on you—this could be a turning point in your life. Pay something to your hosts, pitch in with the yard work and the dishes, and put every spare penny into savings. Set a timetable to get back into your own place. This can be a very difficult step, but it may be just what you need to get the rest of your financial future in balance.

Remember, it doesn't have to be forever. There will *always* be bigger apartments and nicer homes available. If your circumstances change, you can move into a nicer place when the time is right. And in the meantime, you can stay safe, pay your bills, and rest easy.

LITTLE CUTS, BIG CUTS: ADD UP YOUR TOTAL

It is time, now, to add up all your cuts and see where you stand.

WORKSHEET 6. REVISED MUST-HAVE EXPENSES

Total Must-Have Expenses Before Cuts

Enter your monthly Must-Have Expenses *before* you
made any cuts (from p. 39) $ _____

Cuts in Expenses

List each cut and enter your monthly savings (if you saved from a bill
you pay annually, like your car insurance, just divide your savings by 12)

1. _____ $ _____

2. _____ $ _____

3. _____ $ _____

4. _____ $ _____

5. _____ $ _____

6. _____ $ _____

7. _____ + $ _____

Total cuts in monthly Must-Have expenses   = $ _____

Revised Must-Have Expenses

Revised Must-Have Expenses = Total Must-Have
Expenses Before Cuts − Total Cuts in Expenses $ _____

The savings you made here will help you lay a foundation for the rest of your spending plan. You will come back to these numbers again and again as you work with your Wants and Savings. And you will be so glad of all the progress you made here. So give yourself a big pat on the back for every cut on this list—you deserve it!

When It's Okay to Go Higher than 50%

What if you've squeezed, you've shopped, you've pressed and pulled, and you are still not there? Is it ever okay for your money to be out of balance?

There may be times when Must-Haves need to climb above 50% for a while:

- When a new baby comes
- When a loved one faces a serious illness
- When you go back to school
- When you lose your job
- When you launch a new business

Notice something special about this list. What do all these things have in common? They are temporary. *All Your Worth* is designed to give you enough flexibility to manage life's ups and downs, so that you don't have to worry if things go a little awry. It is okay for your money to get a little off-balance when it's temporary.

But when you are working steadily, when everyone is healthy, when everything is *normal*, your Must-Haves should not float above the 50% mark. If they do, the warning flags should be flying.

Who decides whether the reason your Must-Haves are out of balance is only temporary? You do. But we urge you to be honest with yourself. A job that just doesn't pay as much as you're worth does not qualify as temporary—even if you are planning to look for a better job sometime in the future. Divorce isn't temporary. An expensive home mortgage and a big health insurance bill aren't on the temporary list either.

If you have a temporary circumstance that makes it necessary to keep your money out of balance for a while, here are the steps you should take to stay safe:

• *Build a super-strong safety net.* You have opted for life on the high wire, so you need a really, really strong safety net. Savings in the bank is your best line of defense in case anything goes wrong.

This means you still need to make room for Savings. Pay your Must-Haves first, then carve out 20% for Savings. *Then* you can put the remainder toward your Wants.

This probably means that you will be scrimping on the Wants for a while. No vacations, and not much in the way of fine dining or shopping for new clothes. We know that's not much fun, but putting Savings higher on your list is the best possible way to keep yourself safe and start building toward a better future.

• *Set a goal for when you will get your Must-Haves balanced.* Going heavy on the Must-Haves may be the right decision, *for now.* But it doesn't have to last forever.

Try setting a goal for when you are going to be out of the woods. Maybe you can get your money into balance in a year, when the car is paid off. Maybe balance will come in two years, when your youngest child starts full-day kindergarten. Maybe you can get your money into balance (or at least get it a lot closer) when the student loan is paid off next year, or when you move to the next pay grade at work in eighteen months. The point here is to have a clear endpoint in mind, a time when you can finally take a much-needed sigh of relief, and aim toward keeping your money balanced for good.

When to Revisit, When to Relax

It's taken some work to get your Must-Haves in balance, but now it's time for the good news: *You don't have to worry about this for a while.* In general, you should reevaluate your Must-Haves every two years.

Why revisit? Because you just never know. Maybe you will qualify for a better mortgage. Maybe you will be eligible for cheaper car insurance. Maybe a new day-care facility will open up. Maybe there is a better job out there, just waiting for you to apply. The only way to find out is to get out there and look around. Rest assured that every time you check, it gets a little easier, because you've learned the tricks and you know where to look.

You also want to recheck your Must-Haves—and your overall financial balance—whenever you have a major change such as:

- Change of job
- Marriage, birth, or other change in family structure
- Move to a different home
- Significant change in income
- Significant change in expenses (such as sending a child to college)
- Before you make a major purchase (such as a house or car)

When you begin to get your Must-Haves into balance, you have a new way of thinking about your money. You have an easy way to judge whether you can afford something, which can make the big decisions a whole lot easier—and a whole lot less stressful. No more chewing your fingernails about whether the new car will bust your budget or fit in just fine; now you *know*. If you can keep the monthly Must-Haves under 50% the purchase is okay; if not, it's not. That simple.

Balancing your money also makes it easier for you to plan around big changes—a new job, move to a new city, marriage, a new baby—and to integrate them into your financial plan. When you have a clear goal and a plan to get there, you can ease up on the money worries. This means you can focus your real energy on the new job, the new baby, and all the other important things, without wringing your hands over money. In other words, balance can let you relax about money, so you can focus on *life*.

Increasing Your Worth

The task in front of you may be challenging, and you may still wrestle some tough choices. But remember this: Nothing here is impossible. You have lots of options, and you can pursue the ones that work best for you. You are smart enough to look out for your future and you are energetic enough to work hard for what you want. That means you are also smart and energetic enough to get your money in balance.

Significant change is always tough. Shoot, if it were easy, you would have done it already. But here's the kicker: Your hard work *will* pay off. Getting your Must-Have expenses in balance builds the strongest possible foundation for a future of worry-free living and lifelong wealth-creation. And once it is all over—once you have done the hard work, once you are paying your bills without worry, once you are enjoying your fun money and watching your dreams come closer—your worth will grow in many ways, and you will forever be glad you did it.

4

Step Four:
If You Can't Afford Fun,
You Can't Afford Your Life

It's time for fun. How much fun? That depends on your tastes. Saturday at the lake. Strappy sandals. Tickets to the monster truck rally. A mud bath at the spa. A double Whopper with cheese. A dollar for feeding walruses at the zoo, a hundred dollars for advanced tai chi lessons, or a thousand dollars for a weekend at Mall of America. It doesn't matter. This chapter is about whatever is fun for *you*.

Why do you need a step on how to have fun? After all, no one needs to read a book on how to lick an ice-cream cone or when to laugh in a movie. So why a step for spending your fun money? Because you need to make sure that fun is, well, fun.

If you are like most people, you have probably spent plenty of money that just wasn't fun. There you were, sitting at a restaurant or standing in line at Disney World, and then all of a sudden, it hit. Your stomach turned into a knot as you mentally added up how much you were spending. And you thought to yourself, "Oh-no-I-shouldn't-spend-this-much." All of a sudden, the food turned to chalk in your mouth. Talk about a quick way to ruin a fun time.

If you are feeling stretched right now, if you are worried about covering your bills at the end of the month, then it may seem crazy to talk about how to spend money on stuff you don't absolutely need. But remember, *All Your Worth* is a lifetime money plan, not some crash diet that falls apart in a few weeks. You are balancing your money for life, and a critical part of balance is having some money to enjoy. We're dead serious when we say that if you don't have any money for fun, then you can't afford the rest of your life. Making the most of your worth is about building wealth *and* having money to enjoy. So it's time to focus on enjoying your fun money.

CONTROLLING YOUR WANTS SPENDING

In the last step, you focused on *what* you spend your Must-Have money on. You concentrated on how much you spend for each of your Must-Haves, and you looked for the best possible deal.

Getting control over your Wants is very different. It isn't about *what* you spend your money on. Nor is it about getting the best deal on everything you buy. (After all, it isn't much fun to go to the cheapest restaurant in town, even if you can get the best deal on a hamburger there!) The key to getting control over your Wants is to ignore *what* you spend your money on, and to focus on *how* you spend your Wants money.

> Control over Wants money isn't about what you spend; it's about how you spend.

1. Set a Clear Limit—How Much for Fun

Enjoying your fun money is about giving yourself complete, 100% permission to relax. That permission can come from just one place: the utter confidence that you have *enough*. The confidence that you can cover your bills, the confidence that you have put aside enough for the future. In other words, enjoying your money comes from knowing in your bones that it is really, truly okay to spend on something you don't need.

That confidence starts by deciding exactly how much you can spend on all your Wants, without worry or guilt. This isn't about budgeting every penny; it's not about long lists where you write down how much for lipstick, how much for a new socket wrench, and how much for a bagel with cream cheese. No, this is about the big picture: giving yourself some freedom to have fun. Instead of a budget entitled Grim and Grimmer, this is a place in your wallet for Fun and Funner.

> Spending is most fun when you know
> you can afford it.

Calculating how much you can spend on Wants is simple. First, enter your monthly Must-Have expenses, taking into account all the cuts you made in Step Three. Next, take out 20% of your take-home pay, which is earmarked for your Savings. The remainder is your Wants budget.

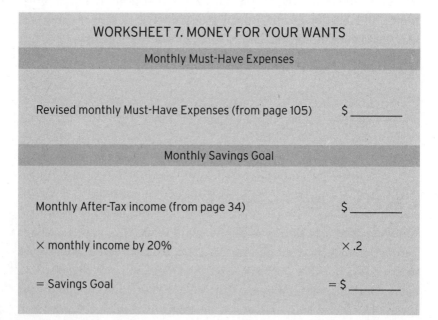

WORKSHEET 7. MONEY FOR YOUR WANTS	
Monthly Must-Have Expenses	
Revised monthly Must-Have Expenses (from page 105)	$ _____
Monthly Savings Goal	
Monthly After-Tax income (from page 34)	$ _____
× monthly income by 20%	× .2
= Savings Goal	= $ _____

Monthly Budget for Wants	
Monthly After-Tax income (above)	$ _____
− Monthly Must-Have expenses (above)	− $ _____
− Savings goal (above)	− $ _____
= Monthly Wants Budget	= $ _____

The last line in Worksheet 7 shows your Wants budget. Cookies or cocktail parties, Cubs tickets or cable TV. This is where you get the money for all the stuff you want, but don't really need.

If your money is in balance, you should have about 30% of your take-home pay left over for your Wants. Of course, the pieces of a balanced budget are interconnected, so if one goes up, another must come down. If you are heavy on Must-Haves, your Wants budget will be skimpier. And if your Must-Haves are lean, it's perfectly fine to spend more on the Wants, so long as you leave 20% for Savings. The calculation is always the same: There should be enough to cover your Must-Haves, enough for your Savings, and plenty left for fun.

Setting Limits: Shane's Story

Shane was one of the poorest kids in a high school full of poor kids. He's proud to have made it out of the old neighborhood, into a respectable job and a nice apartment. A devoted Notre Dame alum, he hopes to settle down someday, but for now he is enjoying the single life. Except for a nagging problem—he worries about his credit card balance, which creeps a little higher every month.

When we helped him calculate his money balance, Shane found that his Must-Haves were under control, but he was having trouble with his fun spending. He lived his own variation on the song: "I'm Just a Girl Who Can't Say No." He *always* dressed nicely, nervous that

his co-workers might think he was "low-class." He *always* paid the entire bill when he asked a woman on a date. And when his buddies invited him to go to a nightclub or to see the Pistons, he *always* said
yes—and always paid more than his share of the tab. None of the out-
ings were wildly expensive—$40 here, $75 there—but his paycheck
wouldn't allow more than a couple a month, and he was saying yes a
couple of times a week.

When we worked out the numbers, Shane immediately knew he
had to scale back, but it unnerved him. "What will they think if I say
no?" So we asked him to practice saying something we've heard rich
people say a thousand times: "I can't afford that." We played drama
coach. Say it with anger. Put some real heart into it—loud and furious.
Now say it with resentment. Fill your voice with bitterness and envy.
And we kept it up: Say it with pain. Say it with disappointment. Say it
with self-pity. We eventually worked our way to the best one: Say it
with good cheer. Laugh out loud about it. Shane said it, and we said it.
We listed all the things in the Wants category that we couldn't possibly
afford. We named $2,500-a-day spas and $1,000 bottles of champagne, and we laughed about them. We named a $19 bar of fancy soap
and $42 underwear. And then we asked Shane to pick one item every
day and then say out loud, "I can't afford that," with a twinkle in his eye
and good cheer in his voice. Over time, it got a lot easier.

We got an e-mail from Shane recently. He said that one of the guys
at work had suggested a Saturday paintball outing, and Shane replied
with a laugh, "Sounds like a lot of fun, but I just can't afford it." One of
the other guys spoke up and said, "You know, I can't either." Then another guy said, "What if we watch the game at my place? We can get
some pizza." The whole day cost less than $10, and he had a good time.
But the best moment was when Shane had said "no," and no one
fainted, walked off, or even raised an eyebrow. Apparently Shane wasn't
the only one who thought fun was a little more fun when there were
some limits.

SELF-TEST: HOW WELL DO YOU SET LIMITS?

Respond with True or False to the following statements:

I can't resist buying certain things.	True	False
I charge things on several different credit cards.	True	False
It's hard to keep track of how much is in the bank.	True	False
When I go out, I usually end up spending more than I planned.	True	False
When my credit card bill arrives, I am always shocked by how big it is.	True	False
I can never make it through the holidays without spending a lot of money.	True	False
Sometimes I buy things, but when I get them home I think I can't really afford this.	True	False
I don't really want to add up how much I spend; I think I'd rather not know.	True	False
I usually buy what I want, even if I'm not sure I can afford it.	True	False

This audit is designed to give you a quick snapshot of whether you struggle with setting limits over your fun spending. If you responded to two or more statements with "True," you would benefit from putting some tighter controls on your fun spending. If you marked "True" for four or more statements, this should serve as a loud wake-up call that you are on a spending binge that is undermining your financial health (and, in all likelihood, your happiness). Keep reading for some simple, effective changes that will help you regain control and rebuild your confidence.

2. Shift to Cash—The Key to Confidence

Dry cleaning, $28. Three frames of bowling and two Cokes, $32. One hardcover and two paperback books, $48. Stereo repair, $124. Dinner and a movie, $59. Orange sweater and matching pants, $83 (on sale!). Replacement shutters, $280. Sunglasses, $42. New bedside lamp, $52. Window-unit air conditioner, $340. Haircut, $26. Heavy-duty soup pot, $66.

Quick! How much did you just spend? If you laid down plastic for all these, you might not realize that you just spent well over $1000. And that is the point: By using credit cards, it becomes almost impossible for anyone to keep track of total spending. Unless you pull out a notebook and calculator every time you lay down a credit card, you will always be a little vague on how much you have spent.

Money is money, but it does matter *how* you pay. Credit cards, checks, debit cards, cash—the method of payment makes a difference.

Credit cards make overspending very, very easy. They are an open invitation to trouble. Even a card with a low limit won't keep you safe; nowadays, credit card companies routinely let you charge more than your limit allows—just so they can hit you with an "over-the-limit" fee at the end of the month.

> Credit cards are an
> open invitation to trouble.

Credit cards also make keeping track of what you've spent very, very complicated. Even if you don't regularly overspend, those cards make your financial life more complex and a lot more stressful. Credit card spending is invisible, so you have to keep a running tally on your own (or just wait and pray). Credit cards always leave you guessing whether you have enough or whether you are already in the hole. If you don't keep track, you risk going over what you can really afford. And if you do try to keep a running total in your head, then you are spending too much time thinking about money, and not enough time having fun.

Credit cards are also ridiculously, unbelievably expensive. Anyone who is working hard to get her money in balance has no business wasting money on these cards. Annual fees? Late fees? Interest charges? Just to spend your own money? That's not smart! If you are someone who clips coupons and refuses to spend more than $1 for a cup of coffee, then you don't want to throw money down the credit card pit.

At this point, you may be smiling smugly, saying to yourself, "Yes, but my credit card doesn't cost me anything. I don't pay an annual fee and I don't carry a balance on my card." Good for you, but that doesn't mean you'll never pay extra money to your credit card company. And here's why: The credit card companies count on the fact that even people like you make mistakes. A few years ago they figured out that they could boost profits by dinging people with more fees—late fees, minimum finance fees, sent-it-to-the-wrong-address fees, returned-check fees, and any other fee they could think of. And boy, did it work! This year, credit card companies will rack up more than $100 billion in fees, interest, and other charges. That's about $900 per household! So give yourself an instant tax cut—don't use credit cards.

Look at it this way: The credit card company makes its profits when you mess up and then pay them for it. You wouldn't agree to carry a bomb into your living room, even if you were pretty sure that it wasn't likely to go off. Using credit cards to pay for the fun purchases is just as dangerous.

But What About the Freebies?

Frequent-flier miles. Ten percent off all your purchases today. A contribution to your favorite charity. A cool T-shirt/cell phone/purple rhinoceros. Come on, you're too smart to fall for that! You wouldn't buy a $500 set of Ginsu knives just because they offered you the free apple peeler, right? Well, credit card freebies are the same kind of con. There are thousands of sharp business types who have full-time jobs aimed at figuring out exactly what gift or gimmick or lure will get their card into your pocket. You get those "freebies" only if the credit card company can make a fat profit from getting you to sign up. And so far, they have it exactly right—credit card profits (freebies and all) keep rising every year. So buy your own plane ticket, make your own contributions to the Golden Retriever Rescue Fund, and live without the T-shirt. But don't send your hard-earned money to MasterCard and Visa!

Besides, economists have demonstrated that when people buy with credit cards, they spend more than if they buy with cash.* That's right: the same people buying the same kind of stuff, but give them credit cards and they blow more money. So use that piece of information to your advantage.

What About a Debit Card?

That other piece of plastic in your wallet may be a debit card, which markets itself as being "just like cash." But is it really? A debit card can have many of the same disadvantages as a credit card. It's just as tough to keep track of how much you're spending, since there is no automatic reminder every time you open your wallet. Worse yet, a growing number of banks are charging extra fees every time you lay down that debit card, so it isn't free. And here's the real whammy: A lot of so-called debit cards are attached to a line of credit. This puts you right back in credit card territory—giving your hard-earned money to a bank and risking high fees and high interest. So if you have any doubts about keeping your debit card spending under control, then treat it like one more credit card—leave home without it.

Just Pay Cash

If you are struggling to keep control over your fun money, then just shift to cash. Put the fun money straight into your wallet. When the cash is there, have a ball. And when it's gone, quit spending. If you want to know how much you have, just open your wallet and count.

---

* Drazen Prelec and Duncan Simester, "Always Leave Home Without It: A Further Investigation of the Credit-Card Effect on Willingness to Pay," *Marketing Letters* (February 2001), pp. 5–12.

No calculator, no complicated record keeping, and no chance to get in a lot of trouble. Simple, neat, old-fashioned.

Cash has worked since Methuselah was a little boy, and it can work today for you. You'll have an automatic budget reminder every time you pull out your wallet because it's right there in front of you—how much you can spend on your Wants. You can know with 100% certainty that you can afford your fun. And you also know ahead of time when it's time to stop. No guesswork, no fudging, and no more running into trouble.

And no more paying someone else for your money. No more late payments because your credit card bill got lost in a pile of newspapers. No more interest payments. No more black marks on your credit report. No embarrassing moments when you get turned down for a purchase. Best of all, cash is accepted everywhere.

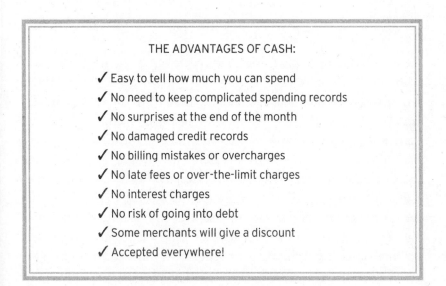

THE ADVANTAGES OF CASH:

✓ Easy to tell how much you can spend
✓ No need to keep complicated spending records
✓ No surprises at the end of the month
✓ No damaged credit records
✓ No billing mistakes or overcharges
✓ No late fees or over-the-limit charges
✓ No interest charges
✓ No risk of going into debt
✓ Some merchants will give a discount
✓ Accepted everywhere!

"But I hate carrying cash." "I could lose it." "I could be mugged." "I don't want to flash a wad of money whenever I'm trying to pay for a loaf of bread." Okay, we get it. The next chapter will explain how your credit card company is about 100 times more likely to rip you off than any mugger in a dark alley. But for now, just stop to consider—is car-

rying cash really that big a deal? Suppose you earn about $30,000 a
year, which would mean your fun budget is roughly $400 a month.
That means you get about $100 a week for Wants. Is it really too much
to carry $100 in your wallet? If you are still worried, then leave half
a week's fun money in your sock drawer, and put the other half in
your wallet. Is it really a problem to walk around with $50 in your
wallet?

The point here is to keep it simple. You may need to continue putting business expenses on your business card, or you may decide to
continue using a gas card (and paying the bill out of your Must-Have
checking account). But for everyday, run-of-the-mill fun stuff, nothing
beats cold, hard cash. No surprises, no extra fees, and no complicated
budgeting. It's the cheapest, easiest, most efficient way to make sure
that your Wants spending stays in balance, every single month.

How to Live Happily Ever After on Cash

"What if I run out?" That's the question we hear most often from folks
who are switching to cash. Once you get the swing of things, it will
happen a lot less often than you might guess. (After all, your grandpar-
ents managed on cash for decades without any problem!)

Even so, you may want to keep an extra $50 (or so) shoved in the
back of your sock drawer, "just in case." This isn't for big emergencies,
like an engine overhaul or a trip to the hospital (we'll show you how to
handle those in Step Six). This is for life's really small emergencies, and
for the fun purchases that can be hard to postpone until the next payday. This is for things like a battery for your watch (no idea that was
coming!); Granddad's birthday present (oops, you forgot!); a trip to the
vet (Fluffy landed in the briar patch); class pictures for the kids (are
those today?); the in-laws come to town (surprise!). That extra $50 (or
so) is there whenever you "need" it (or really, really want it). Just remember to replace that $50 on your next payday.

You may also opt for a little internal budgeting—tucking away
some of the Wants cash so you can save up for a little treat. You may
want to put a little aside each week toward your Christmas fund, or

for a trip to the Grand Canyon, or for the new sofa you've been eyeing. You can stick the cash in your underwear drawer, your bank account, or your piggy bank; whatever works for you. When you have enough for that plasma TV, go get a cashier's check and celebrate all the way to the appliance store. This is your money to put wherever you want. But if you prefer to just "go with the flow" and keep it all tucked in your wallet, that's fine too. So long as you keep your Wants spending in balance, you can section it off or lump it together to your heart's content.

Eating regularly

Food, more than anything else you buy, straddles both the Wants and the Must-Haves. You need it to live. And yet you probably blow a lot of extra money on food that's convenient, or fun, or tasty, or whatever. And that's perfectly fine. This is why you included a modest amount for your basic food needs as part of your Must-Haves. Of course, life isn't that simple; when you go to the grocery store, you aren't going to fill up two separate shopping carts—one with beer and cookies, and the other with dried beans and flour. In reality, you jumble it all into one cart and pay for it all at once. So the easiest solution is to take your food money out of your Must-Haves bank account, and stick it in your wallet along with the fun money. Then just pay the grocery tab in cash, the same way you handle your other fun purchases.

How much cash?

Some of your Wants get paid with a check, instead of cash. The cable bill, your gym membership, your cell phone, and the kids' piano lessons are all Wants. You pay for these items month after month, but you just don't pay in cash, so they need to be accounted for a little differently.

To calculate how much cash to carry in your wallet for fun, you'll need to make a few simple adjustments to account for your grocery money and the Wants you buy with a check.

WORKSHEET 8. CASH TO CARRY FOR FUN

Monthly Wants budget (Worksheet 7, page 113) $ _____

+ Basic food budget (page 39)   + $ _____

− Wants you pay every month with a check (e.g., cable
TV, cell phone, gym membership, long-distance bill,
lessons)   − $ _____

= Monthly Cash to Carry for Fun   = $ _____

If you're writing so many "Fun" checks that you're left with too little cash to enjoy yourself, this may be a clue about realigning your priorities for your fun money. You may decide that premium channels or a cell phone that comes with a tiny television and a popcorn popper are not quite as much fun as having cash in your pocket. Your choice—so long as your total Wants spending stays in balance.

EMOTIONAL SPENDING

Kevin is tall and soft-spoken, with a habit of stooping as if he is trying not to stand out. Everyone calls him a nice guy, although most people would be surprised to learn just how messy his divorce was. His ex-wife placed the whole blame on him—he didn't appreciate her enough, he didn't know how to have fun, he was cold and dull. The fact that she installed a new boyfriend just six weeks later didn't take any of the sting out of her words. Kevin's sons like the new man, and their cheerful chatter about how "cool" the new guy is and how he "knows car stuff" weighs heavily on Kevin.

Kevin takes his boys every weekend, and he works hard to make each outing "fun." They head for the Sharper Image and computer stores. Movies every weekend, complete with tubs of popcorn and giant sodas. Hours at the go-kart track. Trips to Six Flags every month or two. The boys ask Kevin for everything they want—new bicycle helmets, backpacks, a basketball hoop—and Dad always says "sure."

Ten months after the divorce, Kevin finally mustered up the courage to ask a pretty co-worker out for a movie. As they stepped up to the box office to buy tickets, he had to go through three credit cards before he could find one that wasn't over the limit. Mortified, he didn't say a word to his date through the entire movie. He took her home immediately afterward and he didn't call back.

When he came to see us, Kevin's hands shook as he kept smoothing out the credit card bills he had laid on the table. We went through the math on his Must-Haves (okay), Savings (none), and Wants (way over the limit). Kevin immediately started talking about how he doesn't see his boys much and how he wants them to have good memories and— We cut him off. Of course he loves his boys. But that's just not the point.

So we helped Kevin work out his Wants budget. It totaled up to about $140 a week, so he earmarked $120 for the weekends with his kids. (We thought he ought to keep more back for clothes and dates, but this was Kevin's decision, not ours.) The following weekend, when he picked up the boys, Kevin showed them a stack of twelve $10 bills. The boys were impressed. It looked like a lot of money. Kevin explained that this was how much the three of them could spend for the weekend, and he wanted them to decide how to spend it. The boys were heady with power. They considered various possibilities, for the first time pausing to ask, "What would that cost, Dad?" During the entire weekend, Kevin never once said no—he just asked, "Is this really how we want to spend our money?" The trip to Sharper Image ended up as "just looking" when the boys realized that some of those gizmos would eat up their whole weekend allowance. Ultimately, they decided to rent a movie so they would have money for go-karts on Sunday afternoon. On Sunday evening, they blew the last of their money on a pizza with everything, calculating that they could afford extra cheese and extra sausage if they drank plain water. The boys were still laughing about their weekend when Kevin dropped them off.

When we saw Kevin two months later, he looked ten years younger. He said he had asked his co-worker out again, and she had miraculously said yes. The bigger miracle, however, is with his boys. He said that after a couple of weeks, the boys asked when they could go back to Six Flags. The three of them talked about the price, and they decided to start setting aside $40 from each weekend's allowance toward the expedition. Kevin also reported that the boys were getting much more interested in "cheap" fun, combing the papers to find a car club rally or an air show. Kevin says the boys take more responsibility for the weekends now, and they are all having more fun.

Money is a funny thing. You earn it. You pay for your Must-Haves, and put something toward your future. And then . . . The rest should be fun, right?

And yet.

And yet there is money spent because you feel guilty. Money to make up for something. Money to impress others. Money to fight off feelings of sadness or anger or loneliness or disappointment.

The point is, fun money isn't always fun. Money is deeply laden with symbolism and emotion. From the time Granddaddy pulled a quarter from behind your ear, love and money have been intertwined. And ever since punishment for breaking curfew was forfeiting a week's allowance, money has also been about power and punishment. Shane was still trying to fill in the holes left over from adolescence. Kevin felt so much defeat over his failed marriage and so much jealousy toward the replacement dad that he would have blindly spent everything he had for a little relief.

There are no magicians who can wave the wand to make all your emotional baggage disappear. But if you have a problem with emotional spending, then it could be costing you both money and happiness.

Now that you're deep in Wants territory, it's time to ask yourself whether you are really doing what you want—or whether other demons lurk in your spending decisions. You don't have to dive into your unresolved hostility toward your third-grade teacher, but finding financial peace means understanding something about why you spend your Wants money the way you do.

SELF-TEST: ARE YOU AN EMOTIONAL SPENDER?

Respond with True or False to the following statements:

I spend money when I get depressed or lonely.	True	False
When people see me with nice things, they think more highly of me.	True	False
I spend money to relax and relieve stress.	True	False
I worry that people may not respect me as much if I don't have nice things.	True	False
I often pick up the check when I am out with someone so that I look successful or generous.	True	False
It takes a lot of money to look good.	True	False
I spend a lot to make my friends and loved ones happy.	True	False
It takes a lot of money to attract a date.	True	False
Sometimes I am afraid to say no to spending money on someone I care about.	True	False
I am sometimes ashamed or embarrassed by how much money I spend.	True	False
My loved ones expect me to spend a lot of money for gifts at the holidays.	True	False
Sometimes I spend money on things I don't really want because it is expected of me.	True	False

If you marked "True" for two or more statements, you have a problem with emotional spending. It is time for a wake-up call.

Emotions and money are deeply intertwined for you. Sorting through all of it can be very difficult, because it may involve heading into some tough emotional terrain. You can do better—and you will feel better in the long run—once you develop the habit of separating these feelings from your decisions about how to spend your money.

Whatever ails your heart cannot be fixed with money. If you are feeling unhappy, lonely, or insecure, those feelings will linger no matter how much you spend. Spending won't change your feelings about your spouse, your parents, your children, or yourself, and it won't make anyone love or respect you more.

You cannot spend your way out of pain. But you can make every pain worse by trying to treat it with money. Difficulties with money will feed your emotional problems, which will only add more stress to your life. The origin of your problems may lie elsewhere, but out-of-control spending will make the emotional problems worse.

Of course, you already know this. The hard part is figuring out what to do about it.

The perfect answer is to solve the emotional problems head-on, and to keep money out of it. But of course, this isn't a perfect world, and if you're like most people, you'll probably be a "work in progress" for many years to come. Which means you shouldn't have to wait to develop the insights of the ages before you get your spending under control. Here are a few practical steps you can take to get strong emotions out of the middle of your spending.

1. Identify where you're vulnerable. Take another look at your answers to the emotional-spending self-test. Do you see a pattern? Is there a particular type of experience that triggers your emotional spending? Maybe you spend when you feel certain emotions, or maybe you spend when you're around certain people. Identifying the exact moment when you are most vulnerable can help you take steps to protect yourself.

For Kevin, it was weekends with his boys. So we worked on finding a way to keep his money balanced during his vulnerable times, the weekends. For you, the solution may be to avoid the vulnerable situations altogether. Just stay away from the mall or don't go out with the buddies who expect you to pick up the tab. Or you may take Kevin's approach—set some clear limits, and stick with it. You can give yourself a lean budget or a generous one, so long as you make sure to stop when you hit your limit.

2. *Protect yourself from temptation.* If you have a problem with emotional spending, throw out your credit cards. We know, a lot of people think we're a little extreme about getting rid of credit cards. We talk straight about credit cards because we have seen people in a world of hurt over those little pieces of plastic. If you have a problem with emotional spending, you *must* cut up the cards. Right now, this minute. This may cause some anxiety, because you may be using those cards as a crutch to support your emotional spending. But this may be the most important step you can take to improving your financial *and* your emotional well-being.

Using credit cards for ordinary fun purchases is a bad idea for pretty much everyone. But if you are an emotional spender, a credit card in your wallet is just plain dangerous. It is a constant source of temptation, there whenever you feel a moment of weakness.

Think of it this way. If you were trying to give up drinking, you wouldn't keep a bottle of booze on your kitchen table. If you were trying to quit smoking, you wouldn't keep a pack of cigarettes in your jacket pocket. And if you were trying to lose weight, you wouldn't carry a family-pack of Twinkies in your backpack. It's the same here. If you are trying to get control of your emotional spending, don't carry temptation in your wallet. Throw it away. When Kevin cut up his credit cards, he had a much easier time keeping his boys within budget.

3. *Get a little help.* When you want to make important, lifetime changes, you are far more likely to succeed if you have a circle of support to nurture and reaffirm those changes. So think about the people you are close to. Is there someone you can talk to about your emotional spending? The simple act of describing your struggles can help put them in perspective. And you may even get some more good ideas about how to solve them. There's no need to be a Lone Ranger. Reach out for a little help every now and then.

Before leaving this section, take one last look at your emotional-spending self-test. There are dozens of variations on how people spend emotionally. Maybe you spend for others, or maybe you spend alone. Maybe money trickles out day after day, or maybe you go on spending binges. The bottom line is the same: If you are spending emotionally, you are trying to fix something that money can never fix.

So go ahead and feel beautiful or angry or guilty or happy or whatever else you need to feel—but keep your money out of it. You can pull out of this. You can separate spending your money from feeling your feelings, and that separation will help you step more strongly on the road toward a richer life. And you may just find that those sticky emotional situations seem a lot less complicated when you take the money out of it.

How to Share Your Fun Money

An evening at the game or dinner and a movie? Cable TV or Book-of-the-Month Club? A new winter coat or a new table saw? Shrubs for landscaping or curtains for the dining room? These questions (or some variation on them) can bring even the happiest couple to blows. Because sometimes what's fun for you is not fun for your mate (and vice versa).

How to solve it? Simple. Fun money for you, and fun money for your partner. And then (and this is really important) *no questions asked.*

Got that? No asking where the money went. No offering advice on how it should have been spent. No justifying why you got a good deal. Think of it as your own personal Don't Ask, Don't Tell policy.

But we're too broke for me to stand by while he/she blows our money on stupid stuff! It doesn't matter if you are trying to save every penny to buy a new house. It doesn't matter if you think that whatever your mate wants to blow money on is totally ridiculous and dumb beyond belief. Budget an amount you can afford purely for pleasure, and then just let it go. Because *everyone needs fun money.* Period. It may not be much. But no matter how tight the budget, there must be cash for both of you. To spend on whatever you each want, no questions asked.

> Even if your budget is tight,
> each of you should have your own cash,
> to spend on whatever you want.

Why? Because that's the best way to have fun with your fun money. No negotiating over every purchase, no second-guessing each other. And no quarreling over silly little expenditures. It's like personal space; people have different needs, but everyone needs some.

Should it be 50/50? Yes—and no. If your entire relationship is 50/50—if you share the chores, the shopping, the child-rearing, and everything else exactly equally—then go ahead and split your fun money right down the middle. But if things are a little lopsided (which is perfectly normal), then you need to divvy up the cash accordingly. So, for example, if you and your partner have kids, and one parent buys most of the birthday presents, Happy Meals, and new gadgets for the little ones, then that parent should get a larger share of the cash to cover those expenses. Likewise, if one spouse does most of the Wants shopping for both of you—buying a new set of sheets, picking up a pizza, getting Christmas gifts for the entire family—then he should get some extra cash. You may want to set up a cash drawer in the kitchen where you or your partner can grab money that is for the whole family, or you could split the money 50/50 and balance things out as you go. The method doesn't matter. The point here is to find a process for dividing the fun money that feels fair—and a process that works for you. And to make sure that, no matter what, every payday you each get a little cash to spend however *you* want.

Brandi and Brett, the young couple you met back in Step One, are getting the hang of spending for fun. About two months after working out their Balanced Money Plan, Brandi found a tiny pewter elephant on her pillow. Brandi had collected little elephant statues since high school, but she and Brett had been so strapped for money that she hadn't bought one since their honeymoon. They were still fighting their way out of debt, but they each had their own Wants money—$20 a week. When Brandi saw the gift, her stomach did a flip-flop. Was Brett backsliding, spending money they didn't have? It wasn't her birthday. Was he losing his mind? After all, there was so much they still needed. But Brett was firm. "You said I could spend my twenty bucks any way I want. And what *I* wanted was to do something nice for you." Brandi said, "That's when I knew we were going to make it, no matter what."

Brett had crossed over. He had a good money plan, and he had stopped worrying and started living.

Making Room for Fun

Your life is like a big, blank canvas, and you can paint it with whatever colors you choose. The picture is yours. So enjoy your money.

Making the most of your worth is about enjoying life—not thinking about money. *All Your Worth* lets you know how much you can spend on fun, leaving you free to spend it in any way you want. That can make life a lot easier, but it also means it is time to face head-on what spending makes sense for your life. You have a plan that helps you make conscious choices about your money, with no more sweeping everything into a confusion of "gotta-have-it" and "can't-afford-it." You are in the driver's seat, so it's time to decide once and for all what you *really* want.

This may be new territory for you, but if you have come this far—if you have worked through your Must-Haves and thought about your Wants—then you have already moved a long way toward a lifetime of riches. You are ready for the *real* fun to begin.

5

Step Five:
To Build Your Future, Pay Off Your Past

The medical bills from last year's visit to the emergency room. The second mortgage you took out four years ago. The money you borrowed from Aunt Barbara that has been hanging out there for over a year. The credit card balance that has bounced around for more than a decade.

You don't need a scrapbook. Your bills tell your history.

If debt is a big part of your life, you may be wondering, why have we waited until Step Five to tackle your debt? The answer is: *Because now you know where the money to pay your debts will come from.*

If you've followed *All Your Worth* this far, if you've taken the steps and gotten your money in balance, then you know *exactly* where to find the money to pay your debts. You have trimmed your Must-Haves to 50% (or so), and you've set aside 30% for Wants. That means you now have 20% of your income left for saving for tomorrow. And that is where the money to pay your debts will come from: the money for your Savings.

Wait a minute! Isn't that money supposed to go toward saving for the future? What does a ten-year-old Visa bill have to do with the future?

Everything.

Your bills tell your past, but they also tell your future. Every debt, every monthly payment, every dollar you owe is a claim against your future. Debt affects what you can—and cannot—do about your future. And when you pay off the credit cards and IOUs, you open up new worlds of financial possibilities for yourself. You have more to spend, more to save, and a whole lot less to worry about.

Paying for yesterday is perhaps the most important investment you can make in your future. Getting rid of those debts will buy you breathing room. It will buy a future of freedom. And it will bring your dreams—the things you really, really want—into reach.

> Paying off your debts may be
> the most important investment
> you ever make in your future.

Whether you owe $200 to your Aunt Barbara or $2000 to MasterCard or $20,000 to the Mayo Clinic, there is a way out of debt—and a way to a brighter future. Keep reading; this step will help you find the way.

HOW DEBT SWEPT THE LAND

"I owe, I owe, it's off to work I go." Sound familiar?

For millions and millions of Americans, debt has become a way of life. Owing a bunch of money has become *normal* in this country, right up there with playing baseball in the summer and eating turkey on Thanksgiving. In fact, more than *80 million* Americans now owe money on a credit card. And not just a little bit of money: The average family that carries a balance now owes more than *two months' income* on their credit cards.

Maybe your grandpa has told you that "back in his day" if you couldn't pay cash, you didn't buy it. And that was pretty much true: Debt just wasn't a routine part of American life the way it is today. A generation or two ago, almost no one carried any debt except for a home mortgage and maybe a car loan. There were no giant credit card balances, no payday loans, and no home equity loans. In fact, just 35 years ago, the total amount of debt outstanding among all American households was about 1/600th of what it is today. That means that for every dollar your generation owes today, your parents' generation owed less than half a penny!

So how did so many people wind up in the hole? Over the past generation, American families got hit by a one-two debt punch. The first punch came when the laws were changed in the late 1970s. We told you back in Step One that when your parents were young, they had to pay cash for what they wanted because there just weren't any credit cards for regular middle-class people. Why not? It's not because everyone was just so prudent that no one would have *wanted* a credit card. Nor is it that no one had invented the credit card. (In fact, credit cards first appeared more than 80 years ago!)

The real reason that your parents didn't lay down a MasterCard every time they wanted a hamburger was because the *laws* were different. When your parents were young, interest rates were regulated by law, which meant that credit card companies could make money only if everyone paid them back. In other words, because the companies didn't charge a lot for interest, they needed to screen their customers very carefully to be sure they could repay.

But all that changed during the last twenty-five years. The laws that once limited how much interest a company could charge have gone the way of hoop skirts and high-button shoes. Congress and the Supreme Court quietly took the reins off the credit industry in the late 1970s, freeing the way for credit card companies to jack up their interest rates (and their fees).

And the card companies learned something new: They could make higher profits from lending to ordinary, middle-class people than they ever made from the silk-tie crowd. No longer would credit cards be the "exclusive" domain of the well-to-do. Instead, credit card companies would fight to get into the wallets of every man, woman, and child in America. (In fact, we know a little boy who just celebrated his second birthday by tearing up his first preapproved credit card offer! His mom had to intervene before he ate the pieces.)

Why are the card companies so eager to sign everyone up? Because it turns out that if you don't pay off your balance every month, the bank can make an enormous profit. In fact, credit card debt has become the single most profitable line of business for big banks. Banks have found that they can get away with slamming enormous over-the-limit fees, late fees, and interest rates on anyone who gets in trouble.

Josephine can tell the story. She has done administrative work at the Baptist Church for 15 years. When she first got her credit card with Providian Bank, the "introductory" rates were low. But when she started falling behind on her bills, the interest rate flew to 29.9%, and the fees and extra charges started piling on. Two years ago, she owed about $2200; she has since made payments of $2008. So how much does she still owe? With interest and late payments, Providian says she owes more than $2600! In other words, she paid $2008 on a balance of $2200, and it didn't even cover her interest and penalty payments! (The best part was that Providian seemed to think the charges in this case were fairly standard—nothing unusual.)*

And then came the second punch. At the same time that credit card companies started jacking up their rates and sending offers to anyone with a pulse, more Americans found themselves struggling just to make ends meet. Job layoffs started mounting, more people lost their health insurance, medical bills skyrocketed, and the divorce rate pushed upward. As a result, more and more people found themselves looking for a "temporary" fix to their financial problems. And there was that credit card offer, looking just like a life raft to someone who was drowning.

THE TRUTH ABOUT DEBT

The credit card industry is huge, and the messages it beams out are relentless: Debt is good. Debt is sophisticated. Debt is cool. Debt can

---

* For a discussion of Josephine's case, see *In re McCarthy,* case No. 14-10493-SSM (July 14, 2004). The court said that if Providian could provide the right documents, it could collect the whole amount from Josephine even though the charges were more than 100% of what she had borrowed.

make you a good friend/parent/lover. Debt is your friend when you are in trouble.

It's time, now, to bust those myths wide open.

Debt Is Dangerous

Debt is a legal obligation to make payments each and every month—no matter what. No matter what the future holds, debt demands to be satisfied. It is like a big, hairy monster that sits in your living room 24 hours a day chanting "feed-me-feed-me-feed-me." When times are good—when you have plenty of food to feed the monster—this may not seem like much of a problem. You work hard, you earn a decent living, so you figure you can make the payments, no big deal.

But if the tough times come, that's when you realize just how hungry that monster is. Maybe your hours get cut, maybe the transmission falls out, maybe you get lost for months on the interstate highway exchange. Your credit card company doesn't care.

If you've been struggling with your debts for a long time, then you know what we're talking about. But if you're new to the debt game, then you may be thinking, "But credit card advertisements are full of *happy* people!" Smiling couples and giggling babies having those "priceless" moments—in the world of debt commercials, nothing ever goes wrong.

That's because the credit card companies have hired the finest psychologists and the sharpest marketing wizards to achieve just one goal: Make people feel *good* about taking on debt.

Credit card companies found that if they want to rake in the profits, they just need to keep on selling. But think about what they sell: debt. A generation ago, it was seen as perfectly normal not to spend money you didn't have. But that is no longer the case. Our friend Virginia recently lost her mother. The death was sudden, and she was having a hard time getting over it. Virginia confessed that she cried whenever she saw the credit card commercial where the daughter took her mother on a trip to Ireland. "Why didn't I do that for my mom before she died?" The answer, of course, was that she didn't have the money—and her mother would have been appalled if her daughter had gone into debt to take her on a vacation. But the credit card companies won the daughter's heart by persuading her that she should have taken on debt to show her love to her mother.

The truth is, the debt peddlers don't want you to think about what happens when something goes wrong. They don't want you to have that moment of doubt, when you decide *not* to spend "just a little more." Their only goal is to sneak that monster in your living room, in the quiet hope that something *will* go wrong in your life and they can make the big bucks.

That's right: Your credit card company *wants* something to go wrong in your life. Why? Because that's when they make the most money! That's when the interest piles on, the late fees and over-the-limit charges balloon, and the bank racks up big profits from your troubles. If something goes wrong, that monster can eat everything you have. The credit card companies don't want you to know it, but debt is dangerous stuff. And this step will help you slay that beast as fast as you can.

Debt Steals from Your Future

Memories to last a lifetime? Make that bills to last a lifetime! Debt doesn't build a future. Just the opposite: Debt *steals* from your future.

Debt is nothing more than yesterday's spending taken from tomorrow's income. It is a claim against your future. Money that could have gone for future Must-Haves, or future Wants, or future Savings is forfeited—flushed right down the drain. Every payment on an old debt is money that disappears into yesterday.

If you feel stupid for having fallen for the debt game, we're here to tell you that you are not alone. This month more than 80 million people are carrying a credit card balance. Why? Because they can't pay off their debts. They believed they were safe because they were dealing with reputable companies. They believed in the promise of help. They believed that nothing could go wrong.

This step will help you shake off what we call your "Steal-from-Tomorrow" debt. Steal-from-Tomorrow debt includes your credit card balance, but it also includes other kinds of debt:

STEAL-FROM-TOMORROW DEBT

Credit card balances	Back payments on regular bills
Personal loans	Overdue child support payments
Old medical bills	Loans against retirement account
Pawnshop loans	Tax refund anticipation loans
Paycheck advances	Overdrafts on your checking account
Gas card balances	Department store charge cards

You may have noticed that the list of Steal-from-Tomorrow debt doesn't include *all* your debts. The debts that are probably your biggest debts—your mortgage, your car loan, and your student loans—are not included with Steal-from-Tomorrow debt. Does that mean that those loans are somehow "good" for your future? Not exactly. Just like any other debt, you can get in trouble with your mortgage or car loan by borrowing too much or by getting a bad deal. But they have one important distinction from Steal-from-Tomorrow debts: You took these loans so you could build toward tomorrow. You used the money to buy something of lasting value—a home, a car, an education. And once the debt is paid, you will still have an asset, something valuable that you will own outright.

Steal-from-Tomorrow debt doesn't build toward a brighter future. All those credit card bills and IOUs and back-payments aren't about building assets and creating wealth; they are about paying for the past. Yesterday's meals, yesterday's car repairs, and yesterday's trip to Bermuda drag down today's Balanced Money Plan. What you bought may be gone, but the debts linger on. Yesterday's debt steals money that could have gone to today's meals and today's car repairs—or toward tomorrow's new home.

Trying to build your future when you are haunted by Steal-from-Tomorrow debt is a little like trying to write a new story on a blackboard that is already crowded with words from a past story. Until you get the old story erased, you can't write a new one. The first step in investing in your future is to erase the past debts. This step will help you get the blackboard ready for the story you want to write.

Debt Is Outrageously, Unbelievably Expensive

No annual fee! Low introductory rate! Those credit card ads leave you with the impression that debt is so cheap it's almost free.

So how expensive is debt, *really*?

Suppose you're expecting a new baby. You buy a beautiful new $4000 furniture set and layette for the nursery. You put it on your Visa card and never use that credit card to buy another thing. Then you make the minimum payments on your card, month in and month out—never skipping a month and never paying late. Your baby starts walking—you're still making payments. She heads off to kindergarten—you are still making payments. Junior high, high school—still making payments. She heads off to college, earns her degree, gets a job, meets a nice guy, gets married—you are still making payments. In fact, if you have a typical credit card, you will end up making payments for 26 *years* and paying more than $10,000 for that baby furniture. If you are lucky, you will have your baby's nursery paid off just in time for your grandbabies to arrive! In short, debt is very, very expensive. Interest, late fees, over-the-limit fees, more interest—it adds up to a lot of money. A *whole* lot of money. Those "low introductory rates" are no different than the drug dealer who "gives" you your first hit for free; the companies want to get you hooked. So here's another good reason to get rid of your debt: It costs too darn much.

Wherever you are in the cycle of debt, you can take steps now that will make it stop. You can work out a plan that will help you sleep easier, spend smarter, and build a brighter future than all those debt-carrying neighbors of yours. Stick with us, because it's time to get on the road to debt-free living.

1. Stop the leaks

The first move in getting rid of your debt is to understand exactly why you got into debt in the first place. Think of this as akin to finding the hole in the bottom of your boat so you can plug it up before you sail out. You need to know why you got into debt so that you can make very sure you don't end up taking on new debt and making the problem worse.

You may think that understanding your debt is simply a matter of pulling out a few old credit card bills to see what you charged. Not so. In fact, *it doesn't really matter what you put on the credit card.* If you are carrying a balance on your credit card, then it is because your money is out of balance. You could have spent your cash on clothes and used your credit card for groceries; or you could have done just the opposite, spending your cash on groceries and using your credit card on clothes. It really doesn't matter which specific charges show up on the Visa bill. The same is true if you owe money to your best friend, if you took out a payday loan, or if you owe back-payments on your electric bill. What matters is that you are carrying Steal-from-Tomorrow debt, which means that your overall spending is out of balance with your income.

So, it is time to figure out what is driving you into debt.

SELF-TEST: WHERE ARE THE LEAKS?

Respond to the following statements with True or False:

PART A: OUT-OF-BALANCE BORROWING		
I can barely afford my home or apartment.	True	False
Whenever something goes wrong (car repair, minor illness, home repair) I have to put things on the credit card.	True	False
Some months I fall behind on the mortgage/rent, utilities, or car payments.	True	False

(continued)

PART A: OUT-OF-BALANCE BORROWING *(continued)*		
Even though I hardly ever spend money on stuff I don't need, I always seem to have a balance on my credit card.	True	False
By the time I finish paying my basic bills each month, I'm totally tapped out.	True	False
I worry that I can't keep my home/apartment/car.	True	False
When an emergency comes up, there's nothing I can cut out to cover the new expense.	True	False

If you picked "True" next to two or more of these statements, your debt is probably a symptom of a different problem: Your Must-Haves are too high. For you, it doesn't really matter which charges are on your credit card; the real problem is that you are struggling to pay for your basic necessities.

Don't beat yourself up over credit card debt; get your energy focused elsewhere. If your Must-Haves are badly out of balance, you have no breathing room in your budget. Whenever something goes wrong, debt is your only means for coping. Any unexpected expense—a trip to the dentist, a new set of brake pads—winds up on the credit card because you are spending so much on your Must-Haves that there is no money left over for anything else. For you, cutting up your credit cards isn't the most critical move. Nor is vowing to use your card *only* in an emergency. Why? Because when your Must-Haves are too high, any little thing that goes wrong becomes an emergency and you don't have any money left over to handle it. So there will *always* be an emergency to go on the Visa card.

But it doesn't have to be that way. If you follow the path laid out in Step Three and do what it takes to bring your Must-Haves into balance with your income, then you will have money for emergencies (and for fun!). Cutting Must-Have expenses can be hard, but you can't afford not to do it. Those Must-Haves are driving you into debt, which means they aren't just costing you money today—they are robbing from your future. So get your Must-Haves under control. That is your first—and most important—step in getting on the path to debt-free living. And remember the good news—once you get those Must-Have expenses under control, you don't have to struggle with day-to-day spending. You'll have your finances in balance and you can think about things far more important than money.

Part B of the Self-Test deals with a different sort of debt.

PART B: LEGACY DEBT		
I got into debt because of an unforeseen crisis (e.g., a job loss, divorce, an accident, a medical problem).	True	False
I got into debt when I was young and stupid.	True	False
Someone else ran up debts in my name, and I'm struggling to pay them off.	True	False
I'm still trying to pay off bills from a very different time in my life.	True	False
I was a victim of fraud or theft, and I'm still trying to recover financially.	True	False
I made some mistakes a long time ago, and I'm still paying for them.	True	False
Most of my debts are old medical bills.	True	False
If I could just get my old debts paid off, I'm pretty sure I could stay out of debt forever.	True	False
I haven't added any new debt in a long time.	True	False

If you chose "True" two or more times, you have a problem with an old "legacy" debt. You are generally responsible with your money, but you are still haunted by a crisis or mistake from your past. Maybe you made a bad decision (quitting your steady job to launch a fried-Twinkie shop wasn't such a good idea after all). Or maybe you were just the victim of plain old bad luck—an accident, a spell of unemployment, an ex who emptied your bank account and left you with nothing but the hamster. In either case, it's time to dust yourself off and focus on getting that debt paid off, so you can get on with the rest of your life.

Take heart. By now you have already figured out what part of your old life didn't work financially, and you are ready to write a new chapter. Pretty soon you'll be ready to start accumulating some real savings, so you'll be protected from the ups and downs that may come your way. You may have been dealt a bad hand this time around, but as you bring your money into balance, you can get past this and build a strong future.

A word of caution: If you are still in the middle of a crisis, then you aren't ready to begin paying off yesterday's debts. If you are out of work, if a family member is still sick, or if the problem that got you into trouble is still ongoing, then wait until this crisis has passed before you begin tackling your debts head-on. You may have to tread water for a while, or you may even need to take on more debt to keep food on the table until your life straightens out. In that case, skip ahead to "Financial CPR" at the end of the book. When the crisis passes, you can come back to this section and create your plan to get rid of your Steal-from-Tomorrow debt once and for all.

The final section of the Self-Test addresses the third type of debt you might have.

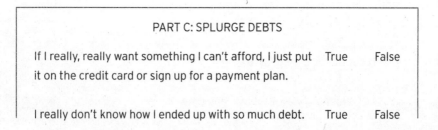

PART C: SPLURGE DEBTS

If I really, really want something I can't afford, I just put it on the credit card or sign up for a payment plan.	True	False
I really don't know how I ended up with so much debt.	True	False

If I didn't have a credit card in my pocket, I would probably buy a lot less stuff.	True	False
My credit card balance usually goes up at the holidays.	True	False
I made a big purchase (e.g., vacation, new TV, furniture) for something that I really wanted, and I'm still paying it off.	True	False
It is harder to say no to someone I care about when I have a credit card in my wallet.	True	False
Sometimes I charge things, and then I later think, "What could I have been thinking? I didn't need this."	True	False

If you checked "True" for two or more of these statements, you have a problem with splurge charging. You struggle to control your spending on Wants.

You have already tackled this in Step Four, when you created a plan for managing your Wants spending. Now that you have a clear budget, all that remains is to get the debt paid off so you can get on with building some real wealth.

If you're still worried that you may slip back into splurging, then consider cutting up those credit cards (if you haven't already). For you, credit cards are not just the mechanism for creating your problem, they *are* the problem. The cards offer a constant temptation to overspend, and a needless complication in your plans to get control over your spending. Cutting up the cards once and for all may be the most important step you can take to stay out of debt.

The Debt Stops Here

You may have discovered that debt isn't polite—it doesn't wait for one problem to pass before another piles on. You may struggle with out-of-balance borrowing *and* legacy debt, or you may be trying to cope with splurge debt from last month *and* legacy debt from a decade ago. That's okay. Remember, the goal is to plug every hole in the boat before you sail off on your new financial plan.

This is the moment to look at yourself in the mirror and say out loud, *"The debt stops here."* Every morning, tell yourself, "I will not take on more debt today." It is vital that you feel this one in your bones: No more debt, no matter what.

If this promise leaves you a little breathless, try a tactic recommended by Debtors Anonymous: Take it one day at a time. Don't worry about the next month or the next year or the rest of your life; just think about today. You have a roof over your head, food in your cupboard, and clothes on your back. You have a spending plan that covers the things you need, gives you room for something extra, and lets you pay off your debt piece by piece. And so all you need to do is to make it through *today* without taking on any more debt.

Over time, it gets easier. As your money comes into balance, the everyday stresses start to disappear. And as you stop the leaks and begin to pay down your debts, you will learn that you really are in control of your financial future. You don't need to be anxious. You are headed in the right direction, and you will start making good time.

2. Add It Up

It is time to get a handle on exactly where you stand. So gather your bills and IOUs, and pull out a pencil. Write down your Steal-from-Tomorrow debts in Worksheet 9. (If you're not sure what goes here, take a look again at the list of Steal-from-Tomorrow debt on page 137.)

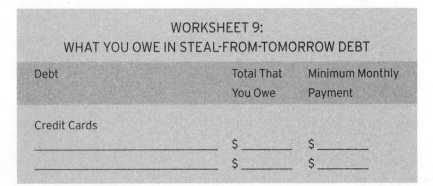

WORKSHEET 9: WHAT YOU OWE IN STEAL-FROM-TOMORROW DEBT		
Debt	Total That You Owe	Minimum Monthly Payment
Credit Cards		
_____	$_____	$_____
_____	$_____	$_____

_____	$ _____	$ _____
_____	$ _____	$ _____
_____	$ _____	$ _____

Loans from friends and family

_____	$ _____	$ _____
_____	$ _____	$ _____
_____	$ _____	$ _____

Overdue or back payments on rent or mortgage, utilities, cell phone, car payment, etc.

_____	$ _____	$ _____
_____	$ _____	$ _____
_____	$ _____	$ _____

Medical bills

_____	$ _____	$ _____
_____	$ _____	$ _____
_____	$ _____	$ _____

Other Steal-from-Tomorrow debts

_____	$ _____	$ _____
_____	$ _____	$ _____
_____	$ _____	$ _____
_____	$ _____	$ _____
_____	$ _____	$ _____

Total	$ _____	$ _____

Take a look at the total amount that you owe. Does it seem like a big number? If you are accustomed to focusing on your monthly payments, then your total Steal-from-Tomorrow debt may surprise you. Don't panic. You can tackle this debt, and we will help you find the way. And remember what Monica said back in Step One—it feels so unbelievably good when these debts are out of your life.

Special Circumstances

If you owe more than a year's income in Steal-from-Tomorrow debt or if your minimum monthly payments claim significantly more than 20% of your income, then you may be in need of some Financial CPR. The Financial CPR section at the back of this book is for anyone whose debts are so high that there may not be a way to pay them all off. Financial CPR will show you how to manage your bills during a crisis, and it will help you decide if bankruptcy is in your best interest. Keep reading and thinking, and at the end of this book we will help you weigh your alternatives.

3. Create Your Personal Repayment Plan

It's time, now, to create your own personal payment plan. The goal here is simple: to get your debt paid off really, really fast.

Drain Your Savings Account

We want you to get really serious about paying off your debt. Drain your savings account, empty your checking account, and sell any stocks or bonds. Liquidate all your accounts except your 401(k) or IRA (the tax penalties make this too expensive). Cash out the bar mitzvah money, crack open Mr. Piggy, and shake out the cushions from the couch. Keep $1000 in the bank, and commit everything else to paying off your debts. (If you don't have $1000 in the bank, Step Six will help you put it there.) It's time to focus some laser-beam intensity on paying off your debt, and that means putting everything you have toward becoming debt-free.

Sound a little extreme? It is. But remember, *there is no saving for the future when you are carrying a load of Steal-from-Tomorrow debt.* If you are in debt, and you think your savings account will keep you safe, you are kidding yourself. You are installing smoke detectors in the hallway while there is a grease fire blazing in your kitchen. If you have Steal-from-Tomorrow debt, you already have an emergency. Put out the fire, and get that debt paid off. You can hang the smoke detectors later.

Consider the math. Your savings account probably earns 3% (or less), while your credit card debt costs you somewhere around 18%. This means that for every $100 you keep in the savings account, you make $3 in interest, but you *lose* $18 on your credit card. That's why the bank has lots of money and you don't! You'll be many dollars ahead if you cash out the savings and pay off that credit card balance. Don't worry too much about that low bank balance; you'll start rebuilding it soon.

You may be wondering, if you're supposed to throw everything into paying off your debt, why keep $1000 in the bank? This is the start of your Security Fund, which you can use to cover any emergencies. This is the money that will keep you from sliding back into the credit card trap when something goes wrong. If you need to dip into your Security Fund, be sure to replace the money as soon as possible.

We've said it before and we'll say it again: Paying off your debt is the best thing you can do to build a secure future. Watching that credit card balance go down month after month is like watching yourself hit one home run after another. The satisfaction comes in proving that you can do it and knowing that you are headed toward a better future. There's nothing quite like it.

Earmark 20% for Debt Payment

Remember how hard you worked to get control over your spending on Must-Haves and Wants? Now you get to reap the rewards of all that effort. Thanks to your Balanced Money Plan, you know *exactly* where the money to repay your debts will come from. No more throwing up your hands in despair because you'll "never have the money to get out of debt." Since your Must-Haves and Wants claim only 80% of your take-home pay, you have 20% left over for Savings. This is the money you'll use to get rid of your debts.

That's it. Clean and simple. Just 20% of each and every paycheck for paying off your debts. No worry, no fighting with your mate, just a steady reduction in your debts, every single month.

The process is extremely simple. Every time you get paid, calculate 20% of your paycheck (multiply your paycheck by .2). Take that amount and put it toward your debts. Keep putting that 20% toward your debts, every single month until every Steal-from-Tomorrow debt is gone.

Tackle Your Debts One at a Time

The best way to get rid of your debts is to tackle them one at a time. Start by picking one debt, and throw everything at it until it's gone. Once the first debt is completely paid off, throw everything you have toward your second debt. In the meantime, keep making the bare minimum monthly payments on your other debts. Keep tackling your debts one at a time until they are all wiped out.

When you pay off a debt, draw a big black line through it on your debt list. That's one monster you've kicked out of your living room for good, so treat yourself to a little celebration! Notice that every time you draw a black line through a particular debt, you've also crossed out a monthly payment. The amount that you save each month on minimum monthly payments will be plowed right back into paying off the other debts. As you pay off more and more debts, you free up more and more money to pay down the remainder. This works a little like riding a bicycle down a gentle hill—you need a hard push to get started, but the longer you roll downhill, the faster you will go.

Pay the Debts That Bother You Most

What should you pay first? Whatever you want. Okay, it isn't quite that simple, but it's close. If you owe any back-payments on your rent or mortgage, pay those first. Keeping a roof over your head is always first priority. And, if you owe back-payments on your car or child support, pay those next. You don't want to lose the car or have the sheriff show up because you violated a support order. But once those are covered, it really is up to you whether Visa comes before MasterCard or vice versa.

So how do you decide? *Pay the debt that bothers you most.*

Is there a bill that makes your blood boil every time it appears in the mail? Is there a debt that always seems to spark a quarrel with your mate? Is there an IOU that is keeping you away from family picnics because you're embarrassed about the $500 you borrowed from your mother-in-law? Then pay that debt first. Would it feel good to get just one thing crossed off? If so, start by paying off the smallest debt. Does it make your stomach knot up when Gargantuan Bank dings you with another $35 over-the-limit fee? Then pay that debt first.

The point is to make your life happier and richer—as fast as possible. So don't get too caught up in comparing interest rates. Every debt you wipe out is a proud achievement that will make your future brighter. Which means that it just doesn't matter very much which debt you pay off first. So you might as well pay off the debt that will add a little bounce to your step at the same time that it improves your balance sheet.

When Should You Borrow Against Your Home? Never!

"Tap into your home equity!" "Consolidate your debt!" "Lower your interest payments and save money on taxes!" The drive toward second mortgages and home equity lines of credit is practically a national fever. And if you are facing a mountain of debt, it can certainly sound tempting.

"Tapping your equity" sounds so sophisticated, like a new kind of Morse code or an elegant ballroom dance. But it should be called what it really is—"going deeper into debt and putting your house at risk." There are lots of people (including a number of so-called financial experts) who will tell you that it's smart to "cash out" your home equity. Well, it isn't smart. In fact, it's dangerous. Really, really dangerous.

Taking out a second mortgage to buy your house or to make a major renovation leaves you with something valuable at the end. But using your home equity to pay off Steal-from-Tomorrow debt just trades one kind of Steal-from-Tomorrow debt for another. Borrowing against your home to pay off other debt violates the first principle of debt-free living: *You can't borrow your way out of debt.* Ever.

> You can never
> borrow your way out of debt.

The experts have touted home equity borrowing for so long now that it seems like heresy to say it's a bad idea. So here are three good reasons to steel your resolve to stay away from home equity loans.

1. Home equity loans put your home at risk. "Tapping your home equity" isn't tapping anything; it is taking on more debt, plain and simple. The only thing that makes a home equity loan any different from borrowing money from MasterCard or your cousin Judy is if you can't make all your payments, the lender can take away your home.

This makes a home equity loan one of the most dangerous forms of debt in existence. Every time you borrow against your house, you are putting the place you live on the roulette wheel, betting that you'll be able to come up with every single payment. Maybe everything will work out, and you'll pay off the loan. But if anything goes wrong— anything at all—and you can't make the payments, then the bank takes your home and you're on the street.

Of course, those cheerful advertisements with the smiling couples never mention that you could lose your house. They don't show those couples on the day the sheriff comes to serve them with a notice of fore- closure. If you think that doesn't happen to hardworking folks like you, think again. Right now, 1 in every 11 subprime debt-consolidation loans is in foreclosure. That's 1 in every 11 families who believed they were being clever when they "tapped into their home equity." You wouldn't try to save a little money by taking a medicine that had a 1 in 11 chance of giving you a heart attack. Treat home equity loans the same way: Just say no.

2. You probably won't save very much. The advertisements keep blar- ing that a home equity loan will save you money. But how much do you really save? Not as much as you might think.

Taking a home equity loan to consolidate your debts is a lose-lose proposition. If you can get your debt paid off in a year or two anyway, the money you save on interest is pretty small, often less than the fees you paid just to set up the loan. And if you *can't* get your debt paid off within a couple of years, you'll keep paying interest on this loan, year after year after year. In fact, many home equity loans last 15 years. Think about that: You could spend 15 *years* paying off that trip to the mall. Fifteen years of interest payments, 15 years before you become debt-free. That's not building a brighter future! If you can't pay off your credit card balance in 15 years, then you have BIG financial problems. And when you have BIG financial problems, the last thing you want to do is to put your home on the line!

And there is one more catch. If you are already in financial trouble, you will probably be steered into a super-high-cost second mortgage. Like the credit card companies that offer teaser rates to get you in the door, the mortgage companies offer good quotes in the ads—and much worse quotes in reality, especially if you have a less-than-perfect credit history. So, using a home equity loan will just put your home at risk without saving you much money. You are a lot better off buckling down to pay off the credit cards—while keeping the vultures away from your home.

3. The only way to tap your home equity is to sell your home. You may be looking at your home and thinking, "Gee, we bought this place 6 years ago for $200,000 and now it is worth $300,000. Just think what I could do with $100,000 . . ." And that's when solicitation for a home equity loan slides into the mailbox.

But your home equity isn't free money that is just lying around, waiting for you to "tap" it. It isn't cash in a savings account, or money in your sock drawer. In reality, your home equity is more like the "equity" in your grandmother's jewelry. There it sits in your jewelry box, something you hang on to and plan to pass down to your children. You realize it has some value, let's say $1000 on the open market. But there is only one way you can have $1000: Sell the jewelry. Sell it or keep it, but "tapping" is just a fiction.

Of course, you could pawn your grandmother's jewelry (which is like taking out a mortgage on it), but that just means you have borrowed money; you'd have to pay the money back (with interest) if you want to keep the jewelry. In short, there is no such thing as "tapping your equity." If you want to make some money, you have to sell your house and move to a cheaper place.

So don't get sucked in by all the fancy talk about "putting your equity to work for you." You don't sit around worrying over how to make your grandmother's jewels "work harder for you." Likewise, you should rest easy that you are putting your home equity to work exactly as you should be: You're keeping a roof over your head.

What if you already have a home equity loan?

What if you already took out a second mortgage on your house to pay off your other bills? The first obligation is, of course, to stay current on your second mortgage or home equity loan, the same way you keep up with your basic mortgage. Payments on your second mortgage should already be accounted for in your monthly Must-Have expenses, and you want to be 100% sure that you get it paid every month, no matter what.

Once you've paid down your other Steal-from-Tomorrow debts, Step Six will outline a plan to help you pay off your mortgage. In your case, you should pay off the second mortgage first, since that mortgage has the higher interest rate. It may take a while, but paying off your home equity loan is a smart, safe move. It will lower your debt load and free up more money for other uses. And, more important, it will make your home safer.

DIRTY TRICKS TO WATCH OUT FOR: HOW NOT TO GET OUT OF DEBT

When you get into financial trouble, life can be just like one of those bad horror movies. All that is missing is the creepy music. You know you're in danger with your debts, and then . . . miraculously, a stranger comes out of nowhere offering you a helping hand. Maybe the stranger calls on the phone, or maybe he shows up on an advertisement on late-night television. The message is always the same: "I understand the danger, and I can help." The stranger always seems like such a nice person. But if this were a real horror movie, the creepy music would start getting louder and scarier. Because this stranger is not your friend.

When you get into debt you become a target for some very nasty scams. You are worried, distracted, and anxious for help—the perfect mark. The "helpers" will pretend to look out for your best interests, but they are really looking out for their own profits.

They wear different disguises. Here are the main ones.

Credit Counseling

If you are really stressed about your debt, "credit counseling" can sound so appealing. It evokes images of a helpful conversation with a wise, friendly ally. And your bills can get so confusing, with shifting rates of interest and convoluted legal terms. It would feel so good to have an expert on your side. But the sad fact is that credit counseling has become an industry thick with slick operators who do little more than take your money and leave you deeper in a hole. Some of them may even try to talk you into paying your credit card bill (and thus your credit counselor) instead of your rent! When you have nothing left to pay to your counselors, they stop the "counseling" and move on to the next sucker. There are some decent credit counselors out there, some good people who run upstanding outfits that really help people. But just like the horror movie with no creepy music, there is no easy way for you to separate the good guys from the bad ones—until it is too late.

What about not-for-profit or religious counseling agencies? Their ads make it sound like these outfits are run by the Boy Scouts, with no other motive than to "help others." Unfortunately, that just isn't so. Again, there are a lot of good organizations, but too many operations are run by crooks who have set up bogus nonprofit shells that funnel money to their owners. Worse yet, they are hiding behind a false identity, pretending to be charitable or religious, when they are secretly trying to steal from the good-hearted people who believe in them.

Even the counseling agencies that claim to charge only a "voluntary" fee—or no fee at all—can be dangerous. Many of them get their operating money from the big banks and credit card issuers. This means that they look out for the big corporations, not for you. They get paid when they talk you into borrowing from your mom or selling your engagement ring. And they don't tell you all your options; some of these agencies will fire any "counselor" who even *speaks* the word "bankruptcy." They sure won't tell you when you are a victim of a credit card scam or when consulting a bankruptcy attorney might be in your best interests. Moreover, they deal only with credit card and similar debts; they won't help you with your mortgage or car loan.

Nonprofit status is no guarantee of trustworthiness, and neither is no-fee or low-fee counseling. Right now several of these nonprofits are under investigation by the government, and some of these guys may end up in prison. There are some good operations out there, and there are groups like the Consumer Federation of America that are leading the charge to clean up the industry. But it hasn't happened yet, and until there are stricter regulations, you don't have any protection if you wind up swimming with a shark. So if you need advice, read a good book. If you just want someone to talk to, call your best friend or talk to your clergyman. But for now, stay away from the credit counselors.

Debt Consolidation

This is the "help" most commonly peddled by credit counselors—which should be your first clue about how bad it is. Debt consolidation promises to roll your debts into "one easy monthly payment!" In reality, the company is just offering to lend you money to pay your debts. This violates rule number one: You can *never* borrow your way out of debt.

There are no shortcuts to paying what you owe. In all likelihood, your "consolidated" debt has no better interest rate than you would have gotten with a little shopping on your own.

So how do they claim to lower your payments while still making a profit for themselves? Three ways: 1. Buried in the fine print in some of these contracts are extra points and fees that you pay up front for the consolidation services. 2. They stretch out the payments forever and ever. 3. They don't mention in the upfront advertising that they are planning to take a second mortgage on your house—a terrible financial mistake that could cost you your home. The effect, of course, is to keep you in debt longer and leave you paying a lot more interest than you have to—and maybe put your house at risk. Debt consolidators can leave you worse off than if you'd never called them. So just make the payments yourself. In the long run, you'll save a lot more money.

Credit Repair and FICO Repair Kits

The ads promise to "repair" your credit as if it were a broken-down furnace spewing out dust. They make your credit score sound like complex machinery that is crucial to your financial survival, and something only an expert can safely fix.

They will make some big promises:

- *We can erase your bad credit—100 percent guaranteed.*
- *We can remove bankruptcies, judgments, liens, and bad loans from your credit file forever!*
- *Create a new credit identity—legally.* (That's a good way to end up in prison!)

These guys are just selling another brand of snake oil. They get your money and whatever "upgrades" they can sell you, and you get some routine advice readily available on the Internet, along with a copy of your credit report (which you could have gotten on your own for free or a small fee). More important, they get your name and e-mail address, which they pass along to the credit counselors and anyone else who might turn a profit from your troubles.

There are no quick fixes for your credit score. It's just a matter of paying your bills, month in and month out. You should double-check your credit report once or twice a year (and before you apply for a new home or car loan) just to make sure there are no errors. (For the names of the credit bureaus and a list of common errors, see page 81.) You can correct most errors on your own. If there is a serious problem, you may need to talk to a lawyer. But either way, forget about the "repair" folks.

Otherwise, put your credit score out of your mind. You need to stay focused on paying off your debts. Don't waste your money on these repair kits, and don't spend a lot of time worrying about your score.

Fee Hikes

Keep a sharp eye on your credit card interest rates. Most credit card issuers put a clause in the fine print that gives them the right to change the interest rate whenever they want—even *after* you borrow the money. It isn't fair, it isn't right, and, at least in our opinion, it shouldn't even be legal. But right now, you need to protect yourself. Do not assume that last month's 9.9% credit card will still be 9.9% when this month's bill arrives. And do not assume that just because you're paying your bill on time, you can let your guard down. They can change your rate pretty much any time they feel like it, regardless of whether or not you've been a model customer. So keep your eyes open.

If your rate jumps unexpectedly, call the card company and complain. Often, the company is counting on people to overlook the increase, and they're willing to roll back the rate hike for anyone who makes a fuss.

If your card company is unwilling to bring your rate back down, then it is time to start shopping. This may be a good time to do the Credit Card Hustle (see page 157). Or you may just want a new card with a plain old solid interest rate that is better than the one you currently have. Either way, never forget that the credit card companies can switch rates on you any time they want. Credit card companies are in business to lift as much out of your pocket as they possibly can, so watch them every month.

TOP 5 MYTHS ABOUT GETTING OUT OF DEBT

Myth	Fact
Debt consolidation can reduce your debts.	There are no shortcuts to getting your debt paid off!
A not-for-profit credit counselor can be trusted to give you good advice.	Many not-for-profit credit counselors steal your money and ruin your credit rating.
Tapping into your home equity is a smart way to pay off your credit cards.	Home equity loans put your home at risk.

A credit repair kit (or a FICO repair kit) can improve your credit score.	There are no quick fixes. The best way to improve your credit score is to pay your bills, on time and in full.
So long as you make your payments, the interest on your credit card will stay the same from month to month.	Credit card companies can increase your interest rate whenever they want, so watch your bill carefully.

CAN YOU PAY LESS?

In some circumstances you may be able to reduce the amount you owe with some clever maneuvering.

Play the Credit Card Hustle

It shows up in the mail with an enticing promise: "6% APR!" Six percent—sounds good, right? Especially if you're paying 19.99% (or more) on that big credit card balance. But should you bite? Should you switch your outstanding balance to a lower-rate card so you can save some money? And when those "low introductory rates" disappear, should you switch again? In other words, should you start dancing the Credit Card Hustle? The answer is: It depends. Take this self-test to see if the Credit Card Hustle will work for you.

SELF-TEST: CAN THE CREDIT CARD HUSTLE SAVE YOU MONEY?

Will it take you 6 months or more to pay off your debt?	Yes	No
Are you paying more than 12% on a large part of your debt?	Yes	No
Will you commit the time to read all terms and conditions carefully, before you shift to a low-interest credit card?	Yes	No

(continued)

SELF-TEST: CAN THE CREDIT CARD HUSTLE
SAVE YOU MONEY? *(continued)*

Will you commit to making your payments on time, every single month, no matter what?	Yes	No
Will you commit to double-checking your interest rate every single month?	Yes	No
Will you commit to keeping detailed records on how much money you transferred, when you transferred it, and how much you have paid?	Yes	No
Are you willing to stand up for yourself if the credit card company charges you the wrong amount, and to back yourself up with copies of all your records?	Yes	No
Will you stick with your commitment not to add any new credit card debt?	Yes	No

---

If you answered "yes" to every question, then the Credit Card Hustle can save you money. But if you answered "no" to any of the questions, then just don't go there. The risks aren't worth it. The reason these companies put out low-interest (and no-interest) cards is not because they are trying to save you money. They issue those cards because they know that most people who switch balances aren't careful, and they end up blowing a lot of money on that credit card when the interest rates shift upward. They also hope you'll charge new purchases on the card—for which that "low introductory rate" doesn't apply. So if you are not committed to dancing the Credit Card Hustle with everything you've got, then just don't go out on the dance floor.

How to hustle safely (or at least as safely as possible)

Start with an offer for low-interest credit (typically 8% or lower). This may come in the form of a flyer or a "blank check" from your existing credit card, or it may come as a mailer for a new low-rate card. If the good offers are not showing up in your mailbox, call your credit card company and ask for a low-rate balance transfer or do some hunting on the Internet.

1. *Read the terms and conditions.* Find out the following information:

- *How do you qualify for the low rate?* Even if you are "preapproved," the credit card company may put you through another screening process before giving you the low rate. This means that even though the big print advertised 6%, you could wind up being charged 26%. So don't do the transfer until *after* you've gotten approved and read the final terms and conditions.
- *How long does the low rate last?* If it lasts less than 3 months, don't bother. Look for a minimum of 6 months.
- *Are there any transfer fees?* Some credit card companies charge extra fees to transfer your money—hoping you won't notice. If the company wants more than a few dollars, walk away.

2. *Pick the best deal, and transfer your balance.* Find the lowest interest rate, and take the plunge. Move all your high-interest debt to one low-interest card. Resist the temptation to sign up for several new credit cards (even if they all have a low interest rate). Taking out several new cards at one time can lower your credit rating even more, so keep the number of cards to a minimum. The goal is to keep things as simple as possible, and to minimize the risk that the Credit Card Hustle could hurt your credit rating.

3. *Follow the rules like a Boy Scout.* Make every payment *on time.* Remember, the company is looking for the slightest excuse to bump the rate up, so this is the time to be practically perfect in every way.

4. *Check your statement carefully, every single month.* The minute something goes wrong—the interest rate rises unexpectedly or an extra fee appears—be ready to call the company to challenge the charge. And if that doesn't work, jump to a different card, and do it fast.

5. *Transfer to the next card before your low rate ends.* Mark the date on your calendar when the low-interest card will turn back into a high-

interest pumpkin, because the Credit Card Shuffle works only if you get this card paid off or transfer the balance somewhere else before time runs out. So watch the date, and be ready to move.

6. *Keep meticulous records.* Keep a copy of the credit card application and the billing statements, and record every payment. If you talk to a company representative by telephone, write down the date and time of the call, the name of the person you spoke with, and what you agreed on.

7. *Don't put any new charges on the card!* Many credit card issuers give you a low interest rate on the balance transfer *only,* which means you pay a super-high rate on any new charges. And here's the rub: They won't even let you pay off your new high-rate charges until *after* you've paid off all your low-rate debt. So don't make a single new charge on the low-interest card, even if you "plan to pay it right away."

Does the Credit Card Hustle sound like a lot of work? It is. If you are carrying a lot of debt, the hustle can save you hundreds of dollars—and it can help you get out of debt months earlier. So it may be worth the effort. But never forget that the dance is dangerous, and you must look out for yourself.

Negotiate the Medical Bills

If you do not have health insurance, you should *always* try to negotiate the price of your medical care. Why? We'll let you in on a well-kept little secret: *Sophisticated buyers never pay sticker price for medical care.* Not the insurance company, not Medicare, not even rich people. So you shouldn't pay sticker price either, even if you don't have a big insurance company looking out for you.

Here are a few tips for negotiating your medical bills:

1. *Talk with your doctor.* Your doctor knows you personally, and is more likely than anyone in the health-care system to help you out. So explain your circumstances, and ask for a discount (or a payment plan) on your treatment. (If you have health insurance, you can also ask your

doctor not to bill you for the co-pay. Technically, doctors aren't supposed to agree to this, but many will do it if you ask.) When I (Amelia) worked for a large medical practice, the doctors routinely gave a 40% discount to anyone who asked. If you need outside services (such as hospital or lab services), ask your doctor to negotiate a discount on your behalf; the doctor has a lot more pull with the hospital administrators than you do.

2. *If you need a prescription, ask for a free sample.* At the medical practice where I (Amelia) used to work, there was an entire closet full of free samples that had been dropped off by representatives of various drug companies. For the most part, the free samples just sat there, forgotten. But whenever a patient told a doctor that she was hard up for cash, the doctor cheerfully handed over a month's supply. If you are struggling to pay for your prescriptions, ask your doctor for a free sample; there's no point in paying at the pharmacy if you can avoid it.

If your doctor doesn't have any free samples, there are other ways to get a break on your drug prices. Check online to find out whether the drug company offers discounts for people with moderate incomes. Look into getting your drugs through Canada. (Our doctor friends tell us that it really is cheaper, and quite safe.) Or sign up for a medical discount card.

And be sure to ask your doctor to write a prescription for the generic drug; it's just the same as the brand-name stuff, only a lot cheaper!

3. *Make an offer.* If you can't enlist your doctor in your cause, then your best bet is to accumulate a little cash, and then call the billing department with an offer. I knew a hospital billing director who would slice 30% off the bill of anyone who would send in payment right away. Of course, the discount was only given to people who asked for it, so be sure to ask. If your first offer is rejected, then call back and ask for a supervisor, who may have more latitude to negotiate.

4. *Don't put it on your credit card.* If you make a direct payment to the medical provider, you will have more negotiating leverage than if you put your medical bill on your credit card. And if you need to set up a payment plan, the provider will probably give you better terms than Visa or MasterCard.

STAYING DEBT-FREE—CUT UP THE CARDS

Now that you have your debt repayment plan, you may find it easy to get out of debt. On the other hand, you may worry about the danger that faces anyone who is working his way out of debt: backsliding.

You promised yourself you wouldn't take on any new debt, and you meant it. And yet, seeing the advertisement for a weekend getaway after 54 straight days of frozen slush can weaken the resolve of even the most determined person.

If you struggle with—or just worry about—backsliding, then make the big step: Get rid of the credit cards. Melt them over the stove. Take out the pruning shears and cut them to little bits. Fold them back and forth until they pop apart. Once your debt is paid off, call Visa or MasterCard, and tell them to cancel your account. You can't afford these cards.

A credit card in your wallet is the surest path to backsliding. Whenever you find it a little tough to stay the course, there is the card. Whenever you face temptation, there is the card. It sits in your wallet, constantly reminding you that you don't *have* to deny yourself; you can always take on just a little more debt and get whatever you want.

You have lived with the consequences of credit cards. You have paid the price. And the best way to make sure you never pay it again is to take the cards out of your wallet. You have nothing to lose and a lot to gain.

But don't you need *a credit card?* Not really. You may be worried about repairing your credit, and you may think a credit card is the best way to accomplish that. Not so. Want to build your credit? Mail a check for your phone bill. Pay down your student loan. Make your car payment on time. (According to a new study, making car payments on time is the best way to build a healthy credit rating.) Build up your Savings. In short, do all the things you should be doing anyway to build toward a lifetime of riches. But don't keep using the credit cards. They don't improve your credit, they cost you a lot of money, and, if you are not extremely careful, they can leave your credit rating worse off than before.

What about the things that you can get *only* with a credit card, like renting a car, buying over the Internet, or ordering from a catalogue?

Get a debit card that takes money straight out of your bank account. It will cover most of what you need. And for the rest, you can always use a credit card to reserve a hotel room or secure a car rental, and then pay the tab in cash.

TOP MYTHS ABOUT CREDIT CARDS

Myth	Fact
Credit cards are a good way to keep track of what you spend.	Credit cards make it really easy to lose track of how much you have spent and what you can actually afford.
It's easy to use your credit card without getting in trouble.	The credit card company hires thousands of savvy businesspeople whose sole job is to get you in trouble. Almost no one outsmarts them forever.
You need a credit card to build your credit.	Credit cards are more likely to get you in trouble and ruin your credit. Paying your bills on time is the best way to build your credit.
It is smart to use credit cards because you get frequent flier miles.	Most frequent flier miles never even get used. With the fees and interest credit cards charge, you are better off buying your own ticket.
Credit cards are a smart way to pay your other bills automatically.	You aren't paying your bills; you are just shifting from one outstanding bill to another—usually with higher interest.
Credit cards are a good way to donate to your favorite group.	Most credit card companies give only a tiny fraction of what you charge to the charity you designate. Get your money in balance, and write your own check directly to your favorite charity.

(continued)

TOP MYTHS ABOUT CREDIT CARDS *(continued)*

Myth	Fact
If you get approved for a higher limit, you can afford to spend that much.	Credit card companies want you to charge more than you can afford; that's how they make money.

Can you keep a card for emergencies? Okay, we're not fanatics (although we're close). One credit card may be okay for emergencies. But it is important to be crystal clear on what qualifies as an emergency. When someone is in the hospital, when your boss hands you a pink slip and you need to put food on the table, or when you need to get to your grandmother's funeral—those are emergencies. And that's pretty much it. Christmas is not an emergency. Soccer shoes are not an emergency. A 2 for 1 sale is not an emergency. In-laws coming to town unexpectedly is not an emergency. If you keep a card for emergencies, it has to be for real, honest-to-goodness emergencies.

How to make sure that you never, ever slip up? Make it really hard to use the card. Bury it in a canister in the backyard. Stick the card in a tub of water, and put it in the freezer; you'll have to wait for the block of ice to melt before you can use the card. Get a big adhesive label, write "For Emergency Only" on it, and stick it across the front of the card so you'll have to peel the label off to use the card. Whatever method you choose, the point is to force yourself to ask one more time: Is this a real emergency? If it isn't, then put the card away. Spending is over.

If you are not sure you will be able to resist temptation, then just scissor all the cards up and throw them away. You will build up plenty of savings as part of your balanced spending plan, so you will be able to manage life's little crises without the cards. And besides, if anything ever goes very, very wrong, we can promise you this: There will *always* be someone trying to sign you up for another credit card.

You are working hard to get out of debt. Make it easy on yourself: Take the cards out of your wallet.

LIVING DEBT-FREE

Monica (from Step One) got her spending into balance pretty quickly, but paying off the old bills was tough. "It wasn't so much that it was hard to write the checks; with the balance thing, I had the money. The hard part was seeing how stupid I was." She described how she would walk around her apartment and see some little trinket. "I'm still paying for this stupid glass paperweight, and I don't even like it! How dumb is that?" And there were moments when she got discouraged, thinking that no matter how much she paid, she would *never* get out of the hole.

After 5 months, however, the Citibank balance was paid in full. Four months later the Capitol One balance was gone, and a month after that she finished paying off the Gap card. In 14 months, she was debt-free. "That debt was like a bad tooth that just keeps aching. It hurt so long, I just learned to live with it. It wasn't 'til it was gone that I knew life didn't have to feel like that."

When she made the last payment, she called her mom and dad and asked them out to dinner. She took them back to the same place where they had been on Mother's Day a little over a year earlier. They had a good time, laughing about pictures of a cousin's new puppy and talking about a trip her folks were planning. When the check came, Monica swooped it up again. Her mom looked at her, a smile frozen on her lips; no one said anything.

When Monica pulled out three $20 bills, she saw her mother's face relax into a genuine smile. "I'm a cash-only girl now. I don't owe a cent to anyone, and that's the way it's going to stay." They sat in silence for a bit. "Mom smiled and patted my hand, and my pop said, 'You are one tough cookie.' You know, my dad doesn't say much, so that felt really good."

Paying off debt can be tough. It takes hard work and discipline and a real dedication to your own future. But Monica is right: This may be the most feel-good step you can take. Getting these debts paid off will change your whole outlook, making each step a little lighter.

As you pull out of debt, you are building a firm foundation to start building some serious riches. And that's where the real fun will begin.

6

———————— ■ ————————

Step Six:

Build Your Dreams a Little at a Time

Until now, we have asked you to keep your feet firmly planted on the ground and your eye trained on the bottom line. No idle daydreams, no trips into things-will-work-out-somehow territory. The first priority was to get very clear about how to take control over your spending and get your money in balance.

And now it's time to reward yourself for all that hard work. It's time to dream.

This is the last step in *All Your Worth*—and the one that's the most fun. This step will consider all the things you *need* to save for and all the things you *want* to save for. Saving to buy a home, saving for retirement, saving to give a generous donation to your favorite charity, saving for a rainy day, saving to sail around the world or to send your kids to college or to buy a new Harley-Davidson. When you finish this step, you will have a comprehensive road map to a richer, more secure future.

A LITTLE AT A TIME

How do you eat a huge meal? One bite at a time. How do you make a long trip? One mile at a time. How do you build a big house? One brick at a time. You wouldn't say, "I can't possibly eat the whole meal!" or "I'll *never* get to Milwaukee!" You would just keep at it, one step at a time—and not think much more about it.

Okay, you already know this. So here's the next question: How do you get $500,000? Here's a hint: The answer is *not* "Win the lottery" or "Inherit a bundle from a long-lost uncle." The answer is that you will get $500,000 by saving a little at a time. Save, and keep on saving, and you'll make it sooner than you think.

Gradual savings is not the stuff of the six o'clock news. A lifetime of riches—*Nightly News* Style—comes when you strike oil in the back-yard or when you discover a Picasso stashed in your attic. According to the evening news, riches are like lightning—an accident that just happens when you are standing around thinking about what to fix for dinner. The *Nightly News* version holds that steady saving has little to do with getting rich.

Somewhere deep in your heart you may be thinking that if you don't win the lottery or stumble upon a diamond mine, wealth will never come your way. We're here to tell you that is just plain wrong. Savings, the kind that happens bit by bit, doesn't make the news because it is *common*—not because it is rare. Folks all over America are doing it, and you can too. It isn't hard, it isn't rare, and it can add up to a whole lot of money.

Our Uncle David loves to tell the story about when he started selling airplanes as a young man. Even 30 years ago, private airplanes were mostly the toys of well-to-do doctors and company presidents. But David's first sale was to a department store clerk, a man who fell in love with flying when he was a pilot in the air force. After he left the service, he married and had a family, and took a job selling appliances. And through it all, he saved a little each week—tossing all his change and sometimes a few bucks into a big mayonnaise jar. When the jar was full, he carried it down to the bank, counted it all out, got a money order, and mailed the money order to his mutual fund. Then he took the empty jar home and filled it up again. Sometimes the trips were a few weeks apart, sometimes a few months, but he kept on going. And when he came to see Uncle David, the store clerk bought a brand-new airplane for cash. Last we heard, he was still flying it.

How Far Can You Go?

Still not persuaded that you can build that mansion one brick at a time? Maybe the math will convince you. Suppose you earn $50,000 a year. Now suppose you keep your money in balance, setting aside 20% of every paycheck for your future and investing it carefully (later in this step we will show you how). In 15 years, you'll have more than $250,000. And in 25 years, you'll have nearly $1 million. That's right, a million dollars. Not bad, huh?

Take a look at Table 1 below, which shows you how much you can save if you put aside 20% for Savings. We'll call that your Twenty for Tomorrow.

TABLE 1. HOW MUCH CAN YOU SAVE?

Your annual income	Your Twenty for Tomorrow (20% of estimated after-tax income)	Amount you will have saved in 25 years*
$30,000	$4,320	$576,002
$40,000	$5,760	$768,003
$50,000	$7,200	$960,004
$60,000	$8,640	$1,152,005
$70,000	$10,080	$1,344,005
$80,000	$11,520	$1,536,006
$90,000	$12,960	$1,728,007
$100,000	$14,400	$1,920,008

* Assumes an average 12% annual return (same as U.S. stock market, long term). To keep this example simple, it doesn't adjust for taxes or inflation, which may overstate your real returns. On the other hand, this example also assumes that your income doesn't increase by a single dollar in the next 25 years. In all likelihood, your income *will* increase, and as your income grows the amount you invest will at least keep pace with inflation—or better.

Do those savings numbers look big? They should! Once you begin to add to your Savings, the effects of compound interest begin to kick in. Your Savings produce interest, and that interest becomes more Savings. After a while, the interest on your money is working harder than you are, pulling in interest and dividends faster than you invest every month—all because you started saving a little at a time.

THE 4 STAGES OF YOUR LIFETIME SAVINGS PLAN

The hardest part is behind you. You have already made the tough cuts to make room for a lifetime of savings, so all you need to do is to reap the reward. It is time for all that hard work—getting your Must-Haves into balance and your fun spending under control—to pay off. Because you now have the money to save for your future.

You have already earmarked 50% (or so) for Must-Haves, and another 30% for Wants. And so you have 20% of your paycheck left over at the end of every month, ready to save. That 20%—your Twenty for Tomorrow—will become the cornerstone of your Lifetime Savings Plan.

Savings is not like the other parts of the balanced money plan. For your Must-Haves, the balanced money rule is that so long as you cover your necessities (like health insurance) and keep your expenses under 50%, you can spend the money on whichever Must-Haves you want. If you want a nicer apartment and a beat-up old car, that is okay; likewise, if you prefer a hot car and a tiny apartment, that is okay too. And the Wants are even more open—you can spend the money on anything under the sun, so long as you stay under your limit.

But Savings are different. If you put your money in the wrong place—if you invest poorly or you don't put something aside for retirement—you can wind up shortchanging your future. In order to make the most of your Savings, you need to follow certain guidelines; it is *not* okay to just "go with the flow" and do whatever you want with your Savings.

The following pages will show you the four stages of your Lifetime

Savings Plan. These stages will help you make smart decisions so you can make the most of your Savings and start building some real wealth.

TABLE 2. THE LIFETIME SAVINGS PLAN

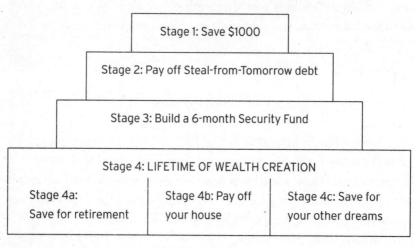

The four stages are designed to be taken one at a time. You may fly through some stages and spend several months in others; that's perfectly fine. These stages are designed to help everyone, no matter where you start, so take as long as you need to get through them. Stage Four—the final stage—is designed to help you build savings for the rest of your working life, so you will be in this stage for a very long time!

STAGE 1: SAVE $1000

Your Lifetime Savings Plan starts with $1000. That's it, just a thousand bucks.

If you already have $1000 in the bank, then congratulate yourself, you've already made it through the first stage in your Lifetime Savings Plan and not even mussed your hair. You are ready to fly on to Stage 2.

If, however, your bank account runs toward empty, then it's time to concentrate all your energy on getting that first brick into place. Put in some extra oomph here. Hold a garage sale. Sell off your CD collection and put your ski equipment on eBay. Cash in the bottles and cans. Offer to work an extra shift. And put every dollar of your Twenty for Tomorrow toward getting that $1000 into place. The goal is to put everything you have into jump-starting your Savings, so you can get some momentum toward some real wealth creation.

That $1000 will be the start of your Security Fund (see page 172). It goes in the checking account you use to pay your Must-Haves, where it will always stay, "just in case." This is the money that makes sure you can manage life's little ups and downs. You can call on it if you blow a tire on the interstate or if the kids hit a baseball through the sliding glass door. This is the money that keeps you from turning back to credit cards whenever anything goes wrong. It is okay to spend this money when you need it; just be sure to build it right back up the next time you get paid.

The $1000 not only creates a cushion for your life, it can also do something more: It can make money for you. The $1000 is there so you never, ever pay another bounced-check fee. With a $1000 buffer in the bank there will be no more returned checks because you accidentally paid the electric bill before your paycheck cleared. You'll be able to pay your bills right on time, each and every month, and that means no more extra charges from the electric company, Visa, your landlord, or anyone else. No more late fees of any kind. Now *that's* a smart way to manage your money.

Best of all, a cushion of $1000 is the start of your Relaxation Money. You can stop checking your bank balance every day, waiting on pins and needles for your paycheck to clear. You can stop holding your breath while you wait to see how fast the rent check gets deposited. Once you get ahead a little, you can pay your bills when it is convenient for you—without all the fuss. You can be confident that you have created enough cushion to manage if your paycheck is a couple of days late or the gas bill is a little high.

So ease back. No more biting your nails until the end of the month. No more waking up at 3 A.M. worrying whether you can get the mortgage payment in on time. No more stress from the payments part of life; it's time to relax a little. Sound good? It should.

STAGE 2: PAY OFF
ALL STEAL-FROM-TOMORROW DEBT

Once you have saved $1000, it is time to focus on paying off your Steal-from-Tomorrow debt. While you are in Stage 2 of your Lifetime Savings Plan, take *all* your Twenty for Tomorrow and put it toward paying off that debt, following the personal debt repayment plan you created in the previous chapter. Don't worry about saving for any other purpose, and don't worry about how long it will take you to get out of debt. The point is that one day you *will* get rid of your Steal-from-Tomorrow debt. Once your debt is paid off, you'll have laid the groundwork on which you can start building your Lifetime Savings Plan.

Once you've paid off your Steal-from-Tomorrow debts (all of them, including Aunt Alice) you'll be ready to move to Stage 3, where the heavy-duty saving begins.

STAGE 3: CREATE YOUR SECURITY FUND

Stage 3 is when you build your Security Fund, or what we like to call the Sleep Tight Fund.

By the time you reach Stage 3, you have a $1000 cushion in the bank, and you have paid off all your Steal-from-Tomorrow debt. (Congratulations!) Your Wants spending is under control, and your Must-Haves are in balance. You are probably feeling better than ever about how things are going.

But maybe you are a little worried about the future. Sure, things are fine now. But what if you lose your job? What if the foundation on the house cracks? What if something big comes up?

That's where your Security Fund comes in. When your Steal-from-Tomorrow debt is paid off, it is time to start putting all your Twenty for Tomorrow into an ordinary savings account that will grow into your Security Fund. This will be your personal defense fund in case something really goes wrong. And it is nothing more than a simple savings account.

That's right—an ordinary savings account. No fancy investments, no special tax breaks. Your Security Fund should be easy to reach, but not *too* easy. Keep it separate from your regular checking account so you won't be tempted to dip into your Security Fund for regular expenses. And don't get an ATM card or a debit card for the account. The rule here is "Hands Off" except in times of real need. Set up your account so that you have to make a special trip to the bank to get your hands on this money.

Why? Because this is the money that will let you sleep easily each and every night. This is the money you can call on whenever you need it. It is there if you get sick, it is there if you lose your job, it is there if the car conks out or the roof caves in. Your Security Fund will stand as the shield between you and whatever life throws at you.

What if you need to spend it? If an emergency comes along, then use this money. If you take a serious blow and can't make ends meet, then you can turn to this account. That's what it is there for. But just as soon as the crisis has passed, you need to start building it up again. This is the cushion you create for all your life—the backstop that is always there for you.

How much should you put in your Security Fund? The general rule of thumb is put enough in your Security Fund to cover your Must-Haves for 6 months.

WORKSHEET 10: SECURITY FUND TARGET	
Total monthly Must-Have expenses (from page 105)	$ _____
Multiply by 6	× 6
= Security Fund Target	= $ _____

How do you build your Security Fund? One dollar at a time. During Stage 3 of your lifetime savings plan, take your Twenty for Tomorrow and just put it in a money-market or savings account. If you are starting from scratch, it should take you just over a year to finish out your Security Fund. That may sound like a long time, but think of it this way: You are changing your life. Real, lasting change takes a little time.

In a little more than a year, you will be in a different place. You will have moved past the vast majority of Americans. Instead of feeling like your financial future is stalled, you will be able to see a tremendous accomplishment—a hefty bank balance in your name. This will become the strong foundation on which you can build your future and your dreams.

STAGE 4:
A LIFETIME OF WEALTH CREATION

This is the last tantalizing moment as you execute your plans and begin your new financial life. It is a little like building a rocket to go to the moon. After all the designing, planning, coordinating, and building, the moment is here. The rocket is finally on the launching pad. The hardest work is finished, and your trip is about to begin. All you have to do now is hit the "Launch" button. This is when you start building the kind of real wealth that goes beyond keeping you safe—this is the wealth that can make your dreams become a reality.

Once you've created your Security Fund, you'll be ready to move into Stage 4. This is the stage you'll stay in for the rest of your working life.

Because Stage 4 lasts for so long, it has more than one piece. The first piece is your retirement fund. The second piece is paying off your house. And the third piece is saving for your other dreams. Just those three pieces, and you have the formula for building wealth, securing your future, and making your dreams a reality.

The future starts here, and it's time to start building the life you deserve.

1. Create a Retirement Fund

It's time to start saving for your golden years. The money you set aside now can mean so much down the line. It can mean travel, a vacation home, helping out the kids, making a big contribution to your church—whatever it is that will make you happy. Now's the time to start making that possible.

But saving for *retirement*? Okay, we've heard it before. Retirement looks sooooo far away, and there are so many things you need *now*. And you like your job so much that you never want to retire. And you plan to strike it rich somehow, so there's no need to save for old age. And if you never ever think about retirement, you'll stay young forever. And if you kiss a frog, it will turn into a prince.

Yeah, right.

You know that you need to save for retirement, but the reality isn't as tough as you might think. In fact, there is some good news. The government gives out a pile of tax breaks to help you save for retirement. Your employer wants to help you save for retirement. And you have years and years for your retirement account to grow, which means that a little Savings goes a long way.

In other words, this is really easy. You just need to *do* it.

You may be wondering what all the fuss is about. So, just in case you're not persuaded that saving for retirement is all that important, here are a few Scary Statistics to remind you that the future is coming, ready or not. One in eight older Americans lives in poverty. The average Social Security payment is about $10,000 a year—not even enough to live in safety in many places, let alone comfort. The elderly are now the fastest-growing group in bankruptcy. And the people who study this stuff think it's going to get even worse: Economists now predict that today's workers will be a whopping $45 billion short of what they will need to live on when they retire.

Now that the scary stuff is out of the way, think about the happier side of retirement—what life can be like if you're financially prepared. Maybe you have something luxurious in mind, like plenty of money for travel or a villa nestled in the hills. Maybe you want to spend your golden years on the golf course, or strolling along the beach. Or maybe your goals are more modest—just a paid-for house and plenty of time with the grandkids.

No matter what the details, *All Your Worth* will help you create a retirement fund that enables you to accomplish the most important objective: *When the time comes, you can retire in comfort and dignity.* This means having money to cover your basic needs, money for your care, money to let you pay your own way. It means there will be no need to call on the charity of others, and no need to continue working longer than you are physically able. And, with a little luck, it means having money for your dreams—however you dream them.

TOP FIVE MYTHS ABOUT RETIREMENT SAVINGS

Myth	*Fact*
You can count on Social Security to see you through old age.	Social Security benefits are not enough to live on.
You don't need to save for retirement if you plan to keep working.	You need to be prepared in case you're not able to keep working.
You can wait to start saving until the kids are grown.	The earlier you start, the bigger your rewards will be.
If you keep working and don't retire, your retirement savings will be wasted.	The money is yours, no matter what. If you don't need it for retirement, you can pass it on to your kids, use it for an emergency, or buy something nice with it.
If you don't think about getting old, you'll stay young forever.	You wish!

Entire books have been written on retirement planning, so if you want to learn more, there is plenty of information out there. (AARP is a very good place to start.) But if you'd rather get your teeth drilled than spend the afternoon reading up on retirement planning, we've boiled it down to a couple of smart, easy moves. Remember, these are *easy* moves, so there's no excuse for not doing them.

• *Sign up for your retirement plan at work.* If your company offers a retirement plan, belly up to the bar and sign on the dotted line. Your boss has already done the hard work by getting the plan set up, so it is really easy for you to get started. Just fill out the paperwork and have the money taken out of your paycheck, each and every month. You'll get automatic tax breaks for every dollar you put in, so the government gives you an immediate boost. And your company may give you matching contributions, which really is free money lying on the ground. Reach over and pick it up.

• *Create your own retirement plan.* If your boss doesn't offer a retirement plan, open an IRA (Individual Retirement Account) on your own. (If you are self-employed or if you run a small business, open a SEP-IRA or an individual 401(k), which offer higher limits and extra tax breaks to small-business owners.) IRAs are easy to set up; you can open one through your local bank or through an online financial institution. Look for an IRA that has low fees and plenty of investment options. Once you've opened your account, just start contributing. The government will help you fund your IRA by chopping down your taxes, so take advantage of it—it's better than walking around with a bucket when it's raining money.

How much should you put in your retirement accounts? Roughly half of your Twenty for Tomorrow—in the neighborhood of 10% of your take-home pay. (Remember, this is once you're in Stage 4; don't worry about saving for retirement until *after* you've paid off your credit card balance and built your Security Fund.) If your employer contributes to a pension, you can put in less than 10%. If you are over 35 and you are just now getting started on saving for retirement, you should put in more. That will give you a good footing for a comfortable retirement, while still leaving plenty left over for your other dreams.

Once you have put some money in your Retirement Fund, sit back for a minute and congratulate yourself. Nearly half of all Americans never make it this far. If you have a retirement account and you are putting money in it, then you have just made it into the upper half (financially speaking) of all adults in the U.S. Hot dog!

2. Pay Off Your Home

Imagine a home of your own. Not just a house that you live in, not just a place that you pay a mortgage on. A home that is *all yours.* No mortgage payments, no rent checks. A home that is completely, 100% paid for, free and clear.

Sixteen years ago, Stephen Acosta broke his back in a motorcycle accident. He was lucky to regain the use of his arms and legs, but his days climbing around on construction sites as a licensed electrician were over. Between the medical bills and the lost income, he was pretty much wiped out. He was just out of rehab when his house was posted for foreclosure. "I limped around and around, just staring at the place. The hedge I put out front, the extra shelves I built in the closets." Even now, Stephen's voice cracks when he talks about how he felt. "It was *mine.* And someone was fixing to take it. No way could I just lay down for that."

Stephen got a repair job in an electronics shop, and then took a second job working weekends as a security guard in a downtown office building. He cut his Wants spending to the bone, and pretty soon he was caught up on the mortgage. "I kept picturing that orange sign on my front door, saying someone else was gonna take my house. And every time I thought about it, I got mad all over again, and I sent another hundred bucks to that damn mortgage company. I figured they could take my whole paycheck, but I'd never let them take my home."

Not long ago, Stephen threw a big party at his small ranch house in the outskirts of St. Louis. He invited all his friends, and his mom drove up from Tulsa. After everyone arrived, he thumped his fist on the table, telling them to be quiet because he had an announcement. He directed everyone's attention to a big green bowl with some papers in it. Stephen explained that this was his mortgage, all paid off. He had gotten it back from the bank, and now he wanted everyone he loved to witness while he burned it. "Everyone cheered while I fired it up. Then my mom cried, and I even choked up a little. Damn it, I pulled myself out and now this place was mine forever—no matter what."

Paying off your home is the double whammy of the Savings world—a tremendously smart financial move that is also tremendously satisfying. After all, where else can you build substantial wealth *and* smile over your flower bed?

The most obvious reason to pay off your home is that you get a great return on your money. Suppose you are paying 7% on your mortgage. Every dollar you pay on your mortgage earns 7%—guaranteed, no matter what. That is a lot more than you can earn in just about any other no-risk, guaranteed investment. Plus, unlike the interest you earn on your savings account, you don't have to pay taxes on that 7%.

Paying off your home is also a great part of your retirement plan. When it comes time to stop working, you can live rent-free, which means that your Social Security and retirement Savings will go a lot further. If you need a lot of cash, you can sell your house and move to something smaller. And if you stay in your home until your last days, the house will be a wonderful legacy to pass along to your children or to your favorite charity.

Paying off your home also does something many financial planners neglect to mention: It gives you freedom. Once that mortgage is gone, just imagine all the freedom in your wallet. Freedom to spend more money on fun, freedom to give more to the people you love, freedom to work a little less and play a little more. Think of this as yet another form of sleep-tight insurance.

But what about . . .

But what about the mortgage interest tax credit? A tax credit is no reason to prolong your mortgage payments! Think of it this way—if you were a professional gambler, your gambling losses would be tax-deductible. But does that mean a gambler *wants* to lose money? No way!

Still not convinced? Consider the math. Let's say you're paying $1000 a month, out of which $700 goes to interest and $300 goes to principal. You would save somewhere around $200 on your taxes. So you want to keep paying $1000 to the bank so you can save $200? Of course not. Math like that will drive you to the poorhouse in a hurry. As a friend of ours once said, "The problem with tax credits is that they are like paper towels. You have to spill your own milk (make the payments) before the tax credit helps you sop up some of it."

But what if you plan to sell your house? If you sell your house, you walk away with the equity—and the equity increases for every dollar you pay down on the mortgage. When you sell the house, the cash is yours, whether you plow it into another home or just shove it in your pocket.

But doesn't it make sense to borrow against your home when interest rates are low? Whether you are borrowing to pay down your credit card debt, play the stock market, or travel to Tahiti, borrowing against your home is still borrowing—period. It is not saving, it is not smart, it is not savvy. A second mortgage or a home equity line of credit is plain old Steal-from-Tomorrow debt, only with the added twist that if something goes wrong and you can't pay, the mortgage lender can take your house away. So just pay down your mortgage, and bask in the knowledge that one day you will be completely, contentedly debt-free.

But what if you don't own a home? Should you rush right out and buy one? Should you decide your future is hopelessly lost forever and crawl into your apartment bathtub and pull a mattress over you? No and no.

If you don't own a home, it may make sense to buy—or it may not. (If you are trying to decide whether homeownership is right for you, be sure to read Chapter 8 on "The Big Buy.") Buying a home is *not* the right choice for some people. And renting is perfectly fine—on one condition. Renters still need to keep saving. Keep on putting that Twenty for Tomorrow into retirement (which you just read) and other savings (which is coming up), and you can be just as secure as your home-owning neighbors. If a home doesn't make sense for you *and* you are saving 20%, you will do just fine. In fact, you will do better than fine—you will be building toward a lifetime of riches.

How do you pay off your home?

One dollar at a time. Take about 5% of your income (which is one-quarter of your 20% for savings) and use it to pay extra on your mortgage every month.

The amount outstanding on your mortgage is an awfully big number, so you may think that paying a couple hundred dollars extra every month is like trying to bail out the ocean with a teaspoon. But you may be surprised just how far that little extra can go. Suppose you have a mortgage for $150,000, at 7%. Now suppose you make $50,000 a year, and your income increases a little, year after year. (Even jobs where the income is pretty steady usually get at least a cost-of-living raise, so the paycheck keeps up with inflation.) If you keep putting an extra 5% of your paycheck toward your mortgage, you could be mortgage-free in 15 years—or even faster! *And* you could save more than $100,000 in interest. Now *that's* a smart move.

3. Save for Your Other Dreams

You're paying off your home, and you're saving for your golden years. Your money worries are disappearing like yesterday's rainstorm. So what now?

It's time to make your *other* dreams come true! Your dreams can be as heartwarming, as daring, or as goofy as you want them to be. Do you dream of a vacation house by the lake, where you can fish for trout and watch birds? Do you long to remodel the kitchen, and maybe install a swimming pool in the backyard? Do you dream of the day when you can make a generous donation to your church or synagogue or help out your favorite charity? Or maybe your dreams are for your kids. Medical school for Katie? Lavish weddings for the twins?

Take a moment to savor your dream. Picture the sunlight reflecting on the lake while your husband proudly holds up a string of trout. Imagine Katie, all grown up in her robe and cap, proudly accepting her diploma. Picture the twins walking down the aisle in a huge double wedding, preparing to take their wedding vows. Put some flesh and bone on your dreams—enough so you can taste them, enough to put a grin on your face. You have earmarked 10% for retirement and 5% for paying off your mortgage early, which means that 5% of your Twenty for Tomorrow is still available. So what do you do with that 5%? That goes toward whatever takes your fancy. These are the fun dreams, the payoff for a lifetime of Savings. You have built your Security Fund, and so you have enough to be safe. You have launched your retirement fund, and so your golden years are secure. You are paying off your home, and one day your life will be mortgage-free. And so it's time to bring your other dreams to life. Travel or weddings, a new car or a lovely vacation—whatever you want.

Make your dreams part of your life plan today. Write down what you want, and put it in your wallet (right next to your money!). Put another copy in your office drawer. Then add some pictures. Take a photo of your dream house. Cut out a shot of an elegant bridal gown or a racy new car or a touching graduation picture. Get an ad for your dream vacation. When you have the image, stick a copy on your refrigerator, your computer screen, or your bathroom mirror. Make your dreams part of your reality, each and every day. And every time you glimpse your dream, be sure to smile. This is what saving is all about.

Sometimes people who save their money are shown as the colorless folks, the conservative ones who don't dare. But this couldn't be further from the truth. In fact, people who save are the ones who dare to dream, the ones who have big ideas—and who make real plans to make those dreams happen. In our opinion, savers are the ones who taste life at its richest.

Cultivate Your Savings

Now comes the $10,000 question (or, maybe someday, the $10,000,000 question!): How should you make your Savings grow? Maybe you already have your Savings in the perfect blend of mutual funds, and you just need to tweak your precious-metals allocation. Then again, maybe you don't know the first thing about investing, and you're worried that it just sounds *hard* (or at least really, really boring). This section will teach you the Lifetime of Riches investment strategy, which will allow you to make the most of your Savings—*without* having to learn a whole new vocabulary or spend the next 10 years taking finance classes. These guidelines are very simple to follow, but incredibly powerful when put in place.

Picking an investment is not so different from picking a car. There are people who love nothing more than searching for an exotic car. They get into heated arguments over the merits of the 1966 Mustang versus the 1968 Plymouth Fury. They tell stories that have punch lines like "The manifold! Can you believe it!" They dedicate their days and nights to studying muscle cars and antique cars, and maybe, after all those hours, they drive something really cool. It is even possible that some of them make a little money when they happen upon something really special that they can buy for a good price. Then again, most of them lose their shirts at the repair shop.

Of course, most of us are perfectly happy to buy something safe and reliable with good gas mileage and enough room for the groceries. *And there is nothing wrong with that.* If you are the kind of person who doesn't want to study up on compression ratios, you can still pick a car that looks nice, starts every morning, zips along the roads, and gets you where you want to go. Investing is the same. If you think it sounds like fun to spend all your time researching the latest financial whizbangs and the hottest new stocks, go right ahead. About a million TV shows and a billion books claim to hold the secret on how to beat the market and get fabulously rich, so you have plenty of reading to do. Our only advice is that you be sure to read those books with a touch of skepticism; after all, if these people had the magic formula for creating billions, why would they tell you about it?

But if you don't want to spend hours and hours learning everything there is to know about the wide world of investing, *that is no excuse for staying on the sidelines.* Even if you're not a trained mechanic, you still buy a car and get out there and drive. And even if you're not interested in becoming a professional-grade investor, you still need to invest intelligently.

Here are four simple rules to sensible, long-term investing.

1. Take Stock

There isn't any doubt about it: The stock market is the best place for long-term investing.

Over the long run, the U.S. stock market has averaged nearly a 12% return. A whopping 97% of 5-year periods and 100% of 10-year periods have made money. The stock market is easy to get into, and easy to get out of. In short, it's hard to beat the stock market for long-term investing.

But the key phrase here is *long-term*. As we all know, the stock market doesn't just go up—it also goes down. So it is not a place to keep money that you might need next week. If you had to sell in a hurry, you could get burned badly if the market takes a dip.

Here's the rule of thumb: The stock market is where you should keep money that you don't expect to use for at least five years. So, for example, your retirement fund should go in the stock market. Timothy's college fund should go in the stock market, at least while he is little. But your Security Fund should *not* go in the stock market because you just might need it tomorrow. The money you're saving to buy a house should *not* go in the stock market because you hope to use it soon. That kind of Savings belongs in a nice, steady bank account or a short-term CD, not in the stock market.

WHAT SHOULD YOU PUT IN THE STOCK MARKET?	WHAT SHOULD YOU PUT IN AN ORDINARY SAVINGS ACCOUNT?
Your retirement fund	Your Security Fund (for emergencies only)
Money for the kids' college (while the kids are young)	Money to save for a down payment on a house
Any money you plan to put aside for 5 or more years	Any money you might need in less than 5 years

2. Try a Little of Everything

What stocks should you buy?

All of them.

Yes, the movies, the dime-store novels, and the get-rich-quick tall tales all start with that one special stock. The hero figured out that the Zoom Company was going to take off, and he bought early. The message is clear—get the inside track on a good stock, hang on for the ride, and get out just in time. These are great stories, but they are just another variation on whether the 1968 Pontiac Firebird was the sweetest car ever made.

Serious investors know the three rules of stock buying: diversify, diversify, diversify. *Diversify* is just a fancy term for putting your eggs in more than one basket. In other words, buy some of nearly every stock listed in the market.

Investing in any individual stock can be risky. Suppose, for example, that the hero of that dime-store novel had bought Enron stock? He wouldn't be feeling quite so smug now, would he? The smart strategy for long-term investing isn't to look for the one stock that will soar to the moon. The right strategy is to buy lots of different stocks in lots of different industries. That way you will get *some* benefit if a particular stock soars, but you'll only take *some* loss if the CEO ends up in jail. You don't get rich overnight, but you don't get wiped out either. Best of all, economists have shown that diversification will give you the best possible return for the least amount of risk. In other words, diversification is really smart.

3. Be Cheap

The third rule is even simpler: Pay as little overhead as possible. This may sound obvious, but you might be surprised by how many people let hefty brokerage fees and a host of other charges steal bites out of their nest eggs. The "classic car" crowd—the guys who love to sit at their computers trading their favorite stocks—is particularly prone to overpaying these kinds of fees (which is another good reason to keep things simple). As for the rest of us, with a little careful shopping we can get nice, low fees.

Do you have to know a lot about the calculation of brokerage fees to be a good shopper? Hey, do you have to know how tuna is canned to know the difference between buying at $2.79 a can and $3.59? Nope. In fact, it is even easier to compare prices and make decisions on your stock investments than it is for the tuna specials—you don't even have to leave the house to do it. Keep reading.

4. Do It All with One-Stop Shopping

What's the easiest way to follow rules 1–3, that is, to get a diversified, low-overhead investment in the stock market? (Drumroll, please . . .) Put your money in an index fund.

An index fund (also known as an "indexed mutual fund") buys stocks from hundreds of different companies, so you get instant, no-hassle diversification. The stocks are purchased according to a preset formula, so you don't blow a bunch of money paying some high-priced specialists to sit around and dream about the next big stock. Instead, the index fund just buys a little bit of stock from all the different companies listed on the stock market, and then sits back and lets the money grow.

The index fund is essentially the Honda Civic of the investment world. Not too fancy, it is a good, reliable vehicle that can get most people where they want to go. The overhead fees on an index fund are typically much smaller than they are for the fancier investments, so it lets you stretch your dollar as far as possible. And here's the best part: Index funds outperform roughly 70–80% of all other stock funds. That means your index fund will do better than the vast majority of brokers on Wall Street. So it is a really good bet *and* it doesn't require you to spend a lot of time shopping.

Are you still not persuaded that index funds are right for you? Think you'd rather play the market? Consider what a few famous investors have to say about index funds:

> *. . . the best way to own common stocks is through an indexed mutual fund.*
>
> —Warren Buffett, self-made billionaire

> *Most individual investors would be better off in an index mutual fund.*
>
> Peter Lynch, legendary stock picker
> and vice chairman of Fidelity

> *Most of the mutual fund investments I have are index funds . . .*
> —Charles R. Schwab, founder of Charles Schwab Corp.
> and one of the 400 richest people in America

> *By day we write about "Six Funds to Buy NOW!" . . . By night, we invest in sensible index funds. Unfortunately, pro–index fund stories don't sell magazines.*
>
> —anonymous *Fortune* magazine writer

Just a month ago, I (Elizabeth) met a woman who was a high-powered investment broker in New York. She was stylish and fun, and very successful in her field, managing more than $500 million in funds for other people. After we had visited for a long time, I asked her where she kept her retirement money. She giggled and lowered her voice, then said "at a low-cost index fund—but don't tell my clients."

In other words, index funds come with good returns, low costs, and the recommendations of some of the smartest people on Wall Street. That's hard to beat.

How do you choose an index fund? Look for an index fund that has low annual fees and includes a lot of different stocks. The most popular index funds are based on the Standard & Poor's 500 index, which includes stock from the 500 largest companies in America. Such a fund is sometimes called just a "500 Index." Together, these firms make up about 70% of the value in the entire U.S. stock market, so you get a nice broad swath of the biggest companies in America. If you want even more diversification (with slightly higher fees), you might consider a "total stock market" index fund (which includes virtually the entire stock market—5000 or so companies). You could also opt for an index fund that includes stocks of companies based outside the U.S., which gives you the most possible diversification. Amelia has most of her retirement money invested in a 500 Index fund, with the remainder going toward a couple of international index funds. Elizabeth is a little more conservative; her retirement fund sits in just a 500 Index fund.

Where should you buy an index fund? Index funds are all the same, so you should choose the place that will give you the lowest possible overhead fees. You can get an index fund though your retirement plan or as a stand-alone investment. If you are shopping on your own, discount brokerages are a good place to start (you can find one online); just hunt for the lowest fees.

If you get your retirement plan through your job, you will have to choose from the list of investment options your employer gives you. If there is an index fund on the list, just sign up for it. But if there is no index fund on the list, look for the most diversified, lowest-cost mutual fund you can find, which is the best way to replicate the benefits of an index fund. And ask your boss to add an index fund next year!

Answers to Your Questions

Can't I just keep my money in the bank?

Still tempted to stay out of the stock market? Consider the earlier example of someone who earns $50,000 and diligently puts 20% of his paycheck in an index fund. In 25 years, he would have nearly $1 million. Now suppose he was a little scared of the stock market, and he decided to just play it safe and keep his money in a savings account where he would earn about 3%. How much would he have at the end of 25 years? A million bucks? Nope. A half a million dollars? Nope. Actually, he would have just $210,000. In other words, sitting on the sidelines would cost him nearly $800,000. Can you afford to give up that much? Of course not! So just get in there and do it.

What do I do when the stock market crashes?

It's all over the news: The Dow Jones is falling! The market is crashing! Brokers are jumping out of windows! What should you do?

Nothing.

Do nothing? Are we serious? Absolutely. The single biggest mistake you can make (other than sitting on the sidelines) is to sell when the market starts to drop. Why? A falling market is the absolute worst time to sell. Odds are, you would get *less* return for your money (since the market is down) *and* you would miss out on the gains when the market rebounds. Both ways, you lose.

If the roller-coaster ride of the stock market makes you a little dizzy, just remember that you're in this for the long haul. You are following the investment strategy recommended by some of the smartest economists and Nobel laureates in the world. And you have years and years before you'll need that money, which means there are years and years for the stock market to turn around. So just sit tight, and keep on investing.

*But I just know Company XYZ will do great—why don't I put all my
money into it?*

They have a great product! Their profits are rising! Why not throw all
your money into the stock of one company? The problem is, you're not
the only one who has noticed that Company XYZ has a great product.
In fact, there are literally thousands upon thousands of professional investors who spend all their waking hours testing products and checking
profits. Odds are, they know that it's a good company, and they've already bid up the price of the stock. Which means that you probably
won't make any more money buying XYZ stock than you would any
other.

Many well-respected economists believe that even the smartest,
most dedicated investors are likely to lose money when they try to pick
individual stocks:

> *It is not easy to get rich in Las Vegas, at Churchill Downs, or at the
> local Merrill Lynch office.*
> —Professor Paul A. Samuelson, Massachusetts Institute of
> Technology, Nobel laureate in economics

> *The stockbroker services his client the same way Bonnie and Clyde
> serviced banks.*
> —William Bernstein, Ph.D., M.D., author of *The Intelligent Asset Allocator*

Don't put all your money in your employer's stock, no matter how
optimistic you are about your company's future. Sometimes bad things
happen to good companies. Remember how thousands of Enron em-
ployees got burned? They lost their jobs *and* their retirement accounts
were wiped out because they hadn't diversified. So don't keep more
than 5% of your retirement savings in your employer's stock (or any
other single stock).

If you are still tempted to try playing the market, remember this:
Tens of thousands of smart, savvy, highly educated professional investors were taken in by Enron. If you want to hunt for the neatest

stock, do that for a hobby. But don't play the market with your retirement fund.

But my financial adviser (or broker) says I should invest in XYZ!

If you are feeling uncertain about your financial planning, you may want to seek the help of a professional. There's nothing wrong with getting a little expert advice—just be careful. Financial planners and stockbrokers aren't so different from car salesmen—they make their money off getting you to buy something. You don't buy; they don't earn. Sometimes they sell you something you really need, like a retirement account. Other times, however, they try to steer you toward high-priced gizmos that yield the fattest commissions for them, not the best returns for you. Financial advisers are slick salesmen, and they can come up with some elaborate reasons why the high-fee mutual fund is better than an index fund. Before you sign on the dotted line, ask your broker what his commission is. If you're not comfortable with the answer, walk out the door.

Investments to Avoid

More than once we've met some perfectly nice guy, a sober sort of fellow who pays his bills on time, always wears a seat belt, and faithfully applies sunscreen. And when the topic of Savings comes up, he explains that he has decided to boost his returns by putting all his money in Mongolian land-title futures. He usually smiles and says, "Getting a great return." And then we smile and nod, thinking, "Did this guy just arrive from Mars? He's going to lose his shirt—and his socks and undies!"

There are a lot of ways to make bad investments. Here are a few.

- *Gold.* Financial sophisticates will tell you that gold is a lousy investment. Don't bother. And that applies to Canadian Maple Leafs, South African Krugerrands, and all other forms of exotic currency (gold or otherwise). Let the guys who have a lot of money to lose play with these investments.

• *Prepaid funerals.* Making arrangements in advance so that your loved ones know your wishes when you die can be an act of extraordinary love and concern. But prepaying your funeral makes you a creditor of the funeral home for years and years, with your money tied up and no way to earn a return on it or shift it to another use if you need it. To make matters worse, two of the largest funeral homes in the country recently filed for bankruptcy, leaving thousands of families with nothing. You wouldn't give your money to a guy at the county fair to hold for you; don't do the same thing with a prepaid funeral. Leave a will, leave instructions, and leave cash—that's the best you can do for your loved ones.

• *Collectibles.* Whether it's Franklin Mint medals, autographed footballs, rare stamps, comic books, baseball cards, antique furniture, first-edition books, artwork, or even classic cars, the message from the sellers is loud and clear—go ahead and indulge, spend more than you think you can afford, because this really counts as Savings. So we want to be very clear: *This is not Savings!* Don't let the occasional get-rich-quick story (which may or may not be true) suck you in. Have fun with the stuff you buy, and enjoy your hobbies. But always be clear in your own mind that these are just for fun, not the cornerstone of your future. Your retirement savings belongs in an index fund, not a comic book!

SENDING YOUR KID TO COLLEGE

Do you want to put a little something aside for the kids? Are you committed to seeing little Herman in his cap and gown? Here's another place where you can take advantage of some nice fat tax breaks. Our favorite is known as a "529" College Savings Plan. (Don't worry, there aren't 528 other plans for you to worry about!) There are 4 main advantages to putting your kids' college savings in a 529 plan:

1. *Tax-free growth on investment.* That's right, the investment grows tax-free. That means the IRS won't take anything out of George's college account: Your family gets to keep it all.

2. *You maintain control over the account.* Maybe you want to put something away for the kids' college, but you have this nagging fear that little Brittany may drop out of school and join a motorcycle gang. Relax. Even though the account is in your child's name, *you* decide when to distribute the money, and how much to give out.

3. *You can take it back.* If you're worried you might one day need the money for another purpose, it's hard to beat a 529 plan. You'd have to pay a penalty (10% of the earnings on the money), but you can take back the gift anytime you want. And if Robbie gets a scholarship or joins the Navy, you can shift the money to his little brother without any penalty.

4. *It's really, really easy.* Each state offers its own 529 plan, and you can sign up for any of them, regardless of where you live (and regardless of where your child ultimately goes to college). Once you've picked a plan, just complete an enrollment form and start saving.

But college is really, really expensive. Isn't that the truth! So start saving what you can, right now. You may not save up enough for the World's Most Expensive College. Sara Sue may need to work part-time in the library to pay for her books. And when the time comes, both you and your child may still need to apply for scholarship and grant money. In other words, your 529 savings may be only part of the picture when your children head off to college. That's okay. Just remember, every dollar you save is another dollar toward bringing this dream a little closer.

This is another one of those places where money is lying on the ground. If college for the kids is part of your dreaming, reach over and pick up some money here.

IT STARTS IN YOUR HEAD

You now have the knowledge and tools you need to get on the road to serious wealth creation. We hope this is a lifelong road of smooth wealth building, month after month. But in just the same way that negative-thinking traps can stop you from balancing your money, these thinking traps can also sabotage your savings plan. In case you run into any traps, here are some tools to help you set yourself free.

IF YOU THINK . . .	YOU SHOULD TELL YOURSELF . . .
I can't afford to save.	I have balanced my spending, so I have enough for Must-Haves, Wants, *and* Savings.
I'll never save enough.	Real wealth is built one dollar at a time.
Figuring out what to invest in is really hard.	An index fund is all I need.
I had a setback, and I'll never get caught up.	Setbacks happen. It's time to push forward on making my future brighter.
The market went down and erased all my hard work.	The market will go up again. I'm in this for the long haul.
I'll start saving next month when my expenses will be a little lower.	I will start now. Today I will begin to move toward the future I want.

And here's one last thinking trap that deserves its own special place: the trap of getting stuck. The trap of telling yourself that you're just not ready, or that if you can't save 20% there's no point in saving anything. So here's a reminder of the first, last, and most important thing you can do to create some real wealth: *Start saving.* Just do it. Really and truly, just start socking some money away.

Good intentions won't get you there; it takes action. Think of this like exercise. You can read lots of books on how many hours to exercise or what kinds of shoes to buy or whether tennis burns more calories than swimming. But all of that is meaningless unless you get off your couch and start moving. The same holds here—take some dollars out of your paycheck and start saving.

Even if you don't get it perfect—even if you don't save the full 20%, or you don't set up your retirement account right away—saving something is *always* better than saving nothing. Every dollar you save is a dollar toward a brighter future.

Looking to the Future

Congratulations! You have made it through the sixth step. You have arrived. You can stand in a place that is a little higher, a place that lets you see a little farther. It wasn't easy to get here. It took some hard work and some tough choices. And you may still be finding your way to the finish line, making progress month by month.

It is time, now, to stop and do something very important: Smile. You deserve a celebration. You are moving past the 63% of credit card–carrying Americans who are lugging around a balance. You have said good-bye to the 50% of Americans who worry about their bills. You are doing better than the 48% of Americans who have not saved one single dollar for retirement. You are taking the best possible care of yourself and your loved ones. You can sleep better and you can laugh louder. You are moving toward a life of security and comfort, with a little less worry and a lot more living. So take a moment to savor all that you have accomplished and all the riches that lay before you. Because you've earned it.

Now take a moment to picture your future. You've mapped out your dreams, and you've created a plan to bring them to life. Your future is safer than ever before, and you have control over where it's headed. Let your smile grow even wider. In fact, you can laugh out loud. You have given yourself the gift of tomorrow.

PART TWO

Powerful Tools

7

---■---

Love and Money:
Having It All

Except for money, we never fight about anything.

I really think we could get our money in balance, except my husband spends too much.

I thought we were okay, and then she went out and bought this new couch, and I just lost it.

You love each other. You are committed to each other. You're married (or practically married). You took those vows, "for richer or for poorer." You share the same home, the same expenses, the same debts—and the same future. Which surely must mean that you both have to fix your money problems together—holding hands all the way. No financial progress until you agree on everything, isn't that the way it goes?

That's certainly the standard advice: You Must Be in Agreement on All Your Financial Decisions. It sounds oh-so-logical. After all, it seems perfectly *reasonable* that you and your mate should be in perfect agreement on money.

But what if you're not? What if you are a normal couple with normal disagreements, and you happen to disagree about money sometimes? What if you get along great most of the time, but conflicts over money creep up when you least expect them? What then?

Most of the financial experts don't offer much help. Maybe they'll tell you to get marriage counseling (as if you could afford that!). Or maybe they'll just leave you on your own, with the clear impression that things are Hopeless until you Reform Your Mate (or file for divorce).

Well, we're here to tell you that is plain nonsense. The truth is, *every couple disagrees over money.* Whether you yell and stomp around or quietly hide the credit card bills, every couple wrangles sometimes. Why? Because money is about choices—hundreds of them every single day—and even people who love each other very much are bound to disagree on some choices some of the time.

Your money choices—and the conflicts that surround them—are probably coming into sharp focus right now. Here you are in the midst of balancing your money, making lots and lots of new choices. This means that there are plenty of new opportunities for conflict with your mate. *But* this also means you have a chance to do something better in dealing with money in your life—and in your relationship.

You *can* improve your money partnership. Right here, right now, this very day. Because getting straight about money in your relationship isn't about waiting for that perfect moment when you and your partner miraculously think alike about everything. It isn't about waiting for the Vulcan mind-meld. It is about working together, every single day, reaching compromises that work for both of you—just like you do for the rest of your relationship.

> You can take steps to improve your money relationship, right here, right now.

Even if you don't have screaming fights over money, out-of-balance spending and worry over money can drive a wedge between you and your partner, adding anxiety to every purchase. We're here to tell you, there is room to improve. And if you have a really bad relationship over money—if you hide things or cry a lot or scare each other—then working out a lifetime money plan is going to pay big-time dividends for you. Not only will you be able to sleep better at night knowing your money is in balance, but you also have a chance here to put your relationship on a much stronger footing. If you can get better on money, you can get better with each other.

Does that mean we promise Nirvana? Will she always look adoringly at you and say, "Darling, I see that you have done an excellent job with the Must-Have spending"? Will he always hold you rapturously while murmuring, "Sweetheart, please spend more on your Wants. You deserve it." Will you live in complete harmoney and never fight again, while violin music swells in the background? Nope. Not only do we not promise that, you probably wouldn't want to live in Nirvana anyway.

But here is what we can promise you: Wherever your relationship is now, getting straight on money will go a long way toward making it better. Agreeing on a basic plan that you can live with will take a lot of pressure off your relationship. But most important of all, when you have some financial peace, you can focus on the things in your life that really matter—including the love and laughter you share with each other.

BUT HE (OR SHE) REFUSES TO CHANGE?

Maybe you are blessed with a willing partner. The two of you are reading side by side, chatting about *All Your Worth* over supper. You are in contended agreement on nearly all your money issues, and all that remains is to iron out a few details.

Then again, maybe things aren't quite so rosy. Maybe you are stuck with all the work, pulling both oars while your partner goes along for the ride. Or maybe your partner is downright stubborn, unwilling to budge even a little, throwing over anchors while you try to keep rowing.

And maybe, somewhere in the back of your mind, you believe it just isn't possible to improve your money partnership. You would like things to get better, of course, but in your heart of hearts, you believe your money problems are really your partner's fault. He spends too much money. She doesn't earn enough. He's not willing to change. She doesn't listen to reason. And if your mate isn't sitting here reading this book, what can you do to make things better anyway? Nothing can improve until your partner changes—and your partner is just sitting on the couch, not willing to lift a finger. What then?

Hold off on your skepticism for a minute. Suppose, just suppose, *you* can make a big difference in your money relationship all by yourself. Yes, your partner is not perfect. And no, your partner is not off the hook. But you are the one reading this book, so we're talking to you—and this is your chance to make the most out of this opportunity.

Here are the 3 keys to working with a partner who refuses to change.

1. Change What You Can

The first key to working with a partner who doesn't want to change comes from the old serenity prayer:

> *God grant me the serenity to accept the things I cannot change;*
> *The courage to change the things I can;*
> *And the wisdom to know the difference.*

Make a promise, right here, right now. "*I will change the things I can.*"

Sounds reasonable, but what does that really mean? It means *taking action* on anything and everything you possibly can. Reshop the insurance. Take the credit cards out of your wallet and start using cash. Start building your Security Fund. Sign up for the retirement plan at your job. Even if you can't make everything perfect, you can make things *better*, all by yourself.

> Make a promise to improve things as much as you can, all by yourself.

You can let your mate be the excuse for leaving things exactly as they are, which of course means that things never get better. Or you can make significant improvements on your own. Yes, it would be easier if your spouse came along, but this isn't about "easier," it is about "better." Don't wait for your mate to be perfect; fix the things you can, right here, right now.

2. No Nagging

You may find the second key even tougher than the first. So here it is:

No nagging. No bitterness. No complaining.

Oh, it's tempting. After all, "You spent *how* much?!" and "When-are-you-going-to-get-those-mortgage-quotes?" may come as naturally to your lips as "Where's the remote?" But you need to give it up. Right here, right now.

Why? Because it doesn't work. You can't nag someone into meaningful change. And you sure can't complain your way into a happier relationship. So take that off the table. Don't use *All Your Worth* as an excuse to increase the conflict and tension in your marriage. This is about making life better, not about making it worse.

> You cannot nag someone into meaningful change.

But it isn't fair. You are right, it isn't fair. It isn't fair that you are working harder than your mate. It isn't fair that you spend less, or that the debt was all hers to begin with. It isn't fair that you have to deal with the annoying insurance agents while he sits on his duff. It just isn't fair. And that's too doggone bad.

So here is what you can do. Every time that "it-ain't-fair" monster pops into your brain, you should pause for a moment, and think of something you love about your partner. Imagine his sense of humor, the way he lights up when he tells a good joke. Remember how she took care of you when you had the flu, and how sweet she is to your batty old grandma. Remember the gentle way he holds your hand when you watch TV, and how gracious he was when you wrecked the car. Picture that wonderful moment, and hold it in your mind.

Because let's face it, a deep and intimate relationship isn't about what's fair, it's about the good, the bad, and whatever works. Money is just one part of your relationship. After all, you may be better at dealing with money than your partner, but your partner may be better at fixing up the house. Or taking care of the kids. Or earning a living, or fixing the car, or just making people smile. If you try to keep everything "fair," if you aim for the perfect "I saved $50 on day care, so you have to save $50 on life insurance," you will never succeed. Worse than that, you won't make your relationship any happier, and you won't get any richer. So let go of the nagging. Let go of the complaints. Let go of the it-ain't-fairs. You'll be a whole lot happier and a whole lot closer to the riches you are striving for.

3. Stick to the Subject

Does that mean that getting your partner to change is impossible? Of course not. While there are no guarantees, with the right approach you can certainly improve the odds of success.

But first, let's talk about what *not* to do. Don't have one of those giant It's-Time-to-Talk-About-Money conversations. Yeah, we know, this is what nearly every financial counselor recommends—"Just Talk About It." Talk is fine, but the grandiose "It's time for massive change, so let's schedule a summit at Camp David" just doesn't work very well, especially for couples who have a tendency to quarrel over money. The discussion nearly always starts when one partner (probably you, since you are the one reading this book) says something like, "Honey, We Need to Change the Way We Deal with Money." No nagging, no complaints, but a heck of a lot of pressure. And your mate, who was just that moment thinking about what kind of ice cream to eat, says something like, "Uh, I think we're doing okay." (Translation: Can I have my ice cream now?) But you are determined to have The Talk, and so the battle begins. Not an argument over anything specific, like what kind of car to buy, but a battle over Giant Abstract Issues. You start throwing around statements like, "We Need to Save More." (But how much more? And where will the money come from?) Your mate responds with things like, "Uh, I work hard, you know." And before you know it, one of you has hurled an accusation ("You shouldn't have bought those stupid parakeets!"), and the gloves are off.

To avoid hurt feelings and broken dishes, try something a little less weighty, and a lot more specific. Stick to the subject. Instead of making a grand pronouncement like, "We Need to Change the Way We Deal with Money," try something a little more modest, like, "I found a good deal on car insurance—what do you think?" Or, "I shifted from credit cards to cash, and it's working pretty well. Would you be willing to try it too? I can stop at the ATM for both of us." Present a simple, straightforward suggestion, preferably one that has a relatively easy answer. And keep it positive; an invitation to something constructive is a lot more likely to produce a good result.

By sticking to the subject, you stay away from all-or-nothing territory. After all, very few moments in a relationship are about complete reversal. How many human beings have ended a fight with the words, "Ah, darling, I've been such a fool. I will never dirty the house again"? Not many. Change comes a little at a time, agreeing to pick up the socks in the living room and helping clear the plates after dinner. So don't demand complete, instantaneous reform, as in: "Either you adopt every part of *All Your Worth* or we start packing right now for our trip to the poorhouse!" Just ask your partner for a piece at a time. You may never get your mate to say "Yes, you are so wise! I am 110% committed to this new financial plan!" But there's a good chance you can get your partner to make a lot of little and not-so-little compromises—as in "Okay, I'll sign up for the 401(k)" or "Yeah, $50 a week sounds reasonable." And when you add them all up, these little changes can add up to big bucks. And a lot more happiness.

THE 8 GOLDEN RULES OF MONEY AND RELATIONSHIPS

Here are the 8 Golden Rules of Money and Relationships. They are for couples of all kinds—those rowing peacefully in the same direction and those bashing at each other with the oars. If your mate wants to read the golden rules with you, all the better. But if you are on your own, start putting them into practice anyway. You may not make things perfect, but you can take the sting out of your money conflicts, and maybe find a better way to compromise. And when it's all over, you may discover that you fight a whole lot less and smile a whole lot more.

Rule 1: What's Mine Is Ours

This is the question we hear most about money and marriage: one bank account or two?

The truth is, it doesn't really matter. Financially speaking, how many bank accounts you have just isn't a very big deal. It isn't a tenth as important as what kind of health insurance you have. And it isn't a hundredth as important as whether you pay off your credit card debt or how you invest your retirement funds. How many checking accounts you have is like how many file folders you want to use—some people organize with just one, and some people organize with a lot. So long as you are organized, it just isn't a big deal.

So why are there so many inquiries about what is, at best, a fairly minor issue? Because nobody wants to talk about what's *really* going on.

When people ask "one account or two," what they're usually asking is some version of, "Is it *all* ours, or can I still have *mine*? If I earned it, do I have permission to spend it how I want?" In other words, talk of "my account" and "your account" is just another way to talk about "*my* money" and "*your* money."

And so here's the *real* answer. If you are not married (legally or spiritually), it is yours. Your lives are somewhat separate (or at least you haven't promised to stay together forever), and so your money stays separate, too. The bank accounts are separate, the bills are separate, and the big decisions are largely separate too. Any financial sharing you agree on is just that—an agreement, to be negotiated (and renegotiated) according to the situation.

But if you are married, things are different. When you get married, the money becomes "ours." By and large, that's the law. More important, that's just the practical truth. If you are like most couples, the assets belong to both of you, the debts belong to both of you, and so the money—and the decisions about money—belongs to both of you.

Realistically, it just isn't possible for one of you to be poor while the other is rich. If this marriage is to last a lifetime, then you are not going to retire in comfort while your mate eats out of a garbage can. You are not going to live in a mansion while your spouse lives in the street. And unless you are a real heel, you are not going to take your vacation at an exotic resort while your mate bunks with the fleas in a third-rate motel. In short, you are married, and so is your money.

"But I earn all the money (or at least most of it)!" Yeah, and your mate does all the child care (or the housework, or both). "But he agreed to support us, so my money is just for me." And why should he be obligated to you while you aren't obligated to him? Keeping score like this guarantees that you both come out losers.

Still not persuaded that the one who earns the money isn't "entitled" to more? Then keep this in mind: Life is very long, and you really don't know how things will turn out. What may seem "fair" today can turn to dust tomorrow. Consider the story of Jim, who spent 20 years working as an executive at IBM. He made a lot more money—and worked a lot more hours—than his wife Debbie, who was an administrative assistant for an insurance company. They never had kids, and they hired someone to clean the house. So, by the laws of "fairness," Jim could easily have told Debbie, "I earn it, so we'll spend it my way."

But he didn't. They spent their money together, and never once did Jim utter the words "my money." And you know what happened? He got cancer. Eat-your-guts-out, bone-crunching-pain, why-is-this-happening-to-me cancer. By the time he got the diagnosis, the tumors had already pushed into his liver, lungs, and spine. Debbie tried cooking everything the doctors suggested—homemade stews, fruit smoothies—but Jim was just too sick from the chemotherapy to eat more than a spoonful or two. Always a heavy man, he lost 100 pounds in five months. Night after night after night, Debbie was up, nursing him. When the tumors spread to his brain, his mind got cloudy, and there were times he didn't recognize her. Ultimately, he couldn't be left alone, and Debbie left her job so she could be there, 24 hours a day.

If Jim and Debbie had subscribed to the "fair" theory of marriage, she would have darted out the door the day he got the diagnosis. After all, what she had to go through in taking care of Jim was about the least "fair" thing imaginable. And Jim certainly wasn't going to "pay her back" (the cancer was terminal). But their marriage wasn't based on "fairness," it was based on sharing. They shared their home, they shared their lives, and they shared their money. And in the end, they shared the cancer.

Which is a long way of saying, we believe that marriage—and life—work out a lot better when you pool the money and don't worry too much about "yours" and "mine."

Usually that translates into a joint checking account. For most couples, it works best when there is one primary account, where all the paychecks and any other income go. The account is under both names, so you both have access to the money and you both know where you stand financially. The joint account is just for the Must-Have expenses (the mortgage, the car payments, and so forth). Neither one of you should worry about bouncing a check, because you won't write checks for anything except the basic bills, and you have already budgeted to meet those expenses. Money for Wants and Savings comes out as a single big check—not individual purchases—in an amount that you have agreed on ahead of time. That way you don't have to squabble over little purchases, or worry that your partner has overdrawn the account. And you should keep your $1000 cushion in the joint checking account, just in case. Every month your checking account statement should look roughly the same. Paychecks going in, a certain amount of cash going out for Wants, and a fixed amount going into Savings.

Does that mean that separate checking accounts are bad? Nope. If you and your mate prefer to keep everything separate, that can be perfectly fine too. There are plenty of couples where one partner has a lot of business expenses, or a tendency to misplace the checkbook, or a twenty-year habit of managing his own bank account. Those couples may decide that separate accounts are the best way to keep things running smoothly. That's okay—if you meet a few conditions.

• You both need to know where you stand financially. It is not okay to use separate accounts to keep secrets.

• You both must accept 100% responsibility. That means it is not okay to use separate accounts as an excuse for "Her credit card balance is her problem" or "*I* covered *my* bills, so why should I worry?" The money and the bills still belong to both of you, even if you find it more convenient to manage from separate accounts.

• You make the big decisions together. It's perfectly fine to splurge on a new pair of shoes without consulting your mate; it is not okay to buy a new car or to empty your retirement account. If you can't agree on the big decisions, that is no excuse; keep on talking until you find a reasonable compromise. Even if your accounts are separate, you have a joint financial future, which means you need to work together on the plans that will have a major impact on your lives.

Rule 2: Be Truthful . . . and Make It Easy for Your Partner to Be Truthful Too

You know that a good relationship is based on trust, but it can seem so *easy* to hide the credit card bill, to overstate how much you've been saving, to "forget" what those new shoes really cost. A few secrets here, a white lie there, and life seems so much smoother. You don't have to explain yourself. You don't have to defend anything. And you don't have to worry that your partner will use the information against you later on.

SELF-TEST: ARE YOU AND YOUR PARTNER TRUTHFUL ABOUT MONEY?

Respond with True or False to the following statements:

It seems so much easier just not to mention what I spend money on.	True	False
I have borrowed money or run up debts without telling my partner.	True	False

(continued)

If you marked True for any of these statements, you have a problem with openness and honesty in your money partnership.

A few little lies don't hurt—or do they? After a while, you have a lot of little threads to keep up with—a lot of things your partner doesn't know about. And even though you never mean to, you may find yourself telling bigger lies, just to keep up. You aren't bad; in fact, you may have the best intentions in the world. But there is more and more in your relationship that isn't quite true.

Vicki Rozier never meant to lie to her new husband. She just slipped into it. Her folks had said they would pay for the wedding, but they didn't come through, and Vicki wound up charging a lot of the expenses. And then the credit card balance kept creeping upward, with all the little expenses for their new apartment. Vicki got in the habit of snatching her Visa bill out of the mailbox before Tyler ever knew it had arrived, just so he wouldn't ask her any questions.

And then it happened—the first real, live lie. Tyler had said he was a little worried about money, so Vicki tried to stay out of the stores altogether. Then she saw this really elegant little rug, perfect to set off the entry area—and 33% off. She put the $162 on her credit card, and when she got home that evening she had every intention of telling

Tyler. "I mean, jeez, there was this horrible stain on the floor I was just trying to cover up. But he came in all tired and cranky, and he sees the rug, and his face gets all red and he goes kind of stiff." So she quickly blurted out, "It's from the thrift store. $10 cash." He immediately relaxed and laughed, and never noticed Vicki's guilty look.

But Tyler had his own secrets, or at least that's what Vicki suspected. "He gets tips, and I know he doesn't tell me how much. And he'll say things like, 'Oh, we don't have enough money for that,' without me ever seeing a bank statement or anything."

Mistrust and evasions over money can be one of the most difficult cycles to break. After all, if your partner isn't honest about money, why should you be? There is just one reason: Because it's the only way to save your relationship. Really and truly, mistrusting your partner about money is no different from mistrusting your partner about anything else: Suspicion will eat away at your relationship, day after day.

So what can you do? Sure, you can't control your partner. But *you* can decide that from now on, you will be totally honest with him or her about money, no matter what. No more lying, no more covering up, no more hiding receipts or holding back on how much overtime pay you got. Just the truth, plain and simple.

And here's the other half of your commitment, the one that makes all the difference between good intentions and real success: Make it easy on your partner to be truthful. You may not be able to force him to tell the truth, but you *can* promise that you will never belittle him, never make him feel bad, never criticize him when he tells the truth.

Vicki remembers the exact evening that it all turned around for her, the day Tyler came home early and opened her credit card statement:

By the time I got my key out of the lock, he was screaming—I mean, I was scared, I never saw him so mad. I gotta admit, I wanted to lie, just to make him stop. And then I thought, this is so stupid. He has it in black and white for pity's sake. So I told him everything. All of it. What I'd bought and not told him. How my dad couldn't pay for the wedding, but I was too embarrassed to say. I swear, I just cried and cried. I never felt so small in all my life.

But Vicki didn't stop with a good cry. "I knew, I just knew we had to get it out there. So I was like, 'How much money do we really have? Have you bought stuff I don't know about?' " She tried hard not to hurl the questions as accusations, but really to ask. And then it started to slip out—his secret stash, his hidden purchases. "I was so mad at first. I mean, he made me feel so bad, and he was screwing up too. But then I thought, this is what marriage is all about, right? Sticking it out, for better or for worse. And then I really was sympathetic—I mean really. This stuff is hard for him too."

Get honest. Ultimately, you can't hide money decisions from your most intimate partner. You have the things you bought. You owe the money you borrowed. If you keep adding to the lies, someday it will all crash down around you. So make the decision, right here, right now, to tell the truth. And then resolve to make it easy for your partner to tell the truth too. If you do, you'll do better with money. And you'll do better with each other, which is what it's all about.

Rule 3: Stop Playing the Blame Game

Question: Which one of you is responsible for your money—you or your mate?

Answer: Both of you.

You already knew this, of course. And yet, it can be so easy (and so satisfying!) to blame your partner for all your money troubles. In the blame game you aren't responsible—either for what went wrong or for making things better.

SELF-TEST: ARE YOU CAUGHT IN THE BLAME GAME?

Respond with True or False to the following statements:

My partner spends too much money on things we don't need.	True	False
My partner blames me for our money troubles.	True	False

My partner should earn more money.	True	False
Sometimes we spend money when we get angry with each other, maybe partly to get even.	True	False
I feel like I need to justify how much I spend or how much I earn (or don't earn) to my partner.	True	False
My partner thinks only about himself or herself when spending money, not about my needs or wants.	True	False
When I see the bills my partner ran up, I get really angry.	True	False
Deep down, I believe our money troubles are primarily my partner's fault.	True	False

If you marked True for any of these statements, you and your mate have a problem with shifting responsibility and blaming each other for your money problems.

Let's get it all on the table. Your partner got a bad deal on the car. He took a new job thinking he would make a lot of money, and instead he got fired. She splurged on a brand-name purse that she really couldn't afford. He never balances the checkbook. She spent money on something stupid just to get even with you. The list of sins goes on and on.

What should you do about it?

Let it go.

Let the past be past. Take a deep breath, and put it out of your mind.

Sure, it's hard to be that magnanimous. This book is not just for saints. So if you're not up for "Forgiveness is divine," then try this on: Be selfish! Get over it because this is best for *you*. You are not forgiving your partner because you're so high-minded, you're forgiving your mate because you can't afford not to. The blame game is the fastest road to the poorhouse. Eye-for-an-eye-style spending will leave you both blind—and broke. You need to get over it so you have a chance to get ahead financially.

Forgiving your mate means taking 100% responsibility for *your* actions. That means that you decide to do what you know is the right thing with your money, *no matter what your partner does.* No more giving yourself "permission" to do things you know aren't smart, just because your mate has also blown a bunch of money you can't really afford. And no more telling yourself it is his job to shop for the mortgage (or balance the checkbook or pay off the credit cards), so you can just look the other way while your finances tumble downhill. You are in this together, and stupid decisions times two just makes for more stupid decisions. Get straight what you can get straight.

But what if your mate isn't quite so willing to let go of the past? There's nothing like your partner shaking the long finger of blame in your direction to send the best of intentions flying out the window. Instead of battling it out, try this. The next time your spouse brings up a mistake you made, try saying "You're right, I made a mistake. I really blew it. If I had it to do over again, I would do it differently. I really wish I hadn't done that." And mean it. An honest confession can suck the wind right out of the sails of self-righteousness.

The next time you get tempted to sink into another round of tit-for-tat spending battles, remember this. The blame game is about mistakes from the past. But if blame causes you to compound past mistakes by making more stupid decisions, then you are letting yesterday's mistakes poison your future. You can't change yesterday, but you can decide what to do about tomorrow. You can decide to let yesterday's mistakes infect your decisions today, or you can decide to learn whatever lesson you needed to learn and move on. You can decide to let blame eat away at your happiness, or you can decide that you care more about living a good life today and about making tomorrow better.

No matter who earns the money, no matter who spends it, you are both 100% responsible. It is time to let go of the blame game, time to let go of the past. It's time to get on with the future you deserve.

Rule 4: Give Each Other Some Free Money

Renee and Samuel fight like wildcats over every little purchase. Carlos and Melissa haven't quarreled in ages. And Renee and Samuel make a lot more money. So what's the difference?

Free money. Back in Step 4, we laid out the principle that each partner should get a stash of cash to spend on whatever he or she wants. A little bit of personal financial space, where nothing gets reviewed by your partner.

Does that make it okay to hide purchases or deceive your partner? Of course not. Free money is premised on honesty. It starts with the two of you sitting down together and agreeing on what you can really afford for fun and how you want to divide it up. Only then can you banish the worry that "overspending" may drive you into bankruptcy or that your partner may be guzzling the champagne while you're sipping weak tea. The amount has been fixed, you've decided together what is reasonable, and you trust each other to live within the bounds you've both agreed on. *That* is a real act of trust.

The amount of money doesn't really matter; it's whatever you think you can afford. But resist the temptation to skip over this. If you think you can't afford any fun money, then we're here to tell you that you can't afford *not* to have some fun money. No matter how tight your budget—even if you are down to shaking nickels out of the couch cushions and redeeming soda cans—every person and every relationship needs to make a little room for individual fun money.

Once you have agreed on some free money, make it really and truly free. Joe can blow it all on fancy power tools and Lisa can indulge her fascination with high-style shoes, even if the garage and the closets are already full. Let it go. If it makes Joe happy and if Lisa feels a thrill, that's all that matters. There are no right purchases and wrong purchases, and no one should be pointing out how the money could have been spent better. Give each other the space to do the things that make you both happy.

Rule 5: Keep Money Issues Separate from the Real Stuff

Sometimes money is the real problem, and sometimes it isn't. Sometimes money is just the most familiar weapon available to fight over something entirely different.

SELF-TEST: IS IT REALLY ABOUT MONEY?

Respond with True or False to the following statements:

Sometimes my partner buys expensive things for me to make up after a fight.	True	False
My partner sometimes uses money as an excuse for not doing something nice for me (like going out for the evening or buying me a birthday present).	True	False
No matter how a disagreement starts, it always ends up as a fight about money.	True	False
I think an expensive gift is a good way to say "I'm sorry."	True	False
Money fights seem to come from nowhere; we're talking about something else and then suddenly we're yelling about money.	True	False
Sometimes I spend money when I'm angry with my partner.	True	False
Sometimes I say we can't afford something, when the truth is I just don't want it.	True	False

If you marked True for any of these statements, you and your mate have a problem with substituting money for the real issues in your relationship.

Picture the last time you had a knock-down drag-out money fight. What were you feeling before the battle? Was the kitchen a mess? Did your back hurt? Were you mad because you felt your mate doesn't appreciate you? Were you feeling insecure or hurt over something else?

These are honest emotions, and they can figure in even the best relationships. Sometimes the problem isn't even with the relationship, but with something else entirely—stress at work, a dispute with your brother, worry over aging parents, and on and on. Unfortunately, there is no magic formula to make those bad feelings go away. But substituting money for the real issues won't resolve any of the deeper problems. Worse yet, it sure can create a bucket of new ones that just compound whatever else is wrong.

Ryan Young and his wife Ellie had fought over money so often that he could recite every accusation from memory—on both sides. "She'll say I blow too much at Greene's [the local Irish Pub], and I'll say she spends too much on her stupid hair, and then we're off and going, like a couple of mad dogs in a thunderstorm." But once they agreed on how much they could both have for free money, the arguments sounded a lot different.

> So I hit Greene's one night with the guys like usual, and she's furious, all over again, harping on how much I blew on beer. And I was about to get all wound up, when I just said, "It was just the cash you said I could have, baby." And she stares at me, still so mad, I could tell. And then those little tears start to leak out. And I go, "Why are you mad at me, baby? I thought I'm doing things your way." And she goes, "Why's it always them? Why don't you take *me* out, someplace nice, you know? You look at me like I'm some boring old hag, and I just want to be your *girl*."

There it was. This fight had never really been about money. It was about whether Ryan was considering Ellie's feelings, and whether Ellie was willing to let Ryan have some time on his own. But they had slipped into so many fights about money that neither could find the real issue under all those layers of money-money-money.

If every conflict turns into a battle over your finances, try keeping the word *money* out of your quarrels. Remember, you have made the decision to get your money in balance, and you are getting on the road to a brighter financial future. You have forgiven the past mistakes, and you have decided to put an end to the blame game. You have agreed to give each other some free money, so there is no need to quarrel over the little purchases. At the end of all that, there just shouldn't be very many money issues left to fight about.

So go ahead and laugh, live, and even fight—but keep money out of it. You may discover that if money is no longer the first weapon in your arsenal, you get a better understanding about what is really wrong. Which means you get a better chance to make things right.

Rule 6: Fight Fair

What happens when money really *is* what you're fighting about? After all, you have different tastes, different priorities, and you may disagree with your mate's choices. And if you're a normal couple, you will argue about it, at least once in a while.

So here are the ground rules for fighting fair about money:

- *Don't hit below the belt.* If you know your partner feels deeply humiliated over losing his job, then you must never, ever use this to your advantage in a fight. If you know your mate still cries over the money her sister stole, then you must *not* rub her nose in it. If you even suspect that your mate is deeply, mortally sensitive on a certain topic, then, no matter how mad you get, don't touch it. You wouldn't say something hurtful about your loved one's failing grades in high school or the ugly burn on her back, so don't bring up old hurtful things when you fight over money. Even when you get mad, there are limits.

- *Don't blame your partner for joint decisions.* If you signed your name on the mortgage, then it is too late to attack your partner for getting a bad deal on the house. It may have been your partner's idea to buy, but the moment you agreed to go along with it, you forfeited the right to blame your partner if things don't work out. If a joint deal goes south, then own up to your half of the bum decision.

- *Don't make giant generalizations.* Calling names or making sweeping statements like "You *always* spend too much" or "You are *never* careful with money" is not nice; moreover, it isn't even true. Whatever dumb thing your mate did, there are at least a thousand other dumb things your mate *didn't* do, right? He didn't buy a pet rhinoceros. She didn't use your stock certificates for toilet paper. And he didn't tell his boss to go skydiving without a parachute. Sweeping statements about how someone *always* overspends or is *never* careful aren't true, but they can sure transform something small into something huge. Those words can turn a minor spat into a raging battle quicker than spit hits the ground, so just hold your tongue because you can't take it back.

• *Don't take every difference as a personal insult.* Differences about money are not intended as attacks. If he doesn't want to spend a lot of money on fresh flowers ("they just die"), it doesn't mean he doesn't love you. If she thinks take-out is essential ("I'm a lousy cook"), it doesn't mean she doesn't care about you. Sometimes money decisions are just about money, not an expression of your innermost soul.

Take the sting out of differences by recognizing they are just that—differences. One of you likes imported perfume, the other likes the smell of soap. One of you likes French wine, the other prefers Budweiser. So what? Proving you are right about how money *should* be spent is a victory that will turn to ashes in your throat. Acknowledge differences, and move on.

Rule 7: Divide and Conquer

Financial equality means sharing the decision making and sharing the responsibility. It does not, however, mean that you have to share the chores equally. Let's face it: You and your partner have different temperaments and different talents. One of you is organized, one couldn't find his car keys if they were strapped to his hand. One has a head for numbers, the other can't add 2 + 2 without a calculator—and doubts the answer even then. And one of you is fascinated by finance (or at least mildly interested), while the other experiences a wave of nausea every time the business news comes on.

After a few decades of marriage, your roles tend to sort out on their own. But if you're in a new relationship, divvying up the chores can be a lot more complicated—especially if you aren't married and your financial lives are still separate. So here are a few tips for dividing and conquering when your money is (mostly) separate:

• Start by deciding how much you will each contribute to the joint expenses. If your income is a lot higher or lower than your partner's, consider using the Balanced Money Formula as a guideline. That way, you both contribute the same percentage of your income to the Must-Haves, you both keep the same percentage for Wants, and so forth.

• Next, decide how to divvy up the chores. Unmarried couples often decide that since they're splitting the expenses 50/50 (or so), they should split the chores 50/50. But remember, financial chores are no different than all the other chores around the house; one of you may be better at it than the other. If your partner turns green when faced with a checkbook, don't fight it; just ask him (or her) to take out the trash while you pay the bills.

Just remember, you are not going to change your Scatterbrained Sweetheart into the Organization King (or Queen). You're not going to infuse your Happy Hippie with a love of money. So instead of trying to split all the financial chores 50/50, divide responsibilities in a way that makes sense. If he is more organized, then he should keep the records. If she likes to negotiate, then she should shop for the car.

And if you are the only one willing to do what it takes to get your money into balance, then just do it. You are both 100% responsible, but you can't each do 100% of the tasks. Do what makes sense for you.

Rule 8: Learn the Art of Compromise

You are doing your honest-to-goodness best to have a happy, healthy money relationship. And yet you still disagree. Not on the little stuff, but the big things—the stuff you can't just cover with your fun money. She wants a bigger house. He thinks it's time for a new car. These are really big decisions, and no amount of good intentions can make them go away. What then?

• *Keep talking.* Talk is cheap. So when it comes to the big expenditures—a car, a mortgage, child care, retirement investments—start talking, and keep on talking. Watch out for "whatever you think" or "I've got it all under control"—that's the fast road to "I told you so" and "This mess is all your fault."

One of the nice things about big decisions is that there can be a lot to talk about. Keep the conversation going over time. Look up some studies in *Consumer Reports* and ask your friends about their purchases. Bring more information back to the table, and open another conversation. Once you get it open, keep talking until you both feel 100% responsible for the final decision.

• *Put time on your side.* Sometimes it's just a matter of timing. A nice vacation this year, remodel the kitchen next year. The kids need more room now, but there will be a nicer car down the road. Can you layer the things you want over time? Instead of saying it is a vacation *or* a new sofa, decide that you will save for both. You get something and your partner gets something. Sure, it will take longer, but you recognize that both of you have legitimate Wants and you can work together for them. That realization is priceless.

• *Focus on the big picture.* What if you are still squabbling? Keep an eye on the big picture. Even if you can't agree on everything, there are some very big things you *can* agree on. You both want to keep a roof over your heads. You both want to grow old in comfort and dignity (even if you don't agree on how much money to put in your retirement account). You both want to ensure your children's safety. You both want to stop fighting, and you both want to stop worrying about money. Kind of puts your disagreements into perspective, huh? When a relationship has become bruised over the subject of money, reminding yourself of the common ground can be a healing salve.

THE HEART OF A RELATIONSHIP

Money can be the hardest kind of intimacy. Money is wrapped up in attitudes and values shaped from infancy. ("We always put Edgar in designer outfits because a child who looks good feels better about himself." "We never wasted money on fancy clothes because kids just grow out of them.") It sometimes feels as if everything we stand for can be expressed in terms of how we spend our money.

Negotiating the shoals of money intimacy can be as difficult as anything you will ever face together. The differences between you and your partner can be subtle and hard to interpret, and the land mines are everywhere. Worse yet, money issues are pervasive. Even if you never talk about money, you *will* develop a money relationship—for better or for worse. Whether you discuss it every day or shroud it in silence, you and your mate *will* decide who works, who spends, who pays which bills, how much debt you carry, and how much you save—all of which forms your money relationship.

Every money relationship can be made better. No matter where you're starting from, it really is possible to improve the role that money plays in your relationship. So give it a try. Even if you're not convinced that all of these ideas will work in your relationship, give it an honest effort. Get on the path to balancing your money. And get on the path to the joyful, fulfilling, rewarding relationship that you and your partner deserve.

The Big Buy: Purchasing the Home That Is Right for You

Homeownership. A little patch of earth, all your own. (Or, for condo owners, a little patch of sky all your own.) When you own your own home, you can do it *your* way. Paint the walls bright orange or build a catwalk on the roof or convert the backyard into a skateboard park; it is entirely up to you. As Robert Frost said, "Home is the place where . . . they have to take you in." There is nothing on God's earth quite like sinking your toes into a bit of grass that is all yours. Not the landlord's, not your parents', but *yours*.

Entire books have been written on home buying. This isn't one of those, and we're not here to cover everything you could possibly want to know about buying a home. Instead, we're here to answer one question: How do you buy a home while making the most of all your worth?

ALL YOUR WORTH RULES FOR SMART, HAPPY HOME BUYING

Whether you are buying your first home or your fifth, if you think there may be a moving van in your future, then this chapter is for you. We have boiled down our years of study into 5 rules for smart, happy home buying.

Rule 1: Pay Off Your Steal-from-Tomorrow Debt Before You Buy

If you still have credit card and other Steal-from-Tomorrow debt, get that paid off before you buy a new home. This is the best way to get yourself on the right financial footing, so you will be completely ready to take on the financial responsibilities of homeownership (or the responsibilities of a bigger mortgage).

If this advice makes your heart sink because you think, "Oh, no, that means it will be years before we can buy," then take that as a sign. There is a message beaming your way, and you need to hear it loud and clear. *You cannot afford to buy a house right now.* There is a hole in the bottom of your boat, and now is not the time to add the weight of a mortgage.

Karina Beaupre knows what it's like to receive that message. A single mom, she was really anxious to get her son Eugene "out of an apartment and into a real home—a place with grass and nice kids next door." Karina had a good job as a claims adjuster, but her credit card debt, along with a couple of late payments and a dispute over a water bill, had bruised her credit score. And she didn't have two nickels saved for a down payment. Even so, she got a real estate agent to show her dozens of houses, and she finally found one she was crazy about. The mortgage company was glad to offer financing, but they wanted 14.75% interest—more than double the going rate for people with good credit. When Karina heard that, she cried for days.

> I thought, no way can I pay that, and now I'm gonna lose that house, and my boy's never gonna have a yard. But then my mom said, "What are you bawling about? You act like that's the last

house in the whole world!" I was kind of mad, but really, there's no one like your momma to knock sense into you.

Karina swung into action. She got her mom to keep Eugene two weekends a month, while she took extra shifts at the office, putting every extra dollar into paying off her debts. She got dead serious about paying off her credit card balance, and then she started saving for a down payment. Twenty-six months later, she called her real estate agent back. "I said, 'This time I'm ready. Show me my house.' And you know what? I found something I liked a lot—maybe even better."

Paying off your Steal-from-Tomorrow debt will put more money in your pocket. When the debt is paid off, all the money that was going to monthly payments will be *yours,* not Capital One's. Getting rid of those debts will make your credit score rise, which means you will qualify for a better interest rate on your mortgage. As Karina learned, that can add up to hundreds of dollars that stay in your pocket, every single month.

And there's one more reason to pay off your Steal-from-Tomorrow debt before you go house hunting: You'll be safer. Without all those debts, you will have a lot more flexibility in your budget if anything goes wrong. You'll be able to focus on getting your house payments made, and not have to worry about Visa, MasterCard, JCPenney, or the IOU to Uncle Roy.

So what should you do? Follow Karina. Pull up your socks and get that debt paid off, one dollar at a time. Every time you pay off some Steal-from-Tomorrow debt, say out loud, "I am one step closer to owning my own home." And when you get there, you'll be so, so glad you bought your home with a clean slate.

Rule 2: Save Until You Have at Least 10% for a Down Payment (Better Yet, 20%)

Sure, there are plenty of lenders who will give you a mortgage with no money down. And there is no shortage of people who will stand on a soapbox and tell you this is smart.

But here is something those no-money-down guys don't tell you:

100% financing costs more—a lot more. Buyers who have no down payment are often classified as "subprime," which means they pay the highest interest rates, the highest fees, *and* they get stuck with high-priced mortgage insurance. If Karina had bought her house with no money down, her monthly payment would have been $1870 instead of just $1005—that's an extra $865 a month! In thirty years, she would have paid $309,000 *more* on the no-money-down mortgage—enough for Eugene's college, four brand-new cars, and a good start on a retirement fund for herself.

Think of it this way: If you buy a house with no money down, the house isn't more valuable, but you will end up paying a heck of a lot more for it. This is a little like going shopping and deciding to buy from the store that charges the *most*.

And there is one more thing the no-money-down crowd won't tell you. People who buy a house with no down payment are up to *20 times* more likely to lose their home in foreclosure. Just imagine what that would have meant to Karina. She would have moved into a house that she loved, only to be moved out when the sheriff showed up to dump her things on the lawn and auction her home to the highest bidder. She would have lost all her payments, ruined her credit for years to come, and said good-bye to the vegetable garden and the kids in the neighborhood. There are a lot of financial steps that can hurt, but few hurt as much as being forced to turn your house over to the bank.

You may be thinking, "But nice, hardworking people never lose their homes in foreclosure!" Guess again. Over the past 25 years, the home mortgage foreclosure rate across this country has *tripled*. Last year alone, more than 800,000 homeowners filed for bankruptcy in a last-ditch attempt to hold on to their homes. And for every family suffering through a foreclosure or bankruptcy, there were many more who handed the keys over to the bank and quietly moved out—just to keep the words *foreclosure* and *bankruptcy* off their credit records.

It is happening today in your town. People try to keep it quiet, but don't let that fool you. Good, hardworking people can get upside-down financially and lose their homes. And it is much more likely to happen to people who took out mortgages that had no down payments, mortgages that were at high interest rates, and mortgages that were too big to fit into a balanced money plan.

So play it safe, and save until you have a sizeable down payment. This will make your home a whole lot more affordable, and a lot more secure. It will also mean that you own a big piece of equity, right from day one. And with Twenty for Tomorrow you'll get there sooner than you might think. That down payment will be your first step toward making your home the best part of your long-term plan to create a lifetime of wealth.

Rule 3. Buy a Home You Can Afford

Ready to go shopping? Great! Just keep your money in balance.

Spending what you can afford sounds simple, but staying within your means isn't as straightforward as it used to be. When your parents bought their first home, the rule of thumb for how much you could afford to spend on a house was easy: You laid out all your financial information on the banker's desk, and he told you what size mortgage you could manage. That was it: If you make this much money, you can get a mortgage this big. In those days, banks wanted to be very, very sure people could repay, so they did a lot of math before they lent any money. You couldn't get into trouble by borrowing too much because the bank wouldn't let you.

Today the world is upside-down. Getting approved for a mortgage is no guarantee that you can actually afford the house, because banks routinely approve mortgages that are way more than you can afford. The mortgage company has exactly one goal—sell the maximum number of mortgages at the highest possible price to as many people as possible. Now the burden is on you to do your own math. You wouldn't take advice from a car salesman on how big a car to buy. Don't take advice from a mortgage company on how much mortgage to buy either. Make your own decision.

How do you know what you can afford? Just follow the Balanced Money Formula. Add up all the monthly costs of the home you are considering. That should include the mortgage (a fixed-rate mortgage, so the costs won't go up in a few years), the homeowners' insurance, the property taxes, and the utilities (the real estate agent should provide some of that information). And don't forget to include *all* the utilities, including things like sewer and gas that you might not have paid for in your apartment.

Be careful about buying too much house. Real estate agents are notorious about steering clients to homes that are just "slightly" above their price range. Even good friends will nod wisely as they tell you to "stretch to buy the biggest house you can." Mortgage brokers will push you toward variable rate or interest-only mortgages so you can "lower your monthly payments." This can sound great—pay less now. Of course, you'll be at the "pay-more-later" stage as soon as the interest rates rise. No matter how you slice it up, "stretching" to buy a bigger home is just another word for getting in over your head. So just stick to your guns and buy a house you can really and truly afford, with no fudging on the mortgage payments.

Calculate what your total Must-Have expenses would be if you bought the home. So long as you can keep your *total* Must-Haves under 50% of your take-home pay, you can afford the house you want.

Rule 4: Get the Cheapest Mortgage

You have found a great place with wonderful cabinetry and the perfect backyard for your schnauzer. You have made an offer, and the seller has agreed. So your shopping is over, right? Wrong! Your shopping is just beginning. What most people don't realize is that the rate on your mortgage is at least as important as the price of your home—maybe more so. So don't make the mistake of bargaining hard to knock $5,000 off the purchase price, and then paying $50,000 extra over the life of your mortgage. Set aside the paint chips, pull out a pencil and paper, and roll up your sleeves. It is time to do some serious shopping for a mortgage.

Getting the best price on your mortgage may sound obvious, but don't kid yourself. Many people end up with a high-priced mortgage for a really simple reason: They didn't shop hard enough. In fact, *half* of all the people who sign up for high-priced mortgages could have gotten a low-priced mortgage—if only they had shopped harder.

So do your shopping! No matter how fantastic the first quote is, get a second quote and keep on getting quotes until you have at least five. It doesn't matter if you were "preapproved" by one bank before you started house-hunting; you still need to shop aggressively and pick the best deal. There is too much money at stake to stop short on this one.

There are a lot of tricks to watch out for when you get a mortgage, so you need to protect yourself. For a list of questions to ask the mortgage lender, go back to "Reshop Your Mortgage—But Be Careful" on pages 80–87. The rules for getting a new mortgage are basically the same as the rules for refinancing, so you can use the earlier section to guide you. And take your time—this is one place where a little bargain hunting can save you tens of thousands of dollars!

Rule 5: Buy a Home That Makes You Smile

And now for the last—and perhaps the most important—rule. Before you sign on the dotted line, stop and ask yourself one last question: Does this home make you smile? Will you be glad to wake up in this place every morning? Will you smile when you open that front door to pick up the newspaper and when you walk across that funny bump in the floor to get your cup of coffee?

I (Elizabeth) have to confess, my husband and I once ended up in a house that did not make us smile. It was a good deal, and we were in a hurry to pick a place. We reasoned that since we were "just renting" it didn't matter so much. But really, we made a dumb decision. The place had dinky windows, the walls had dark paneling, and the shag carpet seemed, well, *ominous*. (I always wondered what was buried down deep in that tangled yarn.) I would drive home from teaching classes at the University of Texas every afternoon, and I could feel a cloud settle over me as I unlocked the front door. Frankly, the place depressed me.

Oddly enough, that house was the pride and joy of its owner. He thought the small windows made the place "private," the wood paneling was "cozy," and the shag carpet was "homey." So I learned two lessons: Not everyone likes the same things in a house. And there just isn't anything in the world that's worth feeling lousy in the place where you live.

A home isn't just an investment for your money. A home can be an expression of who you are—the cozy cottage, the formal Victorian, or the hip bachelor says a lot about what makes you tick. A house may be a place to start a marriage, a place to raise children, or a place to grow old. A good house is like a good shoe—it should fit *you*.

Your home will affect you every single day. So use your head *and* your heart. When it comes time to choose, buy a place where lots of sun shines through the windows or where a cozy glow makes you feel safe. Buy a home where the neighbors seem friendly and the kitchen is charming. Never forget that your home is the place where you *live*— and we want you to make the most out of that living.

DEALING WITH THE BUTS

You are armed with the facts. You are ready to go out there and buy the home of your dreams (or wait a couple of years until you're ready). You are motivated, and your mind is made up. And then come—the BUTS! Your real estate agent, your mortgage lender, and even your dear Aunt Lucille will be bursting with a load of *buts*. But-But-But. A zillion reasons why saving your money and buying what you can afford is a bad idea. A zillion reasons why you should act right now before you have any time to think it through. So when the buts get you down, here are a few answers to steel your resolve:

But If You Want to Build Real Wealth, You Need to Start NOW!

Five years ago, this place went for $200,000, and now it's worth a million bucks!

Housing appreciation has become a beloved American story, and there is just enough truth in it to keep the myth alive. The loudest

cheerleaders for the myth are those who make money from it. Real estate agents, mortgage brokers, and bankers all make big bucks when
people buy-fast-at-any-price. This is the cast of characters most likely
to be hollering, "The market will always go up!" and "You can make
millions!"

Even pocket-calculator, sharp-pencil types seem to get a little drunk
on housing prices. Seemingly sensible, well-respected financial advisers
get all ga-ga over housing. These are some quotes from some best-
selling financial advice books:

> *Should you wait to buy a home? The answer is unequivocally no!*
> *Don't wait. Do it now!*

> *No down payment? Borrow from your retirement plan! . . . Try the*
> *Mommy-and-Daddy bank!*

> *You aren't really in the game of building wealth until you get in the*
> *real estate game . . . My single biggest regret is I didn't buy sooner.*

With that kind of advice, is it any wonder that perfectly reasonable
people can get caught up in the frenzy?

All of us know someone who in the murky past paid $10,000 for a
house that is today worth half a million bucks. I (Amelia) live in Los
Angeles, where housing prices rose a whopping 29% in a single year.
With numbers like that, it can seem like homeownership is the working man's best path to riches.

The reality is a lot less exciting. On average, home values usually rise
at roughly the same pace as inflation. That means that putting your
money into a home is a little better than putting it in a passbook savings account—but not nearly as good as putting it in the stock market.
So, for example, if you had bought a typical $100,000 home back in
1977, today you would own a home worth $308,000. Not bad, but if
you had put that same money in the stock market back in 1977, today
you would have just over a million dollars—and you wouldn't have
paid for one single roof repair to keep your fund going.

Moreover, while there have been some phenomenal run-ups in
home prices, there have also been some phenomenal crashes. Between

1989 and 1993, for example, the value for a typical home (when adjusted for inflation) *dropped* by 7%. And many cities have experienced much bigger real estate crashes. I (Elizabeth) bought a house in Austin, Texas, for $204,000, only to get a job in Philadelphia three years later. It took us 16 months to sell the house—which meant we had 16 months of trying to cover *two* mortgage payments every month! The final price? $167,000. Believe me, no one sells you a house with a guarantee that prices will always rise and markets will always stay hot.

The best financial reason for owning a home is *not* so you can resell it for a bunch of money. At best, making big money is a long shot—certainly nothing you should gamble a third (or more) of your paycheck on every month for the next 30 years. The best financial reasons for homeownership are:

- One day you will get your house paid off, and you can live rent-free for the rest of your life.
- Owning your own home is a great safeguard against inflation. Rents keep rising, but a fixed mortgage is just that—fixed.
- Over the long run, the money you would have spent on rent goes toward building something valuable.

If you are trying to double your money, go to the racetrack or the casinos. Homeownership has some ups and downs, but over time it is more like passbook savings—a respectable return on your investment, but not an exciting bet for the high rollers. If you need to wait a few years while you save for your down payment and pay off your debt, don't worry; you'll still have plenty of time to get on the wealth-building train. *And* you'll do it from the strongest possible place.

But Rent Is a Waste of Money!

The logic here seems so rock-solid: At the end of the month, you have nothing to show for all that money you spent on rent. Of course, the same would apply to your heating bill. And your water bill. And your food bill. At the end of the month there are a lot of things you pay for that you don't have anything to show for—nothing except that you lived your life. When you paid your rent, you got what you needed—a roof over your head. Rent is no different from food, but no one is suggesting you buy a cow.

Still not persuaded? Consider the math of buying a home. If rent is a waste of money, then presumably the money you put into owning your home is *not* wasted, because it goes toward something valuable. But how much of that money actually goes to your personal bottom line? The fact is, not much. If you buy today with no down payment, for the first several years that you "own" your home more than 90% of your payments will go to interest, fees, taxes and insurance. That money will be just as "lost" as the money you would have spent on rent. In the early years of home owning, renting can look about the same to your wallet.

Over the long run, it is generally wiser to own your home than to rent, because a part of your money goes toward something valuable (although in the early years, it's only a very small part of your money). But that's over the long run. In the short run, it really doesn't make much difference whether you rent or own. If you wait a year or two until you are stronger financially, a bigger part of what you pay each month will go to *your* bottom line—not the mortgage company's. The wait will be worth it.

But Everyone Should Own a Home!

Here's a quick test:

> What do you do when the toilet overflows?
> A. Call the landlord.
> B. Find a plunger.

If your answer was A, homeownership may not be right for you (at least not right now). Homeownership can be a lot of work, and if you just don't feel like taking it on, then renting may be the better bet.

If you move around a lot, homeownership probably isn't worth the hassle. You can be forced to sell on short notice, just when the market is in the doldrums. Total expenses—real estate commissions, closing costs, inspection fees, and the rest—average 9% of the sale price of the house, so you can be left deep in a hole.

If you live in a market where a home costs more than a Boeing 747, renting may be the only prudent decision (at least for now). Some markets get badly overheated, and waiting for them to cool off a bit may make sense.

Before you sign up for thirty years of payments, it is okay to take a deep breath and ask whether homeownership is right for you—right here, right now. This may not be the time or place, and it is perfectly fine to pull back from buying if you decide you're just not quite ready.

But Prices Are Rising So Fast, If You Wait You'll Get Priced out of the Market!

It's a boom market! There are multiple bidders! The market is so hot, no one can lose! The message is clear: "The train is pulling out of the station, but if you run, you might just make it." This argument is doubly persuasive because it doesn't give you time to think—just run or you'll miss it!

Jarrod and Daniela Ferguson were new to the Bay Area when Daniela decided to attend a seminar on investing at her local bank. The seminar turned out to be a real estate marketing event, full of testimonials on the phenomenal price increases over the past few years. Daniela was shaken by the seminar. She wasn't a risk taker, but what if they *didn't* buy? The speakers said over and over that people who don't get in the market *now* will be closed out forever. She and Jarrod didn't want to live in an apartment for the rest of their lives, so she pushed Jarrod to agree to buy a rambling old fixer-upper.

And then, 5 months after they closed, Jarrod's company was bought out and he was transferred to Chicago. Daniela wasn't worried about finding a new job, and she actually looked forward to living in Chicago. But in the blink of an eye, they didn't need a house in the Bay Area. The really bad news came from the real estate agent. It seemed the market had "cooled off" and that "fixer-uppers are moving slowly." Now they were caught. The agent's estimate for what they could get was about 10% below what they had paid, and closing costs would be another 9%. And because they really needed to move fast, the agent suggested another 10% reduction in price. Four months later they sold the house, borrowing an additional $44,000 to pay off the mortgage on a house they no longer owned. Four years later, they were still living in an apartment—and still working off the debt from their first home.

Hot markets are about hype, and hype can be expensive. If the market cools off and you need to move, *you* will be stuck with the mortgage payments. The real estate agents and mortgage brokers won't give you a dime if you get in trouble. So figure out what you can afford, and stick to your guns. If that means waiting until the market cools down and your Savings fatten up, don't worry about it. Just remember what you already know: On average, home prices rise at about the same pace as inflation. There may be a run-up right now, but odds are in your favor that it won't last very long.

When the time is right, you can find a great house *and* sleep a lot better knowing that your money is in balance and your home is secure. And when you hear the hurry-up hype, just nod your head and smile; you'll be fine, no matter what the market does.

TOP MYTHS ABOUT BUYING A HOME

Myth	Fact
You should buy a home now!	You should buy a home when you're ready.
If the bank approves you for the mortgage, you can afford the home.	Banks are out to maximize their profits—period. *You* must calculate what you can really afford.
Mortgages are all alike, so there's no need to shop around.	Anyone who doesn't shop around for a mortgage is asking to get fleeced.
You can trust your real estate agent to look out for your interests.	Your real estate agent gets paid to look out for the seller's interests, not yours.

(continued)

TOP MYTHS ABOUT BUYING A HOME *(continued)*

Myth	Fact
Everyone should own a home.	Homeownership is great for some people, but not right for others.
Responsible people don't lose their homes in foreclosure.	Hardworking people lose their homes in foreclosure every day.
There is no point in saving for a down payment.	A down payment can save you tens of thousands of dollars.
You can pay off your credit cards *after* you buy the house.	You will save money and make yourself safer if you pay your Steal-from-Tomorrow debts *before* you buy.
You can make big money buying houses and flipping them quickly.	Anyone who needs to sell quickly can lose a lot of money.
Rent is wasted.	Rent puts a roof over your head.
Real estate prices always go up.	We wish!

THE GREAT ADVENTURE

Homeownership is one of life's great adventures. With luck and a little careful planning, your home can become a cornerstone of your financial plan *and* the site of your happiest memories.

For Russell and Diana Creighton, homeownership wasn't exactly trouble-free. They look back today and laugh about how many times they wondered if they could make it. Diana tells about the day they moved in, when their 7-year-old son decided that he could climb the red oak on the edge of the property. Everyone was watching the movers, so no one saw Jeremy make the climb. But they heard him fall—slipping off the lower limb, hollering all the way to the ground, where his arm made a loud "snap!"

Jeremy was still wearing the cast when a rumbling noise woke them up one night. Russell ran to the backyard, just in time to see the earth open up and their septic tank explode, as a smelly, dark-colored ooze rolled across the lawn.

Then came the real shock: When the weather got warm, they learned that the next-door neighbors were nudists, a discovery Jeremy made just before he fell out of the oak tree (again!) and broke his wrist. Russell cut the oak tree back, and things settled down for the next few years, until Diana installed a 24-hour light in the little lean-to shed in the backyard where she was trying to grow seedling vegetable plants. A few days later, the police rapped on the door. Apparently they thought Russell and Diana had gone into the marijuana supply business!

Through it all, they repainted the house, added a new baby—and kept making payments. Once they had recovered from the initial moving and closing costs, they started adding extra money to every monthly payment. By the time Jeremy was a senior in college, the Creightons had paid off their mortgage. They owned their own piece of land—oak tree, septic system, lean-to greenhouse and all. Homeownership was a lot of work, but it was well worth it.

We believe in homeownership—the kind that comes with a smile. *All Your Worth* is your way to buy a home, pay it off, and keep on smiling.

9

■

Financial CPR: Protect Yourself
When Things Get Tough

By now, your plan for a Lifetime of Riches should be well on track. You've worked hard to bring your money into balance. You've created a plan to make your money last a lifetime. You are building a Security Fund and moving toward a future that will be richer and more secure.

But you know and we know, sometimes things don't go according to plan. Sometimes, even when you are doing your best to put everything together, the pieces just don't work. Maybe you get laid off, and it takes months to find another job. Or maybe you get divorced, and your ex leaves you with a cranky cat and a pile of bills. Or maybe your business partner takes off to get in touch with his inner wildebeest or maybe a refrigerator falls on your foot. We get it. There are times when bad things happen to good people, times when it seems like you just can't catch a break.

Most books just end with "here's the plan," and you are supposed to ride into the sunset. But we think it pays to know some financial CPR. Just like real CPR, we hope you'll never have to use your financial CPR training. But we want you to have the knowledge, just in case. We want you to know, somewhere in the back of your mind, that if things ever go really wrong, you are ready to handle whatever life throws your way. You have a *real* plan—a plan for good times and bad, a plan for life.

YOUR EMERGENCY BACKUP PLAN

Any CPR instructor worth her salt will tell you that the most important step in saving someone is to prepare for an emergency *before* one arises. Know how to recognize the danger signs, learn the steps, and run through some practice drills. There may not be time to get out the instruction manual when a person is turning blue, so it is a good idea to give it some thought now, when everyone is breathing just fine. This same lesson holds true for financial protection.

Financial CPR is about creating a strategy for what you will do if things go wrong. It boils down to one question: *What will you do in a financial emergency?*

Here are 4 steps to create your own emergency backup plan:

1. Spot the Dangers

You know what we're talking about—those scary places where you might be vulnerable. You know they're there, but it's more comfortable to look away. Maybe you worry about your health, or maybe you worry about your job. We want you to do something that may feel a little unnatural (and a little frightening!). We want you to look those worries square in the face. Hold your horses, this isn't just about giving you a bad case of insomnia. We want you to focus on what you can do to make things better (and to worry a little less!).

So, for example, suppose you worry that your job could disappear. That may just be a fact of life, but there are things you can do now to prepare yourself. Do a little online job hunting, and dust off your résumé and send it out to a few places, just in case. Or perhaps you are concerned about your parents' health. Now is a good time to talk with them about their wishes, and maybe help them get long-term-care insurance. Spot the vulnerabilities and think about them now when you have plenty of time to take steps to protect yourself.

If you see some real dangers lurking in your future, there is something else you can do now: Don't make it *worse.* Maybe you can't find a better job right now, but you also know that this isn't a good time to take on a brand-new car loan. If your folks are getting along in age, this might not be the time for you to move. We hope things will stay perfect, but life isn't always so smooth. So find the time to review the possibilities, so you can protect yourself—just in case.

Jot your ideas down on a sheet of paper. Include the possible vulnerabilities and your ideas for what you might do. Writing it down will make it real.

2. Make a List of Wants You Could Cut

Ask yourself: If something went wrong, which Wants would I cut first? The point here is not to get rid of the Wants spending right this minute. Just the opposite: as long as you're working and everyone is healthy, you should keep enjoying your Wants to the fullest. Just be prepared, so that if the need ever arises, you'll be ready to move fast.

This is where all the hard work you put into getting your money in balance pays off. You've broken the credit card habit, and you've gotten really, really clear on what you need and what you can live without. So take a moment to think it through. What would you cut first? What would you cut second? For example, you might decide that at the first sign of trouble, you would start cooking every night and skip the trips to Taco Bell. Or maybe you would cancel your cell phone, or get rid of cable TV. (Who needs 154 channels, anyway?) Ultimately, if things ever got really tough, you would probably cut all of your Wants. But for now, think of the cuts that hurt the least, so you're ready to trim if the need ever arises.

This is also a good time to make sure that you can make these cuts. If you think you could live without your cell phone, then make sure that you aren't trapped into a two-year contract. Likewise, find out if there is a penalty for canceling your satellite dish. With a little preparation now, you'll be able to respond lightning-quick if the need ever arises.

3. Make a List of Must-Haves You Could Cut

The next step is to look for places where you could trim your Must-Haves *if* you ever need to. You are probably thinking, "Are these people crazy, there's nowhere left to cut!" But hold your horses; we're not asking you to make more cuts. We're just asking you to *think* about the cuts you could make if you absolutely had to.

It's time for some creativity. If things got tough and you couldn't manage your Must-Haves, what steps might you take? Could you move in with your parents—maybe just until you get back on your feet? Could you sell the car and take the bus for a while? Could you pull the kids out of preschool or after-school activities? Could you rent out the house and move into an apartment? We ask these questions for a very specific reason: Sometimes decisions you make now can preserve options for the future.

Jessie Nowland is living proof. Four years after buying her own little bungalow, she decided to remodel. Her builder tried to talk her into getting rid of the second bedroom so she could make a single, larger master bedroom suite with double walk-in closets and a spa bath. He sketched out pictures and urged her to "go for it." But Jessie hesitated, deciding to keep the two smaller bedrooms and add a second small bathroom instead. Seven months after the renovations were complete (and long before they were paid off), Jessie took a hard fall at work. Even with worker's compensation, she was out of money in about 5 months, and she was looking at 5 more months of rehab before she could return to her job as a cardiac nurse. So Jessie invited her mom to move in. "It was a godsend. Mom drove me around, did the shopping. And she helped out with the mortgage, the utilities, that kind of thing. If I had remodeled my house to fit only one person, this never would have worked." Think now about preserving your options if things go wrong. You may end up keeping some flexibility that could be important later on.

Make a list of possible cuts you could make *if* you ever need to. We've started the list with a few common answers; check those that apply to you.

EMERGENCY TARGETS

Wants

❑ Restaurant meals

❑ Cable TV

❑ New clothes

❑ Cell phone

❑ _____

❑ _____

❑ _____

❑ _____

Must-Haves

❑ _____

❑ _____

❑ _____

❑ _____

4. Practice Every Year and Before Any Major Purchase

It is good to practice a CPR drill every year or so. Do the same with your money. Once a year, set aside an hour to think about what you would do if your finances took a tumble. Pick a special day—the day before your birthday or January 1. (We have a friend who always does this on Halloween—the scariest day of the year!)

And then do a little planning. Update your list of places where you might be vulnerable, and make sure you've done your best to address them. You should also update your list of Emergency Targets, so you're ready to cut your spending if you ever need to.

Once your CPR drill is over, file away the papers and put the worries out of your mind, secure in the knowledge that you have planned ahead and done your best. Then give yourself a treat. You deserve it.

And remember, this isn't about walking around with a black cloud over your head. This is about taking sensible, positive action when you have time to plan it out. Think of yourself as an optimist with a parachute.

What to Do When Bad Things Happen

No time for the drill; this is a real emergency. You've run through your Security Fund and money is getting tight. What should you do? We can't promise that things won't get tough, but we can give you some tools to help you stay calm, and to keep *you* in charge of your own future.

1. Stay in Control

Don't panic. This is important. We once saw a man slump to the floor in an airport, his face rapidly turning purple and his eyes fluttering closed. The woman closest to him shrieked loudly, "Help this man!" then bolted for the women's room. A few minutes later she came back looking wild-eyed and carrying a single paper towel. Fortunately, other folks in the airport hadn't panicked, and CPR was well under way by the time she came back.

Panic can happen any time. A pink slip may leave you pacing the floor all night. A collection notice may leave you speechless. That is when you need to repeat to yourself, "No matter how bad things get, I *always* have options." But to weigh your options carefully, you will need a clear head. Keep your wits about you, and don't panic.

> No matter what happens,
> you always have options.

First, you need to understand that when you are in financial trouble you are still in control. Yes, creditors have rights. But *you* have rights too. More important, *you* are the one who earns the money. And *you* have control over the bank account, the house, and everything else in your name. This means that *you* are the one who decides which creditors get paid, and *you* are the one who decides whether to sell something, to give it back, or to work out a payment plan. These are *your* decisions, and *you* are still in the driver's seat.

So keep calm. You may be forced to make some tough choices, but these are still *your* choices. If you keep your head, you'll get through this.

2. React Quickly

The corollary to "Don't panic" is "Move fast." When something goes wrong, you need to create a plan, and you need to do it quickly (which is why you practiced the Financial CPR drill at the front of this chapter). Just like when someone starts choking, the time it takes to respond can make a huge difference.

It may seem obvious that you need a quick response, but in fact many people delay. The greatest danger when you get into financial trouble is not bill collectors—although they can be the most annoying. The greatest danger is misplaced optimism. We've heard it over and over again: "I'm sure I can find another job right away." "Surely Tim will be feeling better soon." "My wife and I will patch things up after a little time apart." Many job counselors tell people who have lost their jobs to keep up their lives just as before—hit the credit cards and keep everything "normal." Well, things aren't normal. The speed with which you react may make the difference between a fender-bender and a head-on collision.

> When you get in financial trouble,
> respond quickly.

If a crisis comes your way, the first thing will be to trim the spending. Go back to your CPR drill, and look at the list of cuts you decided you *could* make if you had to. Now is the time to start cutting—fast. When rumors of pink slips start flying around the office, that's the time to eat dinner at home and cancel the cell phone.

What's the point of cutting your spending? If you've lost your job, the answer is pretty obvious: Make sure you have enough to pay your Must-Haves. But if the bad news is still just a rumor, that's the time to fatten up your Security Fund a little more. It's also a good time to stop investing in your retirement fund or putting extra payments into the mortgage; you can resume just as soon as the crisis passes. You already know this instinctively; after all, you wouldn't open an IRA or go on a shopping spree the day after you lost your job. But if you take the time to think about this now, you'll be ready to react more quickly if the need ever arrives.

Give yourself a timeline. Since you don't really know when the crisis will end, you should create a schedule for yourself. So, for example, you might decide that if you haven't found a job within 3 months, it will be time to move to a smaller apartment and take a job waiting tables on the weekends while you continue to job-search during the week. The point here is to be proactive, so that *you* stay in charge of your life.

3. Call Your Creditors

If you are in trouble and you know you'll miss a payment, get on the phone. We learned this lesson from Ramón, an old friend of ours. When he was a wet-behind-the-ears accountant who had just hung out his shingle, one of his clients, a small trucking business, ran short on cash. "The owner said to call the people we owe money to and tell them we'd be late in paying." Ramón was appalled, but he needed this guy's business, so he picked up the phone and started calling. "My hands were sweaty, my heart was pounding, and I thought they might start cursing me out. But the first company I called said they appreciated the notice, they worked out a quick plan with me, and actually thanked me for calling. By the third call, I was breathing normally, and I realized I was actually helping get this business back on track." Over the years, Ramón found he had a knack for helping struggling companies. He opened his own turnaround business, and today he runs a multimillion-dollar company that employs more than a hundred people. And it all started with a phone call.

What is good enough for Ramón and his business clients is good enough for you. So get on the phone. Sure, it may be embarrassing, but your creditors will be much more willing to work something out if you call them before they have to call you. Explain what has happened—you've lost your job or you've been attacked by a wild buffalo—and tell them you want to make good. Some creditors, such as student loan issuers and utility companies, have special provisions to accommodate people who are facing a serious illness or a job loss, so be sure to ask. You are much less likely to get hammered with late fees and collection notices if you make the first call.

Ask your creditors if they will work out a repayment plan for you—perhaps just a token payment for a few months until you get back on your feet. (Be sure to keep a record of whatever you agree on; you may need this later on.) But remember this hard-and-fast rule: Don't agree to anything unless you are absolutely certain that you can meet your end of the bargain. If you are out of work and you don't yet have a regular job, just tell them what is wrong and that you'll try to work out a plan as soon as you can. Don't commit to anything yet. Be completely honest, and never make promises you can't keep.

4. Pay the Bills That Matter Most

If things get really tight and you don't have enough to cover all your expenses, then *pay the most important bills first.* For most people, the home comes first, and then maybe the car or the health insurance policy. Figure out your priorities. Sure, you want to pay everything, but this is a little like deciding what to save in a fire. Save the most important things first, then save what you can. Don't try to save everything at once, because it just may be too much to handle.

> When trouble strikes, decide which things you treasure most, and pay those bills first.

After her divorce, Antoinette Ameren was determined to keep everything the same for her two daughters—the house, the SUV, the ballet lessons. She felt that her girls were bruised enough when their daddy left, and they shouldn't have to pay anymore. Before long, she found herself choosing which bills to pay and which to put off another month.

It was a call from a collection agent that finally shook Antoinette out of her fog. The bill collector was really aggressive, calling her "a cheat" and "a stupid cow." She slammed down the phone, her hand trembling and her heart racing. "I thought, Is this where I'm headed? People think they can treat me like *this*?" And that was the moment she decided it was time for a change. She put all her expenses on paper, and realized there just wasn't enough to keep going the same way. Her first priority was to own a home, so she sold the big house she had shared with her husband and bought a smaller place—then she let the rest go. She sold the Ford Explorer and switched the girls to a tumbling class at the local YMCA. Antoinette told us:

> It took me seven months to find a decent full-time job. And then my knee went out, and I had to get surgery, and that cost a lot. But we've done all right. I look at our little house—the girls and I have painted and stenciled every room, we even painted frogs in the utility room! . . . I think about how I could have waited [to move] and ended up in some cheap apartment in [a bad section of town]. I saved what I could, and I'm proud the girls and I are making it okay.

If you have one or two particularly noisy creditors, it may be tempting to send them some money just to get them to leave you alone. This is a mistake. You need to work out the payment plan that makes sense for *you.*

It doesn't matter who makes what demands or what the bill collectors threaten. If serious trouble comes your way, you should be fighting for the things *you* care about, not trying to quiet down the most aggressive bill collector.

5. Borrow only as a last resort—and keep it safe

You have cut out the fun spending, you have drained your Security Fund, and there still isn't enough. What then?

If you don't have enough money to keep bread on the table, to get medical care and keep the lights on, then go ahead and borrow the money. Go into debt—but do it carefully.

The first rule is to make absolutely certain that there is no other way. Could you earn a little extra cash instead? Is there still a little something in the piggy bank? If you haven't exhausted every possible reserve, then don't do it. This borrowing will cost you big-time in the future, so break the glass and pull the alarm only when you are sure that there is no other option.

The second rule is that borrowing is for Must-Haves *only*. You already know this (you wouldn't take out a loan to take a trip to Vegas), but we want to make it doubly clear. Once you start down the slippery slope of debt, it can be so easy to just put any old thing on that credit card. "After all, it is Christmas and I don't want to disappoint the kids. And the lawn mower is on its last legs, and this is such a good deal. . . ." These are not Must-Have expenses! So knit your own Christmas presents and borrow the neighbor's lawn mower. You can take on debt for housing, medical care, and food—and that's it.

The third rule: Safety is more important than interest rates. A home equity loan or a car title loan may seem attractive, since the interest rate is lower and the advertisements are coming thick and fast. But the last thing you should do when you get in trouble is put your treasures on the line. After all, it will be tough enough to keep up with your mortgage and your car loan, so you shouldn't make the payments even bigger when you are staring trouble right in the teeth!

> Safety is more important than interest rates.
> If you need to take on debt, use a credit
> card instead of a home equity loan.

What should you do? Start by stringing out your payments. Request a deferment on your student loans, and hold off on paying the cell phone, the dentist, the doctor, and other outstanding bills for anything besides your utilities, home, and car payment. You may get some dings on your credit report and your cell phone may get shut off, but these creditors probably won't charge you exorbitant interest (especially if you call ahead of time) and they won't kick you out on the street.

Next, take the lowest-interest credit card you can find, and charge the necessities. Yes, credit cards are dangerous, and yes, we told you to cut up your cards. But we also said that the cards are for emergencies, and this is an emergency. Put the groceries on the MasterCard, and make the minimum payments as best you can. The bad news is that you may pay more for this kind of debt than you would for a home equity loan (although not always, if you shop carefully). But the good news is that you won't risk losing the place where you live. If push comes to shove, you can discharge your credit card, medical debt, and so forth by filing for bankruptcy.

What about that money sitting in your retirement account? Should you cash it out? No! The law puts special protection on your retirement accounts so your creditors can't get to that money. Those protections are strong for a very good reason—you will need that money later on, maybe more than you need it today. Moreover, cashing out your retirement account is the most expensive kind of borrowing, since you get hit with extra tax penalties. So don't cash out your retirement account, and don't borrow against it either. Hold on to this money for your future.

And beware of the debt peddlers. When you get in financial trouble, the offers come flying for all sorts of new debt you can take on. It may sound crazy, but bill collectors routinely call to offer *more* debt in the same breath they demand payment on your old bills. They try to convince you that taking out a consolidation loan will somehow solve your problems. Hospitals and other medical providers increasingly collect their fees by steering people to high-interest loans, so be especially leery of their offers. When you owe someone money and they are offering to put you in touch with a finance company or to give you more money, run the other way—fast!

Collection agents can be really persistent about pushing these offers. We knew a man in Tennessee who got behind on his mortgage after he had a heart attack. When the mortgage company called, he figured they would give him a hard time about the missed payments, telling him he had to pay up or else. But they didn't even ask him for a single dollar. In fact, they just wanted him to take on a *second* mortgage. Wisely, the man refused to put his home under even greater risk. But the mortgage company wouldn't take no for an answer. They called day after day, rousing the man from his sickbed. When he finally told them not to call back any more, the company started pestering his *wife*, calling her at the office to tell her that she should "make him sign," since she "deserves a break." Be prepared to say no, and to keep saying it. And don't be surprised if a bill collector tries to put a wedge between you and your spouse. When it comes to collecting money, nothing is sacred. Just hang up the phone, and make a pact with your spouse to do the same.

6. Negotiate Like Crazy

Earlier we suggested that you call your landlord or your credit card company if you were going to miss a payment. Now it is time to think about what happens if you fall way behind on all your bills, and there doesn't seem to be any quick way out of the hole.

If you are behind on your bills and your credit score is lower than room temperature, then there is no point in trying to hide it. Your creditors already know. Which means they also know that you may be thinking about filing for bankruptcy—a situation where they might not get a dime. There is a good chance that if you are in that much trouble with your bills, at least some companies will be willing to negotiate.

Try calling your creditors to see if they are willing to deal. The key is to be firm: Tell them you simply do not have the money to pay in full. Come clean, telling them what went wrong and how you've turned the corner. Tell them you hope to avoid bankruptcy, but only if they're willing to work with you. If a company agrees to deal, make very certain that if you pay, they will erase the debt completely. Get it in writing. Some companies may offer to put you on a monthly payment plan with no intention of ever wiping out the debt. If you get that kind of offer, just walk away. Remember, you don't want to spread out your payments; you want to get rid of your debt completely.

7. If Push Comes to Shove, Call a Bankruptcy Attorney

If you are on the verge of bankruptcy, you may be able to negotiate yourself back off the cliff by getting all (or most) of your creditors to take less. But be realistic: Don't agree to a payment plan that you can't afford, and don't expect miracles. Some companies are not reasonable, and some are not even polite. So if you run into a brick wall, don't keep banging your head against it.

We know it hurts to think about it, but at some point bankruptcy may be the right choice. More than a million and a half families file for bankruptcy every year, and nearly every one of them would tell you that going bankrupt was one of the lowest points in their lives. Even so, bankruptcy can be the best step to get you back on the right track. We'll talk about the ins and outs of bankruptcy toward the end of this chapter.

THE HUMAN SIDE TO MONEY TROUBLES

When you get in financial trouble, your wallet isn't the only thing that suffers. Look out for yourself, and look out for your loved ones.

Be Kind to the People You Love

Financial trouble is one of the most stressful things in life, right up there with divorce and the death of a loved one. So no matter how frightened or exhausted or frustrated you get, you need to follow a basic rule: Be kind to the people you love.

That starts with being honest. Be honest with your mate, and be honest with your kids. Kids are a lot smarter than we give them credit for, and they know when Mom and Dad are worried. But they have active imaginations, which means they can dream up something a lot worse than whatever is really going wrong. When Lupe and Jack Randall finally sat down with their 9-year-old son to explain that they needed to cut expenses because Lupe had lost her job, the boy asked solemnly, "Will I be living with Dad or with Mom?" Lupe and Jack were stunned by the question; divorce wasn't anywhere on the radar screen. But the boy knew something was wrong, and in his world, the worst that he could think of was divorce. When they reassured him that they were all in this together, he cried so hard that Lupe and Jack could barely hold it together. So come clean with your kids. They deserve it.

And be kind to your mate. Consider this: If your family is like most, your marriage is more vulnerable when you get in financial trouble than at any other time in your life. Financial calamity is one of the most frustrating, humiliating, and exhausting experiences a couple can go through. Husbands may feel shamed by their inability to provide, and wives may feel overburdened by the demands of bill collectors, bosses, and children. And if your boss makes you furious or a bill collector calls you ugly names, you may not be able to spit back. Your mate is always nearby, however, and it can be tempting to lash out in that direction instead. Be kind. You are both under enormous strain right now, and taking it out on each other will only make things worse.

Your spouse can be your greatest source of comfort. And you should be the same for your spouse. So make an effort. Do some nice things together. Take a walk. Sneak away for a Big Mac and a Coke. Turn the lights down low and dance to your favorite CD. Promise yourself that at least once a day you will have a conversation that isn't about money. Talk about the weather or something funny the dog did. Anything but money. Remember that financial difficulty should not consume your life or your relationship.

And don't develop 20/20 hindsight. When you get in financial trouble, it is tempting to beat up on yourself (and your mate) about the smarter choices you might have made. Maybe you shouldn't have bought a new car, maybe your mate should have applied for more jobs, maybe you should never have tried skydiving. That 20/20 hindsight can keep you up all night, endlessly reliving past mistakes. In the end, second-guessing leaves you with nothing but bleary eyes and a sore heart. So get over the past mistakes, and focus on making smart decisions *now.* Go easy on yourself and the people you love.

Never Trust a Bill Collector

If your financial problems get really bad, you may find yourself at the center of a lot of attention—phone calls, letters, even visits to your home—all from the people you least want to hear from, your bill collectors.

Bill collectors have a lot of different approaches. Some are friendly and sympathetic, some are cold and clinical, and some are downright scary. No matter what tactic they use, they have only one goal. They want to get paid. Period. You can make deals with them if you have to, but don't forget that they are not on your side. So don't ever, ever take their advice.

> Bill collectors have only one goal: To get your money. Don't ever take their advice.

If you have never been late on your bills, you may be shocked by just how nasty bill collectors can be. We've heard some stories that would straighten your hair and curl your toes. Bill collectors may call late at night, on weekends, and even on Christmas morning. They may call you at work, and they may try to embarrass you by pestering your co-workers or your extended family. Bill collectors will threaten to garnish wages, freeze checking accounts, show up with the sheriff at your house, or even have you arrested. We were told of one debt collector who actually threatened to repossess a woman's mattress and set it on fire in the middle of the street! If you get these kinds of threats, ask for a written letter outlining what action the creditor plans to take. If the bill collector won't write the threat down, then he is probably just blowing smoke—and he knows that if he puts it in writing his company could get sued. So get it in writing.

Many of the practices bill collectors use to intimidate people are outlawed by the Fair Debt Collection Practices Act, and you have a right to defend yourself. For example, the law says that debt collectors are not allowed to call before 8 A.M. or after 9 P.M. and they're not allowed to contact you at work if you tell them your employer disapproves. Most creditors count on the fact that people don't know their rights, and many people who owe money are too ashamed to ask for help. You can do better. Read up on your rights at www.ftc .gov, or call the hotline at 877-FTC-HELP. Don't become another victim.

If you have children, you need to be doubly careful about bill collectors. This may sound shocking, but it's true: There are bill collectors who routinely hassle little kids. Many companies make a practice of starting their collection calls in the mid-afternoon, when Mom and Dad are still at work and the kids are home alone. We have talked with people whose children—some as young as 9 or 10 years old—were told that Mommy would go to jail if she doesn't pay the bill collector. "Just tell her to pay up, and we won't call the police." Never mind that the threats were untrue; the bill collector figured that if he scared the kids enough, Mom would borrow the money from someone else and make a payment just to make the calls stop. So protect your kids, and never, ever let them answer the phone when they might be talking to a bill collector.

Stay Away from Credit Counselors

Remember what we said back in Step Five: Credit counselors sound oh-so-friendly, but many are just slick operators who want to wring every last penny out of you—then toss you on the credit trash pile when they finally decide that they can't get any more.

Until the industry is regulated, just stay away. Even some of the nonprofit counselors have been exposed as shams. Right now, you can't tell the dolphins from the sharks, so stay out of the water.

Don't Hide in Shame

If financial troubles come your way, you may find yourself feeling isolated, overcome with feelings of embarrassment and shame. In a society where people speak publicly about everything from their struggles with alcoholism to their efforts to get pregnant, financial trouble remains the last great taboo. Ordinary, hardworking people just don't talk about overdue bills and repo men. This can leave you feeling like you are all alone, like you are the only one in the world facing hard times.

We're here to tell you that if you find yourself in financial trouble, *you are not alone.* In fact, 1 in 7 families is in serious financial trouble. That's right, 1 in 7. A person is now more likely to file for bankruptcy than to file for divorce! You may not know it, but scattered among the folks in your grocery store, your office, your church or synagogue, and even your own family, are men and women just like you—people who have done their best and who are now in financial trouble. If you find yourself at the end of your financial rope, you are not the only one. Plenty of other hardworking, decent people have found themselves in exactly the same spot.

So don't hide in shame. Find someone you can trust—a family member, your best friend, your minister—and talk about it. Financial trouble can be a giant weight on your shoulders. Don't try to carry it alone.

THE BANKRUPTCY OPTION

When we told Emily and Travis that they needed to file for bankruptcy, there was dead silence in the room. Travis looked as if someone had just slapped him, and for an instant it looked like he might try to hit back. Emily looked a little lost, and it was several minutes before she seemed to notice that she needed to blot her eyes. We had gone over the numbers in painful detail, and we all knew that Emily and Travis couldn't even cover the interest on their debts—much less begin to pay down the loans. The conclusion was obvious. But it still stung to hear it.

Travis eventually stopped clenching and unclenching his fists, and

Emily finally reached for a tissue. After a few hours of talking, they were still a little shaky. Emily said:

> I was raised right, to go to church and pay my bills. But good Lord, it's like I'm choking to death every single day. I can't even drive to work without worrying, how am I gonna pay for the gas for my car? Maybe [bankruptcy] will give us a little air. Maybe we can do it.

That is what bankruptcy is all about—hope for the future. Bankruptcy may sound like the end of the line, and it certainly can be a gut-wrenching experience, one we hope you never have to face. But if you do, you won't be alone. Every fifteen seconds, someone makes the decision to walk into a bankruptcy court. In fact, more people file for bankruptcy each year than graduate from college. If you think you don't know anyone who has gone bankrupt, guess again; bankruptcy is now more common than cancer.

If your financial situation gets really bad, filing for bankruptcy may be your best option. One of us (Elizabeth) has taught thousands of students the laws of bankruptcy, and co-authored one of the nation's leading textbooks on bankruptcy; I have also testified before Congress and the president about the intricacies of the Bankruptcy Code. After more than 20 years of teaching and writing about bankruptcy, I can tell you this: By and large, knowledge about bankruptcy is limited to a small number of highly sophisticated lawyers and bankers. Meanwhile, the people who most need to understand bankruptcy—ordinary people who are in deep financial trouble—are left to grope in the dark. If I had a dollar for every person who makes a giant, costly mistake about filing (or not filing) for bankruptcy, I would be a very rich woman. And so I want to share what I know about bankruptcy, so that if you ever find yourself at the end of your financial rope, you can make the smartest possible decisions.

What Bankruptcy Can (and Can't) Do for You

Bankruptcy is essentially a one-time get-out-of-jail-free card that lets you erase many of your debts. The Bankruptcy Code is designed to achieve two goals. First, when you are at a point where there is no hope of repaying all your debts in a timely way, the bankruptcy process is designed to treat your creditors fairly (or at least as fairly as possible). Bankruptcy prevents a particularly aggressive bill collector from pushing aside the other people you owe money to. The judge makes sure that when you don't have enough money to pay all your debts in full, then the back-payments to your landlord or your dentist get the same treatment as your old bills from Citibank and Ford Motor Credit.

Second, bankruptcy is designed to give you a fresh start. The Founding Fathers inserted a bankruptcy provision into the Constitution (before they added the Bill of Rights!) because they wanted Americans to have an alternative to debtors' prisons and a lifetime of debt. Bankruptcy is based on the principle of second chances. Filing for bankruptcy wipes out many of your debts, giving you a second chance at getting back on your feet financially.

When you file for bankruptcy, the courts take legal control over all your assets—the bank accounts, the house, the car—everything right down to the jar of pennies and the old bike with a flat tire. You can get bankruptcy relief no more than once every 7 years (a period drawn from a passage in the Bible), so think hard before filing.

There are two kinds of bankruptcy: Chapter 7 and Chapter 13.

Chapter 7

If you are like about 70% of all people who are in trouble, you would file under Chapter 7 or "straight" bankruptcy. Chapter 7 is essentially a "clear the slate" bankruptcy: You may lose almost everything of value that you own, but then most of your debts will be erased completely. Under Chapter 7, you might have to sell your jewelry or your newer appliances, like a big-screen TV. You will have to empty your bank accounts and sell any stocks or bonds you might own. But you can usually keep your clothes, your furniture, and your household goods; you also get to keep your retirement fund. You can also keep your car, assuming it isn't too valuable (and assuming you keep up with your car payments). Your house is trickier; we'll explain that later.

Of course, by the time you hit the bankruptcy courts, you may not have any assets worth selling. That's usually the case; most bankrupt people don't have any cash, stocks, bonds or much of anything else. If you do have something worth selling, the judge will appoint a trustee to oversee the sale of your stuff. The trustee will then liquidate your bank accounts and distribute any cash to your creditors. Then, whatever is left of your consumer debts—your credit cards, medical bills, payday loans, old phone bills, and so forth—will be wiped out.

If you rent an apartment, you will be excused from the old, past-due rent payments, and the landlord won't be allowed to evict you. (Of course, you will have to keep up with your rent after you file.) The same is true for utilities—you don't have to pay the past-due amounts, but after the bankruptcy you must stay current on your bills or they can shut off your services. You also have to keep up with your car payments or the bank will be allowed to repossess it.

If you own a home, in most cases you can keep it if you keep up with all your mortgage payments. The rules about home equity (the value of your home that exceeds the mortgage) vary from state to state. A few states, such as Florida and Texas, permit you to keep your home, no matter how much equity you have built up. (That's why O.J. Simpson said he was leaving California and moving to Florida when his in-laws threatened to sue him; in Florida he could buy a mansion and then file for bankruptcy, and no one could take it away from him!) Other states, such as Delaware and Maryland, force you to sell your home if you have any equity at all.

Some debts are never forgiven, no matter what. Taxes, student loans, alimony, and child support must be paid in full, regardless of how long it takes; bankruptcy offers almost no relief. And the interest keeps on ticking on those debts. But your other debts—the credit cards, the medical bills, and so forth—are wiped out, so that at the end of Chapter 7, you get to start with a (mostly) clean slate.

If you don't have much stuff, the whole Chapter 7 process—start to finish—is usually over in a few weeks. The collection calls stop, the debts are erased, and you get a fresh chance to put together a new financial life.

Chapter 13

The other kind of bankruptcy is called Chapter 13 and accounts for the remaining 30% of people who go bankrupt. Under this option, you gain extra time to pay down your debts (rather than to get rid of them altogether). When you file for a Chapter 13 bankruptcy, you and your lawyer work out a repayment plan. The plan lasts for 3 to 5 years. During that period, you commit to live on a sharply restricted budget so you can put as much money as possible toward repaying your debts. Your goal is to repay all your old debts during that period, but if you can't get them all paid, any remaining debts will be wiped out at the end of the repayment period (with a few exceptions).

Chapter 13 has one special advantage: If you are behind on your mortgage, you will get a few years to catch up through your repayment plan. This means that if you own a home and you've fallen behind on your mortgage, Chapter 13 may be a better bet than Chapter 7. But if you don't own a home or if your mortgage payments are up-to-date, Chapter 13 probably doesn't offer any special benefits.

CHAPTER 7 AND CHAPTER 13 IN A NUTSHELL

	Chapter 7	Chapter 13
What it does for you	Erases most consumer debts	Gives you extra time to repay your debts
Which debts are erased	Most consumer debts, such as: Credit cards Medical bills Payday loans Back-payments on rent, utilities, cell phone, etc.	No debts are erased when you file for bankruptcy. After your 3-5 year repayment plan, any unpaid consumer debts are erased.

(continued)

CHAPTER 7 AND CHAPTER 13 IN A NUTSHELL *(continued)*

	Chapter 7	*Chapter 13*
Which debts are never erased	Child support/Alimony Taxes Student loans Mortgage (unless you give up your home) Car payment (unless you give up your car)	Child support/Alimony Taxes Student loans Mortgage (unless you give up your home) Car payment (unless you give up your car)
Biggest advantage	Erases most consumer debts quickly, so you get a fresh start in just a few weeks.	Gives you time to catch up on past mortgage payments.
Biggest drawback	No time to catch up on the mortgage, so you could lose your home. (If you don't own a home, this isn't a problem.)	Most people don't make it through the repayment plan, so the debt piles back on.

At first, Travis and Emily wanted to file for Chapter 13 even though they didn't own a home. Travis thought Chapter 13 sounded more honorable because it involves repaying some bills rather than just getting rid of the debts: "I'm not looking to walk out—I just need some time to turn things around." But we cautioned them that the ideal often doesn't match with reality. About two-thirds of the people who file under Chapter 13 never make it through the repayment process. Typically, they hit another setback, and they just can't keep up with the payments. In that case, all the debts—plus interest and penalties—pile back on. Emily's eyes widened when she heard that, and she quietly reminded Travis that he was still on probation at his new job. "You mean to say we could do all this bankruptcy business and land right back in the same boat? No thank you." They decided to file under Chapter 7.

As a general rule, if you are caught up on your mortgage payments or if you don't own a home, you are usually better off filing for Chapter 7. If your attorney gives you contradictory advice, ask for a specific explanation. If you are not persuaded, get a second opinion. Attorney's fees are larger in Chapter 13, and a few attorneys have been known to steer people into Chapter 13 even when it isn't in the client's best interests. Most bankruptcy lawyers are salt-of-the-earth, good people who genuinely care about families in financial trouble, and they would never deliberately steer you the wrong way. But, like anything else, there are a few bad apples, so if something smells funny, seek help elsewhere.

How It Works

If you think bankruptcy is your best option, start by hiring an attorney. In theory you can go it alone or use a "filing service," but filing services cannot provide legal advice (even though they often charge as much as a lawyer!). The laws have a zillion unexpected traps in them, so you are much safer if you hire an attorney.

Unfortunately, the best attorneys don't usually carry a wand and go by the name Glinda. But there is another good way to distinguish a good bankruptcy attorney: Look for a specialist. Stay away from small outfits that advertise bankruptcy along with divorce, immigration, car accidents, and a bunch of other stuff. Instead, look for someone who does a lot of bankruptcy work and not much of anything else. You can call the county bar association for a referral or check the yellow pages.

Once you have chosen your attorney, don't be surprised if you don't see him or her again until your hearing date. Most of the preparation for filing bankruptcy is filling out forms (lots and lots and lots of forms), a task which is generally handled by a paralegal or one of the attorney's assistants. The forms will ask a lot of questions: What do you own, when did you get it, how much debt do you owe, whom did you pay, what is your income. The list goes on until you think they will ask about your brand of underwear! Save your bills, statements, mortgage papers, and all your other financial papers; you may need them for those forms. It may be tedious, but the paperwork is important. These aren't just a bunch of papers filed away where no one ever reads them.

You must sign those forms under penalty of perjury—just like testifying in court—so you want to get the answers exactly right.

Your attorney will file the papers for you, usually a day or two after you finish the paperwork. Relief is immediate. Once the papers are filed with the court, all efforts to collect from you—telephone calls, car repossession, mortgage foreclosure, wage garnishment—all have to stop. Your attorney will make sure that every creditor is notified about the bankruptcy, and you can call your lawyer if anyone tries to hassle you after the filing.

You will get a notice in the mail to appear at a meeting with the bankruptcy trustee. You and your lawyer will show up, typically at an office building near the courthouse. (Court time is usually reserved for serious problems, and most bankruptcy cases are handled as routine affairs.) The usual gathering place is a big hallway, where lots of people are milling around—husbands looking for wives who are parking the car, mothers trying to quiet crying babies, people glancing furtively at everyone else who showed up on the same day. Lawyers always stand out; their suits and briefcases give them away. Every few minutes an assistant to the trustee will call out another name, but it barely makes a ripple.

When your name is called, you and your attorney will go into a room with the trustee (usually a lawyer) who has been appointed by the judge to review your case. You will be sworn in ("Promise to tell the truth," etc.), and the trustee will make a big show of turning on a tape recorder to record the questions and your answers. For most people, the questions are fairly routine—are these all of your assets, did you leave anything out, etc. Your creditors may show up to ask questions, but most of the time they don't bother. If something unusual happens ("Oh, yeah, I have $10,000 in bearer bonds tucked under my mattress" or "Uh, my wife couldn't make it, but she wants to be included in the bankruptcy too"), you may be held over for further examination. But if you are like about 99% of the cases, when the questions are over, the trustee will recommend to the court that you receive a "discharge" of your debts. The whole process should take roughly fifteen minutes. About 6 weeks later, you will receive a discharge document in the mail, which you can show to any creditor who continues to bother you.

Most people are amazed by how fast it all is. Others remark on how the court people were nice folks. But don't kid yourself—this may look like the waiting room at the Trailways bus station, but it won't feel like it. A master sergeant who had served in both Iraq wars told us he cried so hard during the questioning by the trustee that they stopped the proceeding and told him to come back in an hour after he had calmed down. He isn't alone; trustees tell us that the same thing happens several times a day. Even when there are no tears, most people cannot make eye contact, and the smell of sweat is always heavy in the air. This is a moment when people have to face up to financial failure, and the pain can be sharp.

What It Costs to Go Broke

Emily and Travis were surprised to learn that they couldn't afford to go bankrupt—at least not right away. Their bank account was empty, and their attorney wanted $825 in cash before he would process their paperwork.

Attorneys' fees vary depending on where you live and how complex your case is, but a typical Chapter 7 costs about $800 and a typical Chapter 13 will run about $1600. You will also have to pay a filing fee to the courts, currently about $200.

Where do you get that kind of money if you are on the edge of bankruptcy? Emily and Travis decided to skip the car payment and stop making payments on all their credit cards and personal loans. When they freed up some cash, they paid the lawyer, then caught up on their car loan after the bankruptcy. Their approach was pretty risky, since they got even more behind on some important bills, but lawyers tell us it is pretty common. Only in America would so many people be saving up to go broke!

Not a Secret

You may hope to keep your bankruptcy a secret; most people do. But bankruptcy is not a very private affair. If you file for bankruptcy, all of your financial dealings—your debts, your income, your budget—become part of the public records, available at the courthouse (and now on the Internet in some states) for anyone who wants to look at them. The bankruptcy will remain in your credit report for 10 years, raising the cost of everything from car insurance to house payments. Future employers will discover the bankruptcy if they run a credit check (now a routine screening process for many jobs), which can lead to embarrassing explanations or, worse, a lost chance for a job. Your name may be published in the newspaper under "legal notices," and the fact of your bankruptcy may pop up whenever someone searches for your name via the Internet.

As a practical matter, however, if you aren't a rock star and you haven't flimflammed everyone in town, most personal bankruptcies don't attract much attention. In all likelihood, most of your friends, neighbors, and co-workers won't learn that you filed for bankruptcy unless you decide to tell them.

What the Creditors Do

For most people, the best thing about filing for bankruptcy is that the phone finally stops ringing. Once you file, creditors are legally prohibited from calling you, sending you bills, or adding interest on your loans. Basically, they can't even talk to you about your debts. If you file for Chapter 7, they have to write off the debt and walk away. If you file for Chapter 13, they have to deal with your trustee and your lawyer for their share of the payments. Either way, they have to leave you alone. If you've been dealing with bill collectors for months (or years), the ensuing silence may seem like a gift from heaven.

But the peacefulness isn't guaranteed. The law also has a loophole. (Why should bankruptcy laws be any different?) During a Chapter 7 bankruptcy, a creditor can ask you to "reaffirm" a debt. "Reaffirm" is just a fancy legal word for agreeing to pay a debt that you were about to get rid of in the bankruptcy. It's basically a "Treat me special, don't make the bankruptcy apply to me" deal.

If you go to a bankruptcy court, you may notice people working the crowd—often friendly, gray-haired ladies—who call out various names. Don't let their smiles fool you; these are the representatives from Citibank, MBNA, GE Capital, Bank One, and other major creditors, and they are on the lookout for people who owe them money. They are hoping they can convince you to reaffirm debts that the judge is about to wipe out.

As nice as these people may seem, some will try to bully you by threatening to repossess your furniture or your appliances unless you reaffirm your debt. (We've even heard of one who threatened to repossess the kids' old swing set!) Except for the house or the car, this is nearly always an empty threat. It costs a few hundred dollars to send a truck to your house and cart something away, and most used goods just aren't worth that much.

Other companies try the we're-your-friend tactic by offering to sign you up for another credit card. As if you need more of the poison that you already choked on! If you file for bankruptcy, hang tough. Do not reaffirm anything but your car or home loan, and don't take on any more credit cards. Don't get tricked or bullied into signing away your future before the ink is dry on your bankruptcy petition.

> Do not reaffirm any debts except your car loan or home mortgage.

Credit After Bankruptcy

Do people who file for bankruptcy ever get credit again? Do they ever! Within six months of filing for bankruptcy, *84%* of people had already received unsolicited offers for new credit. Many had received more than 30 offers! If you file for bankruptcy, you will discover that you are *more* popular with credit card companies than ever before. Banks know that you cannot declare bankruptcy again for at least 6 years, and they believe there is a good chance that you could still be so strapped for cash that you will soon end up carrying a balance and making minimum monthly payments—rocketing you to number one on their list of favorite customers. Once again, stay away from credit card companies and all the other debt peddlers.

Why People Go Bankrupt

Does it matter *why* you go bankrupt? Not to the bankruptcy court—or at least, not usually. If you defrauded people out of money, the bankruptcy courts won't let you escape your obligations. Likewise, if you stole or embezzled money, you still have to repay the money you took. But if you promised to try to pay and just didn't come through, the bankruptcy courts don't really care what went wrong. Maybe you got sick, maybe you had a gambling problem, maybe you just made some really stupid decisions. Other people might feel sympathy for you or they might call you a lowlife, but the bankruptcy laws don't distinguish whether you have a good reason or a dumb reason for getting into trouble. Bankruptcy is about getting a capsized boat back upright and letting it sail on, without worrying about why the boat turned over in the first place.

That said, you might be surprised by how many bankrupt families tell roughly the same story. Nearly 90% of people who file for bankruptcy cite just three reasons for going broke: 1) job loss, 2) serious illness, or 3) divorce. That means that all the other reasons combined—natural disaster, victim of crime, gambling problems, drug addiction, identity theft, shopaholism, being called up for the National Guard, or plain old bad judgment—account for only about 10% of bankruptcies. In other words, the overwhelming majority of people are using the bankruptcy courts exactly as the Founding Fathers intended—as a second chance after something bad happens.

Is It Honorable?

You may be wondering: Is it *right* to file for bankruptcy? Is it honorable? After all, these companies lent you money. You made a promise, so aren't you obligated to pay what you owe? Of course you are, and you should do your very best to pay all your debts. But you are also obligated to keep a roof over your head, to put food in your mouth, and to get medical care when you need it. When push comes to shove, you must take care of yourself and your family first. The big banks have proven that they can take care of themselves.

If you find yourself considering bankruptcy, reflect on the fact that most of those lenders *knew* you would have a tough time paying them back. They had your credit reports. They knew how much money you earned, and they knew how much you owed. *They took a calculated risk.* It's not so different from auto insurance. If your car was stolen, would you hesitate to ask your insurance company for a check? Of course not! You didn't plan on getting your car stolen. Likewise, you didn't plan to lose your job or to come down with foot-and-mouth disease. If things had gone according to plan, you would have paid your debts, and the bank would have made a big profit.

Whenever a bank makes a loan, it hopes to make money, but lenders know that there is some chance that the money will never be repaid. The interest charges and penalty fees are designed to cover those risks. Remember Josephine from Step Five? She borrowed $2200, paid back $2008, and Providian said that she still owed more than $2600! The way we see it, she had almost paid her way clear, even if Providian was claiming they "lost" $2600 in bankruptcy. As we write this, a record number of people are filing for bankruptcy—at the same time that lenders are reporting record profits off their interest charges and high fees.

Still not convinced of the morality of bankruptcy? Consider this: Businesses file for bankruptcy all the time. Indeed, sophisticated business people chat about bankruptcy as a "financial reorganization" and a "litigation strategy." In other words, they look at bankruptcy as just another tool for smart business management. Do you imagine the CEO of United Airlines and the president of Kmart were racked with guilt when they took their companies to the bankruptcy courts? We doubt it. They did what they thought best for their shareholders and customers. If that meant that some creditors ended up with the short end of the stick, then so be it. They saw it as simply a smart business decision. And when your survival is on the line, so should you.

You made promises, and so did the bank. The bank promised to lend you the money, but it didn't promise to give you the best possible price. It didn't promise to go easy on you if you got in trouble, and it didn't promise that its collection agents would be honest and polite. The bank promised nothing more than to lend you the money and to maximize its profits within the four corners of the law. You made the same promise—to pay back if you could *within the four corners of the law.* Bankruptcy is there to help if your debts get overwhelming. Don't take it lightly, but don't avoid it if you need the help.

When to File for Bankruptcy

Bankruptcy helps the most if you can wait until the crisis has passed before you file. If you are out of work, wait until you have found a new job. If you have a child who is seriously ill, wait until he recovers and the health insurance pays its share of the bills. It can be extremely tough to hold on that long, especially if collection notices are stacking up and bill collectors are calling you every night. But if you wait, you can make sure that you won't find yourself back in the same trouble after you file for bankruptcy.

> Bankruptcy helps the most if you wait until the crisis has passed before you file.

Unfortunately, there are no do-overs in bankruptcy. It isn't like standing in the supermarket checkout line and saying, "Hold on, I need to add something else." Any debt you take on after you file for bankruptcy stays with you—no matter what. The bankruptcy system gives an extraordinary opportunity for a second chance. If you wait to file until the worst of your problems are over, you will have the best odds of getting exactly what you need from the bankruptcy judge—a fresh start.

How do you decide if bankruptcy is right for you? You can start by taking a realistic look at your overall situation. If you owe more than a year's salary in Steal-from-Tomorrow debt, you may never be able to pay it back. If your mortgage lender refuses to negotiate and you get a foreclosure notice, filing for bankruptcy may be the only way to hold on to your home. If bankruptcy is the only way, then go ahead and file.

Getting Back on Your Feet

What happens when it's all over? You have filed for bankruptcy (or negotiated yourself back from the brink), you are back at work, a paycheck is coming in, and the crisis has passed—what then?

Just get back to balancing your money. Stick to the plan like white sticks to rice. Pay your Must-Haves first, set aside a little something for Wants, and get started on rebuilding your future. Set aside 20% for tomorrow—or a little more, if you can swing it—and use that money to dig your way out of debt and rebuild your Savings, one dollar at a time.

Here are some steps to help you rebuild:

- *When the crisis passes, do an honest assessment of your financial circumstances.* If there have been permanent changes in your money—if your new job pays less, or if you've lost your health insurance, or if the divorce is now final—then you need to make some permanent changes in your life. So ask yourself the tough questions: Is it time to downsize the house? The car? The kids' activities? Watch out for the temptation to look backward. People who evaluate their life in terms of "but we always did XYZ" will stay stuck in financial trouble. If your circumstances have changed permanently, then put the past behind you and get on with building a new life on solid financial footing. Get your money back in balance, and get on with building the wealth you deserve.

- *Be alert to the cheats.* Keep in mind that even if your neighbors don't read your credit report, there are vultures who do. They will try to sell you instant cash, credit repair, or new credit cards (as if more debt is what you need!). They don't have anything you need, so just stay away.

- *Stick with cash.* If your credit is in the toilet, what do you do? Use cash. There are some extra-bad deals out there for people with bad credit, so just say no. We've seen credit cards that charge you $176 in fees—for a card that maxes out at $200! If you need to buy a car, stay away from the car salesmen who specialize in selling to people with bad credit; these guys will stick you with a car loan with interest as high as

25%. If you really need to buy a car, try getting an old clunker for cash; you can replace it as soon as you get a little more cash and a little better credit rating.

• *Don't be shy.* If you are looking for a new place to live, tell the landlord up front that you've had credit problems, but your life is now straight and you can pay your rent on time. The same advice holds true for anyone else likely to run a credit check: Come clean. If you 'fess up ahead of time rather than shuffle around after it is discovered, they will be a lot more likely to listen to you.

• *Rebuild your credit the old-fashioned way—pay for things.* Don't try shortcuts because there aren't any. Just pay your bills on time, and check your credit report to be sure it is accurate. Most important, don't lose sleep over it. Over time your credit rating will improve, but in the meantime you are gaining something much more important—a solid financial future.

And through it all, keep living your life all the way to the limit. Abraham Lincoln went broke. So did Harry Truman. But they pulled up their socks and did pretty well for themselves. Financial trouble is hard, but there is still a lot of living to do.

The Last Word:
It's Not About Money

The rules of the game have changed. Today you have to be *smart* with your money. Not just a little smart, but super smart.

Of course, we told you that back on page one.

So now we have something else to tell you: The hard part is over. Really and truly, the toughest stuff is behind you. You have given up the starve-and-spend cycles. You have learned that there's no need for "Pull the belt a little tighter." And you've moved past telling yourself, "I just don't have enough willpower."

You have learned the new rules. You have mastered the principles of balancing your money. You have sailed past your neighbors, and you *know* how to play it smart with your money. You have a smart plan, and you have put it to work.

So what's next?

It's time for the best part of all. It is time to stop thinking about your money.

You may be a little surprised. After all, we just spent an entire book talking about money, and now we're saying you shouldn't even *think* about money anymore! (Or at least, you shouldn't think very much about money.) Why?

Because money isn't the objective. The real goal is to get control over your money so that you can put it where it belongs: in the background.

You probably already knew that somewhere in the back of your mind. After all, you aren't making all these changes so that money can become the King of Your Life. You are making these changes so your life can get better.

If you have spent most of your adult life worrying about money, it may feel a little strange to let go of all that worry. You may feel like you did when you were a kid and you lost a tooth: You keep running your tongue around your mouth, trying to see if the tooth still hurts when you wiggle it—forgetting that the painful tooth is long gone.

Now is the time to stop worrying and get on with what really matters: *your life*. No more lying awake at night wondering if your paycheck is going to clear before the mortgage payment. You've covered your Must-Haves, and those worries are behind you.

No more torturing yourself over whether you can afford something. You *know* the answer. If you have the cash, then you can buy it.

And best of all, no more wondering whether you'll ever get ahead. You have a solid plan to build your savings, and before you know it, you will be accumulating some real wealth.

So if you feel those old money worries kicking in again, just remember: *You don't need to worry—you have mastered your money.* You have balanced your money so that you can easily cover all your bills. You have created a plan so that you always have some cash in your pocket for some good old-fashioned fun. You are getting rid of your debts once and for all, so that monkey will soon be off your back. And best of all, you have laid the groundwork to start making your dreams come true.

In other words, you have nothing to worry about, and everything to smile about. So give yourself permission to worry less and enjoy more. You've earned it.

BRETT AND BRANDI: A NEW LIFE

The birth announcement arrived in the mail, a blue-and-white card with a blue satin bow announcing the birth of Thompson George Caldwell. The picture showed all five of them lined up on the couch: Brett, Brandi, Tessa, Erin, and the tiny Thompson propped on a pillow. There was a handwritten note in back: "Sorry this is so late—things are hectic from the move. Isn't T. handsome!!!!—Brandi"

Brandi told me (Elizabeth) about the year and a half since I had last seen her. She confides, "It turns out I was pregnant when we came and saw you. A baby wasn't, you know, on the plan at the moment, but . . ." Her voice trails off, a private smile on her face. "Brett always wanted a boy. And Thompson is such a yummy little butter roll."

The past year had brought even more surprises. Not long after we met with them, Brett started applying for other jobs. He didn't tell anyone, not even Brandi. He confesses now that he was a little scared that he wouldn't find anything. So when he bounced in the door on a Thursday afternoon and swept Brandi up with "How about moving to Tucson? More money! More future! A really good job!" she was taken completely by surprise. And the biggest shocker of all: Brett had to start on Monday.

Brandi told me about the move, and about buying the new house. ("I thought we were gonna have to beat the real estate agents with a stick to make them show us the smaller houses, but we stuck to our budget.") They had been in Tucson for six months when their daughter Tessa collided with a grocery cart. Brandi recalls:

It was just before Thompson was born. So I went racing into the emergency room with Tessa's head wrapped in a towel. I looked like I was about to have a baby elephant, and they kept trying to put me in a wheelchair, while I was screaming, "Not me—her!" Brett came running in from work and got it all sorted out. But I was so rattled, when we left the emergency room, I got in my car and I ran over Brett's foot! The girls were crying and Brett was hopping around, and it was all a big commotion. When I went into labor the next night, I told Brett I didn't want to go to the emergency room because they had probably had enough of us!

Brandi had other stories, about how Tessa got left at the church after Thompson's baptism ("I thought *you* had her!") and how the dog pulled an entire ham off the table at the party afterwards. Brandi told her stories with flair, filling the room with her infectious laugh.

Brandi went on for a long time without mentioning money. Finally, she seemed to remember what had brought us together. And with the same enthusiasm that she told every other story, she brought me up to date.

And we've stuck to our money plan like nobody's business. We lost some money when we sold the house in Denver, which was really a bummer after all we'd put in, and moving wasn't cheap since I couldn't do much being pregnant and all. But we got a *great* deal on the new place in Tucson, and our payments are even lower. But mostly, we just stick with the balance thing, and it *works*.

Brandi took a deep, satisfied breath. Brett adds proudly, "For the first time, we're not just keeping up, we're getting *ahead*." Brett and Brandi are putting money away for retirement, and they've started saving for the kids' college. Best of all, they have socked away plenty of money in a savings account, "just in case."

Brandi giggles, "Every time the bank statement shows up, Brett pretends like he's smoking a cigar and goes, 'Get the martinis, dah-ling.' You know, like the rich people on *Gilligan's Island.* I mean, we're not living like we're rich. But it is so amazingly wonderful to *feel* a little rich."

But mostly, Brett and Brandi just don't think about money very much. Brett reflects, "Sure, I do my job, and I get my paycheck. But Brandi and I, we haven't argued over money even once since Thompson was born. It seems like mostly we talk about the kids, or family— did I tell you my sister is getting married?—um, or just stuff. It's like money's just not really there anymore. That part finally got pretty easy."

And then Brandi was back to talking about Tessa's soccer tournament last weekend and how Erin knows all her letters and can count to a hundred. Brett interrupted to tell us that he's agreed to be an assistant coach for the girl's soccer team, and he thinks Thompson is left-handed. And we just smiled right along with them. Because it was clear that Brandi and Brett were going to be just fine. Better than fine—they had put the money worries behind them, and they were living their lives to the fullest.

ALL YOUR WORTH

So here we are at the beginning—the beginning of the rest of your life. We wish you a prosperous and secure future, and most of all, a happy life. We want you to have a Lifetime Money Plan that works for you. But in the end, this isn't about money. This is about your life and your dreams. This is about making the most of all your worth.

Acknowledgments

Our debts are many. We owe a great deal to the people who helped this book along, from the first spark of an idea to the final checks on the manuscript. We can never repay in full, but we wish to thank those who have helped make this book a richer, more complete guide.

We start with Phil McGraw, one of the greatest teachers in the world. Without Dr. Phil, there would be no *All Your Worth*. Thank you, Dr. Phil.

We owe a special debt to the people who helped shape our manuscript. Jean Morse offered thoughtful, detailed comments and provided the sharp insights that she brings to every task. Michelle Crookham read and re-read manuscripts, offering advice as only a terrific math teacher can. Amanda Sidwell helped give shape to the book, providing important input at just the right moment. Randi Segatore gave good advice and critical help as the manuscript evolved. Sandy Sidwell gave us yet another perspective on what we needed to cover. For each of these special individuals, we offer our thanks.

Alex Warren was an enthusiastic colleague from the inception of the idea to the final edits. He volunteered his time, his energy, his critical eye, and his unflagging enthusiasm for the project. He helped bring the book to life.

Eric Stein and Steve Reardon at Self-Help and John Rao at the National Consumer Law Center helped us refine our credit advice; we thank them for the good counsel and for running terrific organizations. Dr. Steffie Woolhandler and Dr. David Himmelstein were valuable resources on health care finance issues. Professor Robert Lawless, Judge Bruce Markell, Professor Katherine Porter, Professor John Pottow, Dean Michael Schill, Dr. Teresa Sullivan, Dr. Deborah Thorne, Professor Susan Wachter, and Professor Jay Lawrence Westbrook helped develop the data for the Consumer Bankruptcy Project, which provided important empirical underpinning for this work. Thanks to each of you.

Dean Elena Kagan of the Harvard Law School deserves a special mention for her unwavering commitment to the belief that academic work should make a real difference in the world. Thanks, Elena.

We thank Jan Miller and Dominick Anfuso for their faith in this project. Wylie O'Sullivan helped bring all the pieces together, and Annabelle Baxter offered endless amounts of good cheer and help. Ana Vasquez provided constant support with her endless patience and ready smile. Thank you to all.

Sushil Tyagi offered tremendous support and intelligent insight. We are grateful.

Bruce Mann was infinitely supportive, patient, and helpful. We recognize that we have been blessed.

Index

About the Authors

Elizabeth Warren is a chaired professor at Harvard Law School. She has written several books, including *The Two-Income Trap: Why Middle-Class Parents Are Going Broke*. She has appeared on numerous television shows, including *Dr. Phil* and the *Today* show. The *National Law Journal* named her One of the Fifty Most Influential Women Lawyers in America. She lives with her husband in Cambridge, Massachusetts.

Amelia Warren Tyagi, along with Elizabeth, is coauthor of *The Two-Income Trap*. She worked as a consultant with McKinsey and Company and cofounded the health benefits firm HealthAllies. She is a regular commentator on the nationally syndicated radio show, *Marketplace,* and she has written for *Time* and *The Chicago Tribune*. She lives in Los Angeles, California, with her husband and daughter.

Elizabeth and Amelia are mother and daughter.